INTELLIGENCE AND COUNTERINTELLIGENCE STUDIES

FUSION CENTERS

COUNTERTERRORISM INFORMATION SHARING CONCERNS AND DEFICIENCIES

INTELLIGENCE AND COUNTERINTELLIGENCE STUDIES

Additional books in this series can be found on Nova's website under the Series tab.

Additional E-books in this series can be found on Nova's website under the E-book tab.

DEFENSE, SECURITY AND STRATEGIES

Additional books in this series can be found on Nova's website under the Series tab.

Additional E-books in this series can be found on Nova's website under the E-book tab.

INTELLIGENCE AND COUNTERINTELLIGENCE STUDIES

FUSION CENTERS

COUNTERTERRORISM INFORMATION SHARING CONCERNS AND DEFICIENCIES

ART M. GERARDI
EDITOR

nova publishers
New York

For permission to use material from this book please contact us:
Telephone 631-231-7269; Fax 631-231-8175
Web Site: http://www.novapublishers.com

Library of Congress Cataloging-in-Publication Data

ISBN: 978-1-62417-336-3

Published by Nova Science Publishers, Inc. †New York

CONTENTS

PREFACE

Sharing terrorism-related information between state, local and federal officials is crucial to protecting the United States from another terrorist attack. Achieving this objective was the motivation for Congress and the White House to invest hundreds of millions of taxpayer dollars over the last nine years in support of dozens of state and local fusion centers across the United States. Congress directed the Department of Homeland Security (DHS) to lead this initiative. A bipartisan investigation has found, however, that DHS' work with those state and local fusion centers has not produced useful intelligence to support federal counterterrorism efforts. This book offers recommendations to clarify DHS' role with respect to state and local fusion centers; to improve oversight of federal grand funds supporting fusion centers; conduct promised assessments of fusion center information-sharing; and strengthen its protection of civil liberties in fusion center intelligence reporting.

Chapter 1 – Statement of the Committee on Homeland Security and Governmental Affairs, dated October 3, 2012.

Chapter 2 – The Highlights of GAO-10-972, a report to congressional requesters, dated September 2010.

In: Fusion Centers
Editor: Art M. Gerardi

ISBN: 978-1-62417-336-3

Chapter 1

FEDERAL SUPPORT FOR AND INVOLVEMENT IN STATE AND LOCAL FUSION CENTERS*

United States Senate

I. EXECUTIVE SUMMARY

Sharing terrorism-related information between state, local and federal officials is crucial to protecting the United States from another terrorist attack. Achieving this objective was the motivation for Congress and the White House to invest hundreds of millions of taxpayer dollars over the last nine years in support of dozens of state and local fusion centers across the United States.[1] Congress directed the Department of Homeland Security (DHS) to lead this initiative. A bipartisan investigation by the Permanent Subcommittee on Investigations has found, however, that DHS' work with those state and local fusion centers has not produced useful intelligence to support federal counterterrorism efforts.

The Subcommittee investigation found that DHS-assigned detailees to the fusion centers forwarded "intelligence" of uneven quality – oftentimes shoddy,rarely timely, sometimes endangering citizens' civil liberties and Privacy Act protections, occasionally taken from already-published public sources, and more often than not unrelated to terrorism.

The Subcommittee investigation also found that DHS officials' public claims about fusion centers were not always accurate. For instance, DHS officials asserted that some fusion centers existed when they did not. At times, DHS officials overstated fusion centers' "success stories." At other times, DHS officials failed to disclose or acknowledge non-public evaluations highlighting a host of problems at fusion centers and in DHS' own operations.

Since 2003, over 70 state and local fusion centers, supported in part with federal funds, have been created or expanded in part to strengthen U.S. intelligence capabilities, particularly to detect, disrupt, and respond to domestic terrorist activities. DHS' support for and involvement with these state and local fusion centers has, from the beginning, centered on their professed ability to strengthen federal counterterrorism efforts.

---

* This is an edited, reformatted and augmented version of the Committee on Homeland Security and Governmental Affairs, dated October 3, 2012.

Under the leadership of Senator Coburn, Ranking Subcommittee Member, the Subcommittee has spent two years examining federal support of fusion centers and evaluating the resulting counterterrorism intelligence. The Subcommittee's investigative efforts included interviewing dozens of current and former Federal, state and local officials, reviewing more than a year's worth of intelligence reporting from centers, conducting a nationwide survey of fusion centers, and examining thousands of pages of financial records and grant documentation. The investigation identified problems with nearly every significant aspect of DHS' involvement with fusion centers. The Subcommittee investigation also determined that senior DHS officials were aware of the problems hampering effective counterterrorism work by the fusion centers, but did not always inform Congress of the issues, nor ensure the problems were fixed in a timely manner.

Regarding the centers themselves, the Subcommittee investigation learned that a 2010 assessment of state and local fusion centers conducted at the request of DHS found widespread deficiencies in the centers' basic counterterrorism information-sharing capabilities. DHS did not share that report with Congress or discuss its findings publicly. When the Subcommittee requested the assessment as part of its investigation, DHS at first denied it existed, then disputed whether it could be shared with Congress, before ultimately providing a copy.

In 2011, DHS conducted its own, less rigorous assessment of fusion centers. While its resulting findings were more positive, they too indicated ongoing weaknesses at the fusion centers.

The findings of both the 2010 and 2011 assessments contradict public statements by DHS officials who have described fusion centers as "one of the centerpieces of our counterterrorism strategy,"[2] and "a major force multiplier in the counterterrorism enterprise."[3] The Subcommittee investigation found that the fusion centers often produced irrelevant, useless or inappropriate intelligence reporting to DHS, and many produced no intelligence reporting whatsoever.

Despite reviewing 13 months' worth of reporting originating from fusion centers from April 1, 2009 to April 30, 2010, the Subcommittee investigation could identify no reporting which uncovered a terrorist threat, nor could it identify a contribution such fusion center reporting made to disrupt an active terrorist plot. Instead, the investigation found:

- Nearly a third of all reports – 188 out of 610 – were never published for use within DHS and by other members of the intelligence community, often because they lacked any useful information, or potentially violated department guidelines meant to protect Americans' civil liberties or Privacy Act protections.
- In 2009, DHS instituted a lengthy privacy and civil liberties review process which kept most of the troubling reports from being released outside of DHS; however, it also slowed reporting down by months, and DHS continued to store troubling intelligence reports from fusion centers on U.S. persons, possibly in violation of the Privacy Act.
- During the period reviewed, DHS intelligence reporting suffered from a significant backlog. At some points, hundreds of draft intelligence reports sat for months before DHS officials made a decision about whether to release them to the intelligence community. DHS published many reports so late – typically months late, but

sometimes nearly a year after they were filed – that many were considered "obsolete" by the time they were released.

- Most reporting was not about terrorists or possible terrorist plots, but about criminal activity, largely arrest reports pertaining to drug, cash or human smuggling.
- Some terrorism-related "intelligence" reporting was based on older news releases or media accounts.
- Some terrorism-related reporting also appeared to be a slower-moving duplicate of information shared with the National Counter Terrorism Center through a much quicker process run by the Federal Bureau of Investigation's Terrorist Screening Center.

In interviews, current and former DHS officials involved in the fusion center reporting process stated they were aware that "a lot of [the reporting] was predominantly useless information," as one DHS official put it.[4] A former reporting branch chief said that while he was sometimes proud of the intelligence his unit produced, "There were times when it was, 'what a bunch of crap is coming through.'"[5]

The Subcommittee investigation also examined DHS' management of the fusion center counterterrorism intelligence reporting process. The investigation discovered:

- DHS required only a week of training for intelligence officials before sending them to state and local fusion centers to report sensitive domestic intelligence, largely concerning U.S. persons.
- Officials who routinely authored useless or potentially illegal fusion center intelligence reports faced no sanction or reprimand.

The Subcommittee investigation also reviewed how the Federal Emergency Management Agency (FEMA), a component of DHS, distributed hundreds of millions of taxpayer dollars to support state and local fusion centers. DHS revealed that it was unable to provide an accurate tally of how much it had granted to states and cities to support fusion centers efforts, instead producing broad estimates of the total amount of federal dollars spent on fusion center activities from 2003 to 2011, estimates which ranged from $289 million to $1.4 billion.

The Subcommittee investigation also found that DHS failed to adequately police how states and municipalities used the money intended for fusion centers. The investigation found that DHS did not know with any accuracy how much grant money it has spent on specific fusion centers, nor could it say how most of those grant funds were spent, nor has it examined the effectiveness of those grant dollars.

The Subcommittee conducted a more detailed case study review of expenditures of DHS grant funds at five fusion centers, all of which lacked basic, "must-have" intelligence capabilities, according to assessments conducted by and for DHS. The Subcommittee investigation found that the state and local agencies used some of the federal grant money to purchase:

- dozens of flat-screen TVs;
- Sport Utility Vehicles they then gave away to other local agencies; and

- hidden "shirt button" cameras, cell phone tracking devices, and other surveillance equipment unrelated to the analytical mission of a fusion center.

All of those expenditures were allowed under FEMA's rules and guidance, DHS officials told the Subcommittee. Yet none of them appeared to have addressed the deficiencies in the centers' basic information analysis and sharing capabilities, so they could better contribute to federal counterterrorism efforts.

Every day, tens of thousands of DHS employees go to work dedicated to keeping America safe from terrorism; federal funding of fusion centers was intended to advance that federal objective. Fusion centers may provide valuable services in fields other than terrorism, such as contributions to traditional criminal investigations, public safety, or disaster response and recovery efforts. In this investigation, the Subcommittee confined its work to examining the federal return on its extensive support of state and local fusion centers, using the counterterrorism objectives established by law, Executive strategy, and DHS policy statements and assessments.

The investigation found that top DHS officials consistently made positive public comments about the value and importance of fusion centers' contributions to federal counterterrorism efforts, even as internal reviews and non-public assessments highlighted problems at the centers and dysfunction in DHS' own operations. But DHS and the centers do not shoulder sole responsibility for the fusion centers' counterterrorism intelligence failures. Congress has played a role, as well. Since Congress created DHS in 2003, dozens of committees and subcommittees in both Houses have claimed jurisdiction over various aspects of the department. DHS officials annually participate in hundreds of hearings, briefings, and site visits for Members of Congress and their staffs. At Congress' request, the department annually produces thousands of pages of updates, assessments and other reports. Yet amid all the Congressional oversight, some of the worst problems plaguing the department's fusion center efforts have gone largely undisclosed and unexamined.

At its conclusion, this Report offers several recommendations to clarify DHS' role with respect to state and local fusion centers. The Report recommends that Congress and DHS revisit the statutory basis for DHS support of fusion centers, in light of the investigation's findings. It also recommends that DHS improve its oversight of federal grant funds supporting fusion centers; conduct promised assessments of fusion center information-sharing; and strengthen its protection of civil liberties in fusion center intelligence reporting.

II. Subcommittee Investigation

The past decade has seen a proliferation of "fusion centers" in states and cities around the country. Congress has defined fusion centers as "a collaborative effort of 2 or more Federal, State, local, or tribal government agencies that combines resources, expertise, or information with the goal of maximizing the ability of such agencies to detect, prevent, investigate, apprehend, and respond to criminal or terrorist activity."[6] Although operated by state, local or tribal governments, these centers typically receive significant financial and logistical support from the federal government, primarily from the Department of Homeland Security (DHS).[7]

A failure among government officials to share timely, relevant information on terrorist threats was widely credited with contributing to the broader failure to protect the United States from the September 11, 2001 terrorist attacks by al Qaeda.[8] In the aftermath of those attacks, Congress and the White House made sweeping reforms intended to improve how officials in agencies at all levels of government share information to prevent future terrorist attacks.

As part of those reform efforts, both the executive and legislative branches have championed state and local fusion centers as critical tools for the federal government to share terrorism-related information with states and localities. In 2007, Congress designated DHS as the lead federal partner for fusion centers.[9]

As state and local entities, the exact missions of individual fusion centers are largely beyond the authority of the federal government to determine. Many have chosen to focus their efforts on local and regional crime. In Nevada, the Southern Nevada Counterterrorism Center tracks incidents of violence in schools.[10] However, federal officials and lawmakers established federal grant programs for the centers premised primarily on involving fusion centers in federal efforts to prevent another terrorist attack. They touted the centers' ability to gather counterterrorism information from local sources and share it with the federal government; in turn, federal officials were instructed to share with the centers threat information gathered and analyzed on the federal level to ensure a common awareness of terrorist threats. Support for the centers grew, funding increased, information networks expanded, and federal officials were sent to work from and assist the centers.

Today, DHS provides millions of dollars in federal grant funds to support state and local fusion center efforts. It details personnel to the centers, and offers them guidance, training and technology. The Department promotes its support or involvement with 77 fusion centers,[11] located in nearly every state and most major urban areas.

DHS funds state and local fusion centers through its Federal Emergency Management Agency (FEMA) grant programs. DHS provides information, logistical support, technology and personnel to the centers through its State and Local Program Office (SLPO), part of its Office of Intelligence and Analysis (I&A). DHS personnel also draft intelligence reports based on information received at fusion centers, which the agency then processes for release through its Reporting Branch (RB), also a part of I&A.[12]

The value of fusion centers to the federal government should be determined by tallying the cost of its investment, and the results obtained. Yet, despite spending hundreds of millions of dollars on state and local fusion centers, DHS has not attempted to conduct a comprehensive assessment of the value federal taxpayers have received for that investment.

Several years ago, when the Department formally committed itself to supporting fusion centers, it made an explicit argument for how the centers would contribute to federal counterterrorism efforts. That argument, contained in DHS's 2006 blueprint for engaging with fusion centers, provides a framework for examining fusion centers' contributions to federal taxpayers. In that plan, DHS identified the benefits it expected to receive from its involvement with the centers.

Known as the "State and Local Fusion Center Implementation Plan," it emphasized the counterterrorism benefits to DHS of obtaining routine access to locally-derived information to support its mission. "Our objective is to create partnerships with . . . existing State & Local Fusion Centers (SLFCs) . . . to improve the flow of threat information between DHS and the SLFCs, and to improve the effectiveness of the Centers as a group," Charles Allen, then DHS

Under Secretary for Intelligence & Analysis, wrote in a memo accompanying the plan to then-DHS Secretary Michael Chertoff.[13]

Mr. Allen began the plan itself with a quote from the 9/11 Commission's final report. It noted the panel had concluded that government officials failed to "connect the dots" prior to the September 11, 2001 attacks, and that "DHS was created, in part, to address that issue."

"Based on the legislative mandate . . . it is DHS's mission to ensure that we effectively collaborate with Federal, State, Local and Private Sector elements to share information concerning terrorist threats," Mr. Allen's plan stated.[14]

Specifically, Mr. Allen's plan listed nine "values accruing to DHS" from fusion center involvement:

- Improved information flow from State and Local entities to DHS
- Improved situational awareness at the Federal level
- Improved access to Local officials
- Consultation on State and Local issues
- Access to non-traditional information sources
- Clearly defined information gathering requirements
- Improved intelligence analysis and production capabilities
- Improved intelligence/information sharing and dissemination capabilities
- Improved prevention, protection, response and recovery capabilities.[15]

In 2008, the Bush Administration also produced a list of the baseline capabilities that every fusion center should have to contribute in a meaningful way to federal counterterrorism efforts.[16]

Given the substantial and growing federal investment in state and local fusion centers, the Subcommittee undertook a review of their activities. The Subcommittee investigation initially set out to answer three questions: First, how much has the federal government spent to support state and local fusion centers? Second, based on benefits anticipated by language in statute, executive directives and DHS's own 2006 plan, what has DHS received in return for its investment? And third, is the return worth the cost?

The Subcommittee immediately ran into several roadblocks in its review. First, DHS was unable to produce a complete and accurate tally of the expense of its support for fusion centers.[17] Indeed, for years it has struggled to identify not only what money it has spent or granted to enhance fusion centers, but also how many personnel it has detailed to the centers.[18] Also, while DHS has made attempts to assess the centers' ability to operate, it has never evaluated the quality or impact of the centers' contributions to federal counterterrorism efforts using the 2006 criteria it specified.

Faced with missing, ambiguous and inadequate data, the Subcommittee investigation refocused its efforts, to answer three more fundamentalquestions: First, how well did DHS engage operationally with fusion centers to obtain useful intelligence, and share it with other federal agencies and its own analysts? Second, how well did DHS award and oversee the millions of dollars in grant funds it awards states and cities for fusion center projects? Third, how capable were state and local fusion centers of conducting intelligence-related activities in support of the federal counterterrorism mission?

Over a period of two years, the Subcommittee reviewed more than 80,000 pages of documents, including reviews, audits, intelligence reports, emails, memoranda, grant applications, news accounts, and scholarly articles; conducted a nationwide survey of fusion centers; and interviewed over 50 current and former DHS officials, outside experts, and state and local officials.

On the first issue, the Subcommittee investigation found that DHS's involvement with fusion centers had not produced the results anticipated by statute, White House strategies and DHS's own 2006 plan. Specifically, DHS's involvement with fusion centers appeared not to have yielded timely, useful terrorism-related intelligence for the federal intelligence community. In addition, the Subcommittee investigation found that DHS has not had the proper policies, training, personnel or practices in place to responsibly and timely receive information from state and local fusion centers, and make it available to its own analysts and other federal agencies.

On the second issue, the Subcommittee investigation found that DHS did not adequately monitor the amount of funding it directed to support fusion centers; failed to conduct meaningful oversight of how state and local agencies spent grant funds DHS intended to support fusion centers; did not ensure the grants it made to fusion center projects were yielding the progress state and local officials promised; and did not attempt to determine whether the end product of its efforts and spending were commensurate with the level of its investment.[19]

On the third issue, the Subcommittee investigation found that many fusion centers lacked either the capability or stated objective of contributing meaningfully to the federal counterterrorism mission. Many centers didn't consider counterterrorism an explicit part of their mission, and federal officials said some were simply not concerned with doing counterterrorism work.

Despite these problems, DHS officials have been consistent in their praise for fusion centers as counterterrorism tools when speaking to Congress and the American public. DHS Secretary Janet Napolitano has described them as "one of the centerpieces of our counterterrorism strategy,"[20] and Caryn Wagner, DHS's top intelligence official, told Congress they are "a vital tool for strengthening homeland security."[21] A May 2012 report from DHS stated that fusion centers "play a vital role in improving the Nation's ability to safeguard the Homeland."[22]

But in internal assessments and interviews with the Subcommittee, knowledgeable officials from DHS and the intelligence community have said that most fusion centers were not capable of effective intelligence-sharing work, whether it is receiving terrorism-related information, analyzing it, or sharing it with federal officials and others. They have also admitted that DHS's own practices have fallen well short of what is necessary for an effective intelligence enterprise.

Meanwhile, Congress and two administrations have urged DHS to continue or even expand its support of fusion centers, without providing sufficient oversight to ensure the intelligence from fusion centers is commensurate with the level of federal investment.

As a result, by its own estimates DHS has spent somewhere between $289 million and $1.4 billion in public funds[23] to engage state and local fusion centers in the federal counterterrorism mission, but has little to show for it.

The Subcommittee investigation did not examine the expense, performance or value of fusion centers to the state and local governments which own and operate them, and makes no finding or recommendation in this regard. Fusion centers may provide valuable local services in other fields, such as traditional criminal investigations, public safety, or disaster and recovery efforts. The Subcommittee confined its work to examining federal support for and involvement in the state and local fusion centers, using the counterterrorism objectives established by law and White House strategy, and DHS policy statements and assessments.

III. Background

Fusion centers, few of which existed before the September 11, 2001 attacks, now number as many as 77, according to DHS, and operate in almost every state and many major cities in the country.[24] Their existence has stirred up concerns about domestic intelligence gathering practices, and questions about the federal government's involvement in state and local law enforcement operations. To understand those concerns, and the design and execution of the Subcommittee's investigation, it is helpful to understand the origins of fusion centers; the evolution of DHS's engagement with the centers; how DHS supports fusion centers, particularly through grant funding; and how DHS gathers counterterrorism intelligence from and shares intelligence with state and local fusion centers.

A. History

Prior to the September 11, 2001, attacks, few states or localities operated fusion centers.[25] The Department of Homeland Security, now the federal government's largest supporter of fusion centers, had not yet been created.

The Homeland Security Act of 2002 (P.L. 107-296), which then-President George W. Bush signed into law on November 25, 2002, created the Department of Homeland Security (DHS). That law did not mandate the new agency provide support to fusion centers – indeed, it does not mention fusion centers at all – but it did give DHS sweeping responsibilities to gather, fuse and share terrorism-related information with federal, state and local entities. Specifically, the law directed DHS to:

- [A]ccess, receive and analyze law enforcement information, intelligence information, and other information from the Federal Government, State, and local government agencies (including law enforcement agencies), and private sector entities, and to integrate such information in order to –
  (A) identify, assess, detect, and understand threats of terrorism against the United States and to the homeland;
  (B) detect and identify threats of terrorism against the United States; and
  (C) understand such threats in light of actual and potential vulnerabilities to the homeland....
- Consult with State and local governments and private sector entities to ensure appropriate exchanges of information, relating to threats of terrorism against the United States....

- Disseminate or coordinate dissemination of terrorism information and warnings (including some law enforcement information) to state and local entities, the private sector, and the public[.][26]

DHS officially opened its doors in March 2003, equipped with that mandate and legal authority.[27] Two months later, President Bush created theinteragency Terrorist Threat Integration Center (TTIC), to centralize threat information.[28] In September, he created the Terrorist Screening Center (TSC), an interagency operation administered by the Federal Bureau of Investigation (FBI), to consolidate the federal government's many terror watchlists.[29] The White House's decision to create these two centers outside of DHS led some to observe that these entities "overlap with, duplicate . . . or even trump" the Department's statutory intelligence duties, as DHS's own inspector general put it.[30]

The following year, 2004, was an important year for the growth of state and local fusion centers, even as developments further constrained DHS's role in counterterrorism intelligence. That July, the National Commission on Terrorist Attacks Upon the United States, better known as the 9/11 Commission, released its public report detailing the circumstances surrounding the September 11, 2001 terrorist attacks. Among its findings, the Commission highlighted the failure of public officials to "connect the dots," or share key terrorism-related intelligence in time to prevent the attack.[31]

Although the Commission did not refer to fusion centers in its recommendations, advocates of the centers, including DHS, have consistently interpreted the panel's recommendations to improve information-sharing as a call for increased federal support for fusion centers.[32]

The Commission's report spurred Congress and the White House to action, passing bills and issuing executive orders which reorganized U.S. government agencies' roles and responsibilities in fighting terrorism. Those moves boosted the importance of federal-state-local information-sharing efforts. They also all but shifted responsibility for facilitating information-sharing, integrating intelligence, and analyzing threat information at the federal level from DHS to a new federal interagency body, the National Counterterrorism Center (NCTC), part of the Office of the Director of National Intelligence.

The NCTC was created by the 2004 intelligence reform law and replaced the TTIC.[33] The 2004 law gave the new center the responsibility for integrating and analyzing terrorist threat intelligence from all sources, as well as the job of assessing the terrorist threat to the United States. That law, and Executive Order 13356, also created a new office, the Program Manager for the Information Sharing Environment (PM-ISE), to help local, state and federal agencies better share terrorism-related information.[34]

As other federal agencies and offices took the lead in compiling and analyzing counterterrorism information at the federal level, DHS's intelligence operations began to focus on a responsibility that received less attention in subsequent reform laws and executive orders: information sharing with state, local and tribal partners.

At that time, DHS was working with 18 state and local intelligence and fusion centers to share threat-related information, and officials were working on how to best develop a coordinated effort to build their capabilities.[35]

In 2006, DHS's then intelligence chief, Charles E. Allen, submitted a detailed fusion center plan to his superior, then DHS Secretary Michael Chertoff, which highlighted fusion centers' potential to aid federal counterterrorism efforts.

"Harnessing domestic information is the unique DHS contribution to the national-level mission to protect the Homeland," Allen's plan read.[36] He called fusion centers "critical sources of unique law enforcement information and threat information," and "the natural entry point into the State and Local 'systems' for critical threat information from the National Intelligence Community."[37]

"These centers are both suppliers and customers to DHS," Mr. Allen wrote. "We need the capability to routinely harvest information and finished intelligence in a timely manner from State and Local sources."[38] The plan, Mr. Allen said in his cover memo to Mr. Chertoff, was "one of the most important endeavors the Department can undertake right now."[39]

In presentations to other agencies and Congress, DHS officials stressed fusion centers' value as sources of counterterrorism intelligence for the federal government. Robert Riegle was a key DHS official involved in the department's fusion center efforts at the time. He told the Subcommittee he gave presentations to Secretary Chertoff, the FBI, and Congress about the important contributions fusion centers could make to the federal counterterrorism effort.[40]

"Every single day interrogations occur, in police investigations throughout the United States," Mr. Riegle recounted to the Subcommittee. "We could train people in these units . . . on the seven signs of terror." Local police weren't the only ones DHS could reach as intelligence sources through fusion centers, Mr. Riegle said. "We had fire [departments] – one of the few people who can enter your home without a warrant is a firefighter." [41]

Mr. Riegle said that he did not believe that access to state and local information was really a principal reason for the federal government to support fusion centers, but it was part of the pitch. "It was a selling point to the Feds," Mr. Riegle said. "I've got to tell them what the benefits are." [42]

DHS Secretary Chertoff approved the plan in June 2006. By the end of that year, at least 37 fusion centers had begun operations in states including Connecticut, Delaware, Indiana, Maine, and North Carolina.[43]

The following year, both Congress and the White House took steps to bolster DHS's involvement with fusion centers. Congress passed the "Implementing Recommendations of the 9/11 Commission Act of 2007," which explicated DHS's role in sharing information with state and local agencies,[44] even as it called the Department's outreach to those state and local officials "haphazard and often accompanied by less than timely results." [45] In the law, legislators directed DHS to provide support and coordinate federal involvement with fusion centers.[46]

In the law, Congress established a DHS State, Local, and Regional Fusion Center Initiative. The law directed DHS to provide to fusion centers "operational and intelligence advice;" conduct exercises with them; provide management assistance; and "review information . . . including homeland security information, terrorism information, and weapons of mass destruction information that is gathered by State, local, and regional fusion centers; and to incorporate such information, as appropriate, into the Department's own such information."[47]

To underscore the point, Congress urged DHS to "increase its involvement with them [state and local fusion centers] and appropriately incorporate their non-Federal information into the Department's intelligence products."[48]

The law also directed DHS to detail intelligence personnel to the centers if the centers met certain criteria, several of which required a center to demonstrate a focus on and commitment to a counterterrorism mission. Among the criteria the law suggested were "whether the fusion center . . . focuses on a broad counterterror approach," whether the center has sufficient personnel "to support a broad counterterrorism mission," and whether the center is appropriately funded by non-federal sources "to support its counterterrorism mission."[49]

Also in 2007, the Bush Administration focused on improving how officials at all levels of government shared terrorism-related information. That October, President Bush released his "National Strategy for Information Sharing: Successes and Challenges in Improving Terrorism-Related Information Sharing," in which he called for fusion centers to be "the focus . . .within the State and local environment for the receipt and sharing of terrorism information, homeland security information, and law enforcement information related to terrorism."[50]

President Bush's 2007 report also directed the Federal government to develop for the first time a set of minimum operational standards for fusion centers, which would allow officials to determine whether a fusion center had "achieved a baseline level of capability."

In response, in September 2008, the Departments of Justice and Homeland Security published "Baseline Capabilities for State and Major Urban Area Fusion Centers." The document outlined the basic "structures, processes and tools" fusion centers needed to have in place in order to functionally participate in sharing counterterrorism intelligence information with the federal government.[51] The capabilities included having a governance structure, a staffing plan, and a privacy policy; installing sufficient physical security; developing a funding strategy; having a plan to provide training to intelligence analysts; and having processes and protocols in place to share relevant information with federal agencies.

"It is recognized that at the time of writing this document, most fusion centers are in the process of achieving these standards and capabilities," the 2008 report stated – underscoring how few, if any, fusion centers then possessed all the minimum capabilities to meaningfully participate in counterterrorism information-sharing with the federal government. The report stated that it expected fusion centers "to take a period of one to five years to achieve all of the baseline capabilities."[52]

Even before the 2008 report was issued, the Bush administration had provided grants to fusion centers to develop their capabilities, but it also made clear that it did not believe it was the federal government's place to sustain the fusion centers forever. "The funding . . . helps fledgling centers get off the ground and start to build fundamental baseline capabilities. This is not meant, by the way, to be sustainment funding," explained then-DHS Secretary Michael Chertoff in his keynote address to the first annual National Fusion Center Conference in 2007.[53] "We are not signing up to fund fusion centers in perpetuity. But we do want to use these grants to target resources to help fusion centers make the capital investment and training investment to come to maturity. And then, of course, we expect every community to continue to invest in sustaining these very important law enforcement tools."[54]

Control of the executive branch changed parties in 2009. At DHS, officials criticized their predecessors' efforts to support and benefit from state and local fusion centers. "DHS has failed to date to institute a well-coordinated, Department-wide approach to supporting and interfacing with state and major urban area fusion centers," wrote Bart Johnson, then the Acting Undersecretary of DHS Intelligence and Analysis, to DHS Secretary Janet Napolitano. "This shortcoming has resulted in a disjointed and ad hoc approach by DHS elements toward supporting and interacting with these centers."[55]

Mr. Johnson proposed that the new DHS Secretary, Janet Napolitano, issue a "Secretarial declaration of recommitment" to the fusion center initiative. In place of previous efforts, Mr. Johnson envisioned "a robust Department-wide initiative to support the establishment and sustainment of a nationwide network of fusion centers." Secretary Napolitano approved the proposal, and made fusion centers one of the department's top priorities.[56] "Fusion centers are and will be a critical part of our nation's homeland security capabilities. I intend to make them a top priority for this department to support them, build them, improve them and work with them," she said in a July 2009 speech, after receiving Mr. Johnson's plan.[57]

The White House also publicly embraced fusion centers as part of its anti-terrorism strategy. In his 2010 National Security Strategy, President Barack Obama wrote:

> To prevent acts of terrorism on American soil, we must enlist all of our intelligence, law enforcement, and homeland security capabilities.
>
> We will continue to integrate and leverage state and major urban area fusion centers that have the capability to share classified information; establish a nationwide framework for reporting suspicious activity; and implement an integrated approach to our counterterrorism information systems to ensure that the analysts, agents, and officers who protect us have access to all relevant intelligence throughout the government. We are improving information sharing and cooperation by linking networks to facilitate Federal, state, and local capabilities to seamlessly exchange messages and information, conduct searches, and collaborate.[58]

Despite President Obama's clear focus on fusion centers as counterterrorism tools, some Administration officials have at times shifted away from defending the centers' value to federal counterterrorism efforts. In recent years, they have emphasized other possible fusion center functions, such as disaster recovery, or investigations of crime, sometimes even to the exclusion of any counterterrorism mission. DHS Secretary Napolitano has alternated between describing fusion centers as a crucial part of the department's counterterrorism efforts, and also as centers which do "everything else."

In March 2009, the Secretary spoke before the National Fusion Center Conference in Kansas City, Missouri. Ms. Napolitano explained what she believed was the difference between state and local fusion centers and Joint Terrorism Task Forces (JTTFs), FBI-led groups that include state and local law enforcement as well as other federal agencies and whose primary mission is investigating terrorist threats. Ms. Napolitano said:

> Fusion Centers are not the same as your Joint Terrorism Task Forces (JTTF). They are different and they have different roles. The JTTF, as those in the audience know, is an FBI-driven group designed to look solely at the issue of terrorism and [the] terrorism dimension. The Fusion Centers are designed to look at many, many more things beyond that . . . . [A] serial kidnapper, a gang or organized crime syndicate in an area, a serial or pattern murderer all have been handled by Fusion Centers. The JTTFs have a very defined specific function, the Fusion Center[s] much broader, and then the Fusion Center also includes the capacity for response and recovery.[59]

Ms. Napolitano concluded, "Fusion Centers to me are going to be key in how we increase our ability to protect the homeland."[60.]

In testimony before the Senate in September 2009, DHS Secretary Napolitano was even more direct. "I think it's good to explain the difference between a JTTF and a fusion center. A

JTTF is really focused on terrorism and terrorism-related investigations. Fusion centers are almost everything else," Ms. Napolitano said.[61] But then two years later, in a 2011 speech at the National Fusion Center Conference in Denver, Colorado, Ms. Napolitano called fusion centers "one of the centerpieces of our counterterrorism strategy."[62]

In March 2012 testimony before the Senate, DHS Secretary Napolitano again stressed fusion centers' work beyond counterterrorism. "Their mission is terrorism prevention, but it's also much broader than that," Ms. Napolitano said during testimony. "And as [Arizona] governor I started one of the first fusion centers in the country. It is an ideal place to co-locate, to share information. We use them in a variety of ways," Ms. Napolitano said.[63]

B. DHS Intelligence and Analysis (I&A)

The Department of Homeland Security's Office of Intelligence and Analysis (I&A) runs the department's operational involvement with fusion centers.[64] On one side, its State and Local Program Office (SLPO) acts as a service bureau to the fusion centers, dispatching liaison officers to fusion centers around the country, helping arrange for security clearances for state and local personnel, and providing other training and logistical support for the centers.[65]

On the other side, I&A's Reporting Branch (RB), receives, reviews and publishes so-called "raw" intelligence obtained from fusion centers, distributing it to assist DHS and its federal intelligence community partners.[66]

Raw intelligence is a report of an event that has not undergone analysis or necessarily verification, but is essentially what its name implies. It is typically a report of a single event, creating the proverbial "dots" of intelligence. For DHS, it could be news of possible terrorist precursor activity, an arrest with details indicating cross-border drug smuggling, or information regarding a suspected terrorist traveling into or out of the United States.

Raw intelligence is expected to be fragmentary and more immediate than analytical products, which tend to be lengthier, draw from multiple sources, and take more time to produce.

(1) Homeland Intelligence Reports (HIRs)

During the 2009-2010 period of reporting the Subcommittee reviewed, raw intelligence from fusion centers came to DHS in the form of an intelligence report known as a Homeland Intelligence Report, or "HIR."[67] Reporting of raw intelligence handled by I&A from all components of DHS used the HIR format.[68] HIRs are the primary method DHS uses to publish and distribute the raw intelligence it gathers to federal intelligence and law enforcement agencies.[69]

I&A required all HIRs, regardless of where they were drafted, to meet the following thresholds:

1. Report information that falls within one of five authorized I&A intelligence activities, showing a nexus to Homeland Security issues. This includes information related to:
   a. Terrorist threats to the homeland.

b. Priorities for protective and support measures in response to actual or potential threats or hazards to the homeland, including critical infrastructure or key resources; a significant public safety, public health or environmental impact; political, societal and economic infrastructure; border security; the proliferation or use of weapons of mass destruction; or other potential catastrophic events including man-made and natural disasters.
c. Departmental support, such as the furtherance of law enforcement activities of a component.
d. General tasks directed by the Secretary of Homeland Security.
e. Specific tasks directed by statute or presidential directive.

2. Satisfy valid IC [Intelligence Community] collection requirements or DHS SINs [Standing Information Needs].
3. Contain information that is generally unavailable via open sources (i.e. mainstream media outlets) or from other Intelligence Community reporting.
4. Contain information that is of interest to federal organizations other than the reporting element.[70]

HIRs from fusion centers are typically composed of information drawn from local law enforcement records.[71] They are often unclassified, but treated as "For Official Use Only" (FOUO), a designation DHS applies to documents to which it cannot restrict access under statute or regulation, but which it nonetheless believes to be "sensitive in nature."[72] They are generally two to three pages in length, not including the list of recipients which accompanies each report. Each HIR not only recounts an event, incident or observation, but also gives data on when that information was obtained, the source of the information, and codes indicating the origin of the report, the author, the existence of sensitive U.S. person information and why it is legal to include it, the date and time it was published, and what intelligence needs the report addresses.

An HIR does not bear the name of the official who collected the information or authored the report, although it does bear a numeric code which corresponds to that official's identity. DHS told the Subcommittee that it considers the reporters' identities classified, and has since 2004.[73] It provided the Subcommittee with a list of reporter codes, known as Field Reporter Numbers (FRNs) or "PREP codes," and it provided a list of reporting officials; however, it declined to provide the Subcommittee any document or information in an unclassified setting that it believed could be used in combination with other information to discern the identities of the authors of specific HIRs.[74]

According to DHS officials, in 2007 and 2008, the department trained state and local personnel, including firefighters and policemen, on how to draft an HIR.[75] "It's true, state and local personnel were issued FRNs . . . . Yes, there are reports in the system [by authors] who are not Federal employees, but were trained," said former Reporting Branch chief Keith Jones, who left the position in 2009. "I recall feeling vaguely uneasy about it . . . people I didn't hire writing reports," Mr. Jones said.[76]

The department confirmed that DHS "does not explicitly prohibit" non-federal officials from filing intelligence reports, and that as recently as 2010, DHS published intelligence reports prepared by non-federal officials.[77] However, in a separate statement the department acknowledged "it would be inadvisable" to allow non-federal officials to file intelligence reports, because DHS "lacks the legal authority to compel State, local, tribal, territorial, and private sector entities to abide by" Executive Order 12333, which regulates national intelligence activities.[78]

(2) I&A Personnel

Although DHS has funded fusion centers since it opened its doors in 2003, DHS had few intelligence personnel at fusion centers until recently. In 2006, when then-Under Secretary Allen's plan was approved, I&A began systematically detailing "Intelligence Officers" (IOs) to fusion centers around the country.[79]

The process was gradual – Allen's plan called for the first three dozen IOs to be in place by 2009. Reporting intelligence to DHS was just one of an IO's responsibilities. IOs were also liaisons to DHS, arranging for training state and local personnel, helping local fusion center personnel get questions answered at DHS, preparing information for briefings to state and local officials, and more.[80]

In 2008, the Reporting Branch began detailing its own specialists to fusion centers.[81] Reporting Branch officials sent to fusion centers are known as Reports Officers (ROs) or Senior Reports Officers (SROs), different from IOs primarily because their focus is solely the reporting of state and local intelligence back to DHS. As of May 3, 2012, DHS said the Reporting Branch has deployed reporting officials to 18 fusion centers around the country.[82]

IO and RO intelligence collection authorities are restricted by executive order to "overt" collection practices,[83] which includes the acquisition of information "from . . . observation, government-to-government dialog, elicitation, and from the sharing of data openly acquired . . . . [T]he sources involved normally are aware of the general collection activity[.]"[84]

While DHS produced a memo explaining I&A's collection authorities and fourteen collection categories, DHS officials told the Subcommittee the department has no written guidance or training to explain to ROs and IOs what specific intelligence collection practices are allowable or prohibited under those authorities.[85]

Harold Vandover was chief of the I&A Reporting Branch from December 2009 to September 2011. He now helps DHS develop training for its intelligence officers. Mr. Vandover told the Subcommittee that I&A does not allow IOs and ROs to recruit people to be human intelligence sources for them. They cannot instigate a conversation for the purpose of collecting information, according to Mr. Vandover. They are generally limited to reviewing documentation such as databases, arrest reports and other law enforcement records. Mr. Vandover said they can participate in interviews conducted by state and local officials at their fusion center, but cannot request those interviews, and can only ask questions in order to clarify information already solicited.[86]

As of May 3, 2012, DHS had detailed Intelligence Officers to 66 state and local fusion centers in addition to the 18 Reports Officers. Eleven fusion centers had no DHS I&A personnel of any kind on site to identify potentially useful intelligence and report it to headquarters,[87] hampering those centers' ability to contribute to the federal counterterrorism mission.

During the period of review, IOs drafted their own HIRs and submitted them to headquarters, where ROs in the Reporting Branch would review the drafts, edit them and shepherd them through a multi-office review process. The Reporting Branch was ideally situated to spot problems with reporting from IOs. However, the IOs worked for the State and Local Program Office (SLPO), a separate entity from the Reporting Branch. This division created a cleft in the chain of command, wherein the Reporting Branch was responsible for the quality of the reporting, but not the quality of the reporter. When an IO routinely submitted useless or inappropriate reporting, the Reporting Branch had no authority to take corrective personnel action. It could only notify SLPO officials that the IO was not adhering to department guidelines.[88]

(3) Drafting Fusion Center HIRs

When DHS personnel at a state or local fusion center obtain information that they believe might assist the homeland security mission, they draft an intelligence report, known during the period of Subcommittee review as a Homeland Intelligence Report (HIR).[89] Until October 2011, reporters filed draft HIRs as Microsoft Word documents and transmitted them to headquarters via unclassified email.[90] The Department has since switched to using an intelligence reporting system developed by the Defense Department, and sharing drafts via a secure network.[91]

At DHS's Washington, D.C. headquarters, an I&A Reports Officer (RO) received the documents when they arrived. He or she reviewed the draft against the source documents to ensure everything necessary was present, conducted additional research as warranted, revised the draft, and forwarded it to a Senior Reports Officer for review.[92]

I&A Reports Officers worked their way through the queue of draft HIRs, typically reviewing each one in order of when it was received, officials said. According to Reporting Branch officials, ROs often had to make extensive edits, including rewriting the entire HIR, adding codes and formatting before the document was ready for publication to the intelligence community.[93]

Once the draft was complete, the ROs sent the final, peer-reviewed draft to a Senior Reports Officer (SRO), who reviewed the document and its changes. If the SRO approved the final draft, the RO placed it in a shared folder for oversight review.

(4) DHS Enhanced Review of HIRs

Prior to April 2009, I&A did not systematically send draft HIRs to be reviewed by the DHS Office of Privacy and Office for Civil Rights and Civil Liberties.[94] However, in April 2009, news outlets reported on a DHS intelligence product which suggested that anti-abortion groups, anti-immigration groups, and groups "rejecting federal authority in favor of state or local authority" could be considered "rightwing extremist" groups potentially capable of acts of terror.[95] Media articles about the intelligence report brought sharp criticism of DHS, particularly from conservative groups and civil libertarians.[96]

In response to public outcry over the report, DHS Deputy Secretary Jane Holl Lute ordered I&A to ensure certain types of intelligence products were reviewed and approved by officials from DHS's Privacy Office (PRIV), Office for Civil Rights and Civil Liberties (CRCL), I&A's Office of Intelligence Oversight (I/O), and the DHS Office of General Counsel (OGC) before release.[97]

Following Ms. Lute's directive, I&A Reporting Branch officials coordinated with these four offices, and within weeks they instituted a new procedure.[98] Under the new procedure, after receiving a draft nomination from DHS personnel in the field, a Reports Officer at headquarters assigned it a tracking number; placed the draft, and any accompanying materials, in a shared folder on the DHS electronic network; and alerted officials at the reviewing offices (PRIV, CRCL, I/O, OGC) that a new draft nomination was available for review.[99]

Reviewing officials from each office read the material and submitted their comments in emails to I&A, advising publication or cancellation, asking questions, or recommending alterations to the draft. All four offices reviewed and approved a draft before it was published; an objection from any reviewer caused a report's cancellation.

From 2007 to early 2010, DHS Deputy Under Secretary for Operations James Chaparro oversaw much of I&A's operations. Mr. Chaparro had serious concerns about how the enhanced multi-office review process was implemented. In his eyes, it was "putting a tremendous workload on [the offices] without commensurate resources. You can see exactly what's going to happen. It's going to slow the process down."[100]

As Mr. Chaparro predicted, the new review process, when it met with a steady flow of poorly-written, sometimes inappropriate reporting, slowed I&A's intelligence publishing by months. "It was horribly inefficient," Ken Hunt, a Privacy Office official involved in the review process, told the Subcommittee. "I remember conversations about the inefficiencies."[101] For the better part of almost three years – from early 2009 to late 2011 – DHS reporting was delayed, sometimes by months.[102]

C. Funding State and Local Fusion Centers

DHS has funded state and local fusion center operations primarily through its Homeland Security Grant Program (HSGP), administered by the Federal Emergency Management Agency (FEMA). Through the HSGP, FEMA provides roughly $800 million annually to states and municipalities for the broad purpose of "building and sustaining national preparedness capabilities."[103]

HSGP funds can be used by states and urban areas for items as diverse as body armor, respirators, diving fins, mass casualty transport vehicles, reference databases, boats, planes, and refrigerators;[104] for training on a wide variety of topics; for preparedness exercises; and for special event planning.[105] Recipients can even use HSGP funds for costs like construction, physical security upgrades, rent and salaries, in proscribed circumstances. They can also use HSGP funds to support a fusion center.[106]

FEMA awards the funds to a designated agency in each state, known in FEMA parlance as the State Administrative Agency (SAA). Each year, FEMA determines how much each SAA will receive in HSGP funds according to a risk-based formula set out in statute.[107] It informs each state of the amount it will receive. Then, the SAAs prepare and submit an application to FEMA that identifies and justifies the broad areas in which they plan to spend the grant funds FEMA has already committed to providing them.

States determine how much of their FEMA preparedness grant funding they will direct to fusion center projects. As explained below, DHS does not track the exact amount each state and municipal recipient directs to each fusion center in their jurisdiction.

After FEMA reviews and approves these applications, also known as "investment justifications" (IJs), it disburses grant funds to the states. Each SAA then distributes portions of the funds to specific projects, including those meant to support fusion centers, through the state and local agencies responsible for implementing those projects. Once an SAA allocates grant funds to an individual project, FEMA expects that SAA to compile progress reports on the project. Those reports, known as the Biannual Strategy Implementation Reports (BSIRs), are filed every six months. They are intended to track the expenditure of grant funds.[108] BSIRs are not used to conduct program oversight. BSIRs reviewed by the Subcommittee provided only a high level overview of grantees' spending.

IV. DHS Support for and Involvement Instate and Local Fusion Centers Does Not Generate Timely, Useful Intelligence for Federal Counter Terrorism Efforts

- Reporting from fusion centers was often flawed, and unrelated to terrorism .
- Some reports had "nothing of value."
- If published, some draft reporting could have violated the Privacy Act.
- Most fusion center reporting related to drug smuggling, alien smuggling or other criminal activity.
- Terrorism-related reporting was often outdated, duplicative and uninformative.
- DHS intelligence reporting officials who repeatedly violated guidelines faced no sanction.
- DHS did not sufficiently train its fusion center detailees to legally and effectively collect and report intelligence.
- Short-staffing and reliance on contract employees hampered reporting efforts.
- Reporting officials aren't evaluated on the quality of their reporting.
- A hastily-implemented and poorly coordinated review process delayed reporting by months.
- Retaining inappropriate records is contrary to DHS policies and the Privacy Act.
- Problems with DHS reporting are acknowledged, but unresolved.

A. Overview

"Fusion centers are and will be a critical part of our nation's homeland security capabilities. I intend to make them a top priority for this department to support them, build them, improve them and work with them," DHS Secretary Janet Napolitano said in a speech before the Council on Foreign Relations in July 2009.[109]

At a March 4, 2010 Congressional hearing, DHS Undersecretary for Intelligence and Analysis Caryn Wagner praised fusion centers as "the linchpin of the evolving homeland security enterprise," "a proven and invaluable tool," and "a major force multiplier in the counterterrorism enterprise."[110]

Central, effective, vital to the federal counterterrorism mission: that was how DHS officials have envisioned and explained fusion centers' importance to the Department and their efforts to protect the country from another terrorist attack.

In 2006, the Department's intelligence chief penned a master plan for how DHS should use fusion centers to contribute to the U.S. intelligence community. "Harnessing domestic information is the unique DHS contribution to the national-level mission to protect the Homeland," wrote Charles Allen, then Under Secretary for Intelligence and Analysis, in the Department's strategy for systematic engagement with fusion centers. "We need the capability to routinely harvest information and finished intelligence in a timely manner from State and Local sources."[111]

Congress and the White House handed DHS the responsibility and authority to share terrorism-related information with state, local and tribal governments; in 2007, both Congress and the White House made clear they agreed with Mr. Allen's plan that such information-sharing should happen via state and local fusion centers.

But five years and hundreds of millions of dollars later, DHS has struggled to turn this vision into a reality. Even as DHS officials and others have used public appearances to emphasize fusion centers' alleged contributions to counterterrorism intelligence efforts, the facts have not supported the weight of their claims.

The Subcommittee's two-year investigation found that DHS's support of fusion centers has yielded little, if any, benefit to federal counterterrorism intelligence efforts. After reviewing 13 months' worth of reporting originating from fusion centers from 2009 to 2010, the Subcommittee investigation found that DHS-assigned detailees to the centers forwarded "intelligence" of uneven quality – oftentimes shoddy, rarely timely, sometimes endangering citizens' civil liberties and Privacy Act protections, occasionally taken from already-published public sources, and more often than not unrelated to terrorism.

While there were times when he was proud of the quality of reporting coming out of DHS's Reporting Branch, former branch chief Harold "Skip" Vandover told the Subcommittee, "there were times when it was, 'what a bunch of crap is coming through.'" [112]

"A lot of [the reporting] was predominantly useless information," one former Senior Reports Officer, who worked in the Reporting Branch from 2006 to 2010, told the Subcommittee. "You had a lot of data clogging the system with no value."[113] Overall, the former official estimated 85 percent of reports coming out of the Reporting Branch were "not beneficial" to any entity, from federal intelligence agencies to state and local fusion centers.[114]

Of the 610 reports reviewed, the Subcommittee investigation identified dozens of problematic or useless HIRs – dated, irrelevant, potentially violating civil liberties protections, even drawn from older public accounts.

The DHS officials who filed useless, problematic or even potentially illegal reports generally faced no sanction for their actions, according to documents and interviews. Supervisors spoke with them about their errors, but those problems were not noted on the reporting officials' annual performance reviews, and did not influence managers' decisions about their salary raises, bonuses or career advancement, DHS officials told the Subcommittee. In fact, the Subcommittee investigation was able to identify only one case in which an official with a history of serious reporting issues faced any consequences for his mistakes – he was required to attend an extra week of reporting training.

The Subcommittee investigation also learned that DHS did not adequately train personnel it sent out to perform the extremely sensitive task of reporting information about U.S. persons – a job fraught with the possibility of running afoul of Privacy Act protections of individuals' rights to associate, worship, speak, and protest without being spied on by their own government.

In May 2009, DHS Deputy Secretary Jane Holl Lute required certain I&A reporting to be examined and approved by a thorough multi-office review process which required signoff from the department's Privacy and Civil Liberties experts. Following that policy, I&A officials submitted all DHS reporting from state and local fusion centers to the enhanced review process.[115] While onerous, the enhanced review compensated for the difficulty DHS intelligence reporters had in consistently adhering to departmental guidelines and federal law, and the difficulties DHS intelligence reviewers had in enforcing guidelines and law in the reporting process. Unfortunately, the offices involved in the review process also radically slowed down the reporting process. A lack of oversight from the highest levels of DHS allowed those delays to continue, slowing the publication and distribution of intelligence reports by several months, on average. Those delays affected the reporting process for the better part of almost three years.

The problems created by poor reporting and an onerous review process were compounded by insufficient staffing at the Reporting Branch, the DHS intelligence unit responsible for reviewing and finalizing drafts for publication. DHS officials said they relied on contract employees to perform these sensitive tasks, some of whom they believed to be under-trained or poor performers. And for most of its existence, the office lacked basic documentation outlining its policies and practices, such as Standard Operating Procedures or a Concept of Operations, which should have clearly defined functions, roles and responsibilities in the reporting process.[116]

Moreover, DHS told the Subcommittee that until 2010 it could not routinely receive intelligence reporting from most fusion centers. DHS indicated that its procedures required all "raw" intelligence reporting originating from fusion centers to be filed with DHS by a DHS official on-site at the fusion center.[117] In 2009, DHS reported it had placed intelligence officers at only 32 of the 70 fusion centers which it claimed operated around the country.[118] That meant 38 of the fusion centers had no DHS official and, thus, purportedly no way to file intelligence reports with DHS. Despite directing federal funding to these 38 centers, DHS had not detailed intelligence personnel to those centers, rendering them functionally disconnected from DHS's intelligence reporting process.

Undersecretary Wagner disagreed that those fusion centers were unable to share intelligence with DHS in her interview with the Subcommittee. If a fusion center lacked an IO or RO, "they can pick up the phone or send us an email," she said. Asked why ROs and IOs were necessary if telephones and email were sufficient to share information, Ms. Wagner said, "I wouldn't say these are sufficient."[119]

Since the period of review by the Subcommittee investigation, DHS told the Subcommittee it had expanded the number of detailees assigned to fusion centers. By May 2012, DHS claimed it had placed intelligence officials at 66 fusion centers around the country.[120]

The Subcommittee investigation found that senior DHS officials knew about the problems with the Department's fusion center intelligence reporting efforts, and with its broader intelligence reporting program. Yet the problems went unaddressed for months – sometimes years – and were largely unknown outside of the Department. Officials chose not to inform Congress or the public of the seriousness of these problems during that time, nor were they uncovered by any outside review until this investigation.

By the end of 2009, DHS I&A officials, led by Deputy Under Secretary for Operations James Chaparro, had identified a handful of what Mr. Chaparro termed "systemic problems" contributing to the extreme delays.[121] Among them: Reports officers "do not always apply sufficient scrutiny" to the information they turn into an HIR, particularly from fusion centers.[122] DHS officials involved in reporting intelligence needed more training, they said. Also, the Reporting Branch was understaffed.[123]

Mr. Chaparro left I&A on February 13, 2010, just two days after Ms. Wagner was confirmed as Undersecretary.[124] Ms. Wagner told the Subcommittee that officials did not immediately share with her the conclusions of Mr. Chaparro and others, although in time she received briefings which highlighted the backlog in raw intelligence production.[125]

According to one person interviewed by the Subcommittee, DHS officials who briefed Ms. Wagner discussed how her division was taking months to publish "raw" intelligence reports from fusion centers as well as from components of DHS like the Transportation Security Administration (TSA), U.S. Immigration and Customs Enforcement (ICE) and U.S. Customs and Border Protection (CBP).[126] "I said, that's not acceptable," Ms. Wagner recalled. She requested a study on how her office received and published raw intelligence.[127]

Amy Kardell, a Ph.D. in Organizational Sociology, oversaw I&A's efforts to coordinate intelligence activities among the Department's many components. Ms. Kardell led the effort to examine the problems with I&A's reporting and publication process, and propose solutions.[128] While it proved to be useful, the new study spent several months diagnosing some of the same problems which had already been identified by Mr. Chapparo and others, particularly the inadequacy of I&A's reports officer training.[129]

In May 2010, at Ms. Wagner's request, Ms. Kardell created the HIR Working Group (HIRWG). The group described the problems it would tackle:

> Currently the HIR process from submission to dissemination is perceived as requiring excessive time to disseminate a HIR; suffering from implementation inconsistency from one Component to another; having little perceived value (clearance times render items obsolete) to include understanding the customer sets; dissemination responsibilities; and issues involving ingest to the IC [intelligence community].[130]

The working group's review took six months, and its findings were sharp. Ms. Kardell told the Subcommittee that when she examined the Reporting Branch, she found it "in a state of disrepair."[131] "The house was not in order," as she described it to the Subcommittee, contrasting the branch unfavorably to a well-ordered intelligence operation. "It was kind of like a MASH unit," she said. "[They] used a lot of practices you wouldn't use in a hospital."[132]

The HIR Working Group found the Reporting Branch lacked basic documentation like Standard Operating Procedures, clear reporting thresholds, policy management, and a Concept of Operations.[133] DHS officials who collected and reported information on U.S. persons were not required to meet any standard of competence, nor required to pass any test or certification.[134]

While problematic and useless reporting was common, Ms. Kardell told the Subcommittee she discovered the unit had never conducted an audit or review to see why problems were so frequent, nor did it maintain records which would allow others to properly oversee the program. Ms. Kardell's team also found that many believed the review process could be "arbitrary" and "inconsistent."[135]

Ms. Kardell's review was completed in November 2010. In March 2011, five months later, Undersecretary Wagner directed her staff to act on the group's recommendations.[136] As of September 2012, more than two years after the initial study was completed, DHS had yet to fully implement several of the review's key recommendations.[137]

B. Reporting from Fusion Centers Was Often Flawed, Unrelated to Terrorism

As noted, the Subcommittee investigation reviewed every raw DHS intelligence report drafted on information from state and local fusion centers from April 1, 2009, to April 30, 2010. The period corresponds to the first year I&A implemented its multi-office review process.

The Subcommittee investigation counted that, during that period, DHS intelligence officers at state and local fusion centers around the country filed 610 draft reports[138] to DHS headquarters for dissemination.[139] During that period, the draft HIRs came from fusion centers in just 31 states; fusion centers in 19 states generated no reports at all. In addition, the vast majority of the 574 unclassified draft reports filed came from DHS detailees assigned to fusion centers in just three states – Texas (186 drafts), California (141) and Arizona (89). Meanwhile, fusion centers in most other states produced little to no reporting.[140]

Of the 574 unclassified draft reports field officers filed, the Subcommittee investigation counted 188 marked by DHS reviewers as cancelled, nearly a third. Reviewers recommending cancellation of drafts faulted the reports for lacking any useful information, for running afoul of departmental guidelines meant to guard against civil liberties or Privacy Act protections, or for having no connection to any of DHS's many missions, among other reasons.

Of the 386 unclassified reports published, the Subcommittee investigation counted only 94 which related in some way to potential terrorist activity, or the activities of a known or suspected terrorist. Of those 94 reports, most were published months after they were received; more than a quarter appeared to duplicate a faster intelligence-sharing process administered by the FBI; and some were based on information drawn from publicly available websites or dated public reports. In one case, DHS intelligence officials appear to have published a report which drew from or repeated information in a Department of Justice press release published months earlier. In short, the utility of many of the 94 terrorism-related reports was questionable.

The Subcommittee investigation found that fusion center reporting that attempted to share terrorism-related information was more likely to be cancelled than reporting on other topics. While the overall cancellation rate of draft intelligence reports from fusion centers during the period of review was around 30 percent, the cancellation rate for reports which alleged or indicated a possible connection to terrorism had a higher cancellation rate – over 45 percent.[141]

(1) Some Reports Had "Nothing of Value"

At DHS headquarters, Reports Officers who reviewed the draft HIRs from fusion centers before they were to be published found many of the reports useless. The officers shared those sentiments in the written comments they made recommending that particular draft HIR reports be cancelled. At times they expressed amazement at the poor quality of reporting. For instance, one draft intelligence report alerted would-be readers that a certain model of automobile had folding rear seats that provided access to the trunk without leaving the car, and opined the feature could be useful to human traffickers. One reviewer wrote, "This is common knowledge."[142] A folding rear seat "is featured on MANY different makes and models of vehicles," the reviewer commented. "There is nothing of any intelligence value in this report[.]" The report was never published.[143]

"I see nothing to be gained by releasing this report," one reviewer commented on several other intelligence drafts that were eventually cancelled. One reported an arrest for cocaine possession; another relayed information about the bust of a methamphetamine lab run by a person who had claimed affiliation with a white supremacist group; and one was on an Afghan-born former U.S. Army translator who had been a passenger in a car involved in an accident.[144] Reviewers could see no apparent link to a homeland security mission for any of the reports.

"This report does not provide the who, what, when, where, how," went a comment on a different draft report that was cancelled.[145] That particular draft HIR, dated July 2009, chronicled the experience of a Texas sheriff's deputy who encountered a man standing beneath a bridge near the U.S.-Mexico border. When the deputy spoke with the man, the draft said the man identified himself as a former gang member. After they spoke, the man left, according to the draft report.[146]

The sheriff's deputy saw "numerous human footprints nearby," the draft stated. A records check on the man turned up numerous arrests, including some for drug smuggling, the draft noted. There was no record of any activity by the man's alleged former gang in the area, according to the draft, and the officer saw no drugs at the site underneath the bridge. Nevertheless, the sheriff's department believed the man "may have been awaiting a drug shipment at the time of the encounter," the draft stated.[147]

"There is no conclusive, reportable information in this HIR," another commenter wrote on the draft. "I don't feel this meets our reporting threshold or provides any benefit to the IC [Intelligence Community]." In February 2010, seven months after the draft was filed, DHS I&A cancelled it.

"This is open-source information," a DHS headquarters reviewer wrote to advocate cancelling another draft report, using the intelligence community's term for public, non-classified information such as news reports. The draft relayed a Mexican news report that a Mexican ambulance service allegedly declined to transport a Mexican victim of drug violence in Mexico. Another reviewer concurred, "This is open source news information and lacks any valuable information for the IC."[148]

"[D]oes not contain any actual intelligence," went a comment on yet another draft. That draft recounted the experience of two state wildlife officials who spotted a pair of men in a bass boat "operating suspiciously" in a body of water on the U.S.-Mexico border.[149] "The bass boat, operating within Mexican waters, was travelling at a high rate of speed towards the international boundary," the draft stated. "After the wardens responded by maneuvering their . . . boat in the direction of the international boundary to investigate, the bass boat stopped abruptly just short of the boundary and the two occupants began fishing."[150]

When the wardens drove their boat closer, "the two individuals avoided eye contact, started their engine, and maneuvered the bass boat approximately 50 yards further away from the international border." A comment by the draft's author stated, "it is unusual to fish at that location based on the depth of the reservoir. Additionally, there were high winds and choppy waters at that time." The commenter included the observation that the suspicious boat "was riding low in the water, as if it were laden with cargo."[151]

"The fact that some guys were hanging out in a boat where people normally do not fish MIGHT be an indicator of something abnormal, but does not reach the threshold of something that we should be reporting," one reviewer stated. "I . . . think that this should never have been nominated for production, nor passed through three reviews."[152]

"I am actually stunned this report got as far as it did," went a comment from a reviewer asking to cancel another draft report, about local police arresting a foreigner with an expired visa and a record in the Terrorist Identities Datamart Environment (TIDE), a U.S. government database it calls its central repository of "known or appropriately suspected" terrorist identities.[153] The foreigner was accused of shoplifting.

"The subject of the report is a TIDE match. Okay, good start. But the entire total knowledge about the subject . . . is that he tried to steal a pair of shoes from Nieman Marcus. Everything else in the report is [commentary] . . . I have no idea what value this would be adding to the IC [Intelligence Community]."[154]

"I actually am surprised that nobody recommended this for cancellation already," a senior reports officer wrote on another draft that was eventually cancelled. That draft reported information about an individual with a record in the TIDE database who was arrested for speeding while driving his brother's van. "As I see it, we have a report about a TIDE match that borrowed a van. That is it. From that I can see no reason why the IC would be interested," the senior officer wrote.[155]

While reporting information on an individual who is listed in the TIDE database sounds significant, the Subcommittee found that DHS officials tended to be skeptical about the value of such reporting, because of concerns about the quality of data contained in TIDE.[156]

(2) If Published, Some Draft Reporting Could Have Violated the Privacy Act

Reporting information of little or no intelligence value may have been the most benign type of failure by DHS intelligence officers reporting from fusion centers. During the 13-month period of reporting the Subcommittee reviewed, DHS officials also nixed 40 reports filed by DHS personnel at fusion centers after reviewers raised concerns the documents potentially endangered the civil liberties or legal privacy protections of the U.S. persons they mentioned.

The Constitutional obligations of I&A reports officers and officials at state and local fusion centers were summarized by the Office of General Counsel in a July 2008 memorandum DHS provided to the Subcommittee. "You are prohibited from collecting or maintaining information on U.S. persons solely for the purpose of monitoring activities protected by the U.S. Constitution, such as the First Amendment protected freedoms of religion, speech, press, and peaceful assembly and protest," the memorandum stated.[157]

It continued, "[T]his does not mean you may never maintain or collect information with some connection to constitutionally protected activities; but the information regarding the protected activity may only be incidental to the authorized purpose for which you collected or maintained the information." [158]

The inappropriate reporting appears to have been a regular problem. An April 2009 email from an alarmed senior I&A official stated: "[State and Local Fusion Center officials] are collecting open-source intelligence (OSINT) on U.S. persons (USPER), without proper vetting, and improperly reporting this information through homeland information reporting (HIR) channels," wrote Barbara Alexander, then director of the Collection and Requirements Division, which oversaw HIR reporting. "The improper reporting of this information through HIR channels is likely a result of a lack of training on proper collection and reporting procedures . . . they are inadvertently causing problems."[159] In an interview with the

Subcommittee, Ms. Alexander said she recalled being told the Reporting Branch was "flooded" with inappropriate reporting. "A lot of information was coming in inappropriately," she remembered. "The information was not reportable."[160]

Two years later, in 2011, Margo Schlanger, then the director of DHS's Office for Civil Rights and Civil Liberties (CR/CL), gave a training presentation based on the "main issues coming up" for her office as it reviewed I&A's reporting.[161]

Ms. Schlanger's presentation, a copy of which DHS provided to the Subcommittee, indicated that areas in which DHS intelligence reporters had overstepped legal boundaries included: Reporting on First Amendment-protected activities lacking a nexus to violence or criminality; reporting on or improperly characterizing political, religious or ideological speech that is not explicitly violent or criminal; and attributing to an entire group the violent or criminal acts of one or a limited number of the group's members.[162]

Examples of those errors were present in the Subcommittee's review of HIRs drafted by DHS officials at fusion centers. To the credit of officials participating in the review process, these reports were for the most part cancelled before publication.[163] However, these reports should not have been drafted at all.

One draft reported on a list of reading suggestions by a Muslim community group, "Ten Book Recommendations for Every Muslim." The report noted that four of the titles were authored by individuals with records in a U.S. intelligence counterterrorism database, the Terrorist Identities Datamart Environment (TIDE).[164]

"We cannot report on books and other writings of TIDE matches simply because they are TIDE matches," wrote a CR/CL reviewer on that draft. "The writings themselves are protected by the First Amendment unless you can establish that something in the writing indicates planning or advocates violent or other criminal activity."[165] The report was not published.[166]

One draft HIR that CR/CL opposed publishing reported on a leaflet prepared by a chapter of the Mongols Motorcycle Club, a California-based biker gang. The organization, which has claimed it is persecuted by overly aggressive law enforcement, saw their notoriety boosted in 2008, when a federal investigation into many of its members culminated in the arrest and conviction of dozens of Mongols for crimes including murder, attempted murder, drug trafficking, money laundering, and racketeering.[167]

At first blush, the activities of this group would seem significant. The subject of the DHS intelligence official's report, however, focused not on their illegal behavior, but on a leaflet the club produced entitled, "Checklist for the Club Members Who Are Stopped." The document did not mention any illegal activities. To the contrary, the checklist directed members, if pulled over by police, to:

- Be "as courteous as possible";
- Try to pull over in a lighted or busy area – "this can provide witnesses to any harassment";
- "always carry a disposable camera";
- document the "date, time and which type cop (police or sheriff) is harassing you," including badge number, as well as "all threats/comments about this being their town, they will run you out, etc."

- "STAY IN CONTROL OF YOUR EMOTIONS – Now is not the time to have problems in bars and public places. Watch each other[']s backs and help one another with this";
- "Clean up your vehicle – make sure it is completely legal –current registration, all lights working – even a license plate light being out . . . is enough to have them pull you over";
- "If possible, have a designated driver who will be alcohol and drug free. If not possible, taxis cost less than an attorney."[168]

"There is nothing illegal or even remotely objectionable [described] in this report," wrote the CR/CL reviewer about the draft. "The advice given to the groups' members is protected by the First Amendment. The organization does not advocate the violation of ANY laws – on the contrary, they tell their members to obey the law."[169] The draft HIR was never published.

One DHS intelligence officer filed a draft HIR about a U.S. citizen who was appearing at a Muslim organization to deliver a day-long motivational talk and a lecture on positive parenting. "Intelligence personnel are not authorized to collect information regarding USPERs [U.S. persons] solely for the purpose of monitoring activities protected by the U.S. Constitution," the DHS Office of General Counsel wrote on the draft. It was cancelled.[170]

"Constitutionally protected activities; no nefarious activity," wrote a reviewer recommending cancellation of a different draft HIR reporting about a Muslim organization hosting a daylong seminar on marriage.[171]

Another cancelled draft HIR reported on a U.S. citizen visiting and giving a lecture at a mosque. The draft contained no derogatory information on the speaker, or the mosque, although it noted that the speaker was once the head of a U.S. Islamic school that had a record in the TIDE database. "There is concern," the drafting officer wrote in his initial submission, "that [the subject's] visit . . . could be to strengthen ties with the . . . mosque as well as to conduct fundraising and recruiting for the sake of foreign terrorist organizations."[172] This assertion was not supported by evidence, however, and was removed from later drafts.

"The number of things that scare me about this report are almost too many to write into this [form]," one reviewer stated about the submission. He noted it was sourced to a fusion center on the other side of the country, as well as to open source information – which required it to go through a reporting team which specialized in open source information. "Secondly, the nature of this event is constitutionally protected activity (public speaking, freedom of assembly, freedom of religion)."[173]

Markings on the drafts appear to indicate that half of the draft HIRs which appeared to overstep legal restrictions on government monitoring of protected activity came from one intelligence officer. DHS confirmed that officer "received informal counseling," but faced no other penalty, reprimand, formal counseling or other consequence.[174]

(3) Most Fusion Center Reporting Related to Drug Smuggling, Alien Smuggling, or Other Criminal Activity

Of the 386 unclassified HIRs that DHS eventually published over the 13-month period reviewed by the Subcommittee investigation, a review found close to 300 of them had no discernable connection to terrorists, terrorist plots or threats.[175]

Most draft HIRs that were accepted by DHS headquarters for dissemination relayed information from arrests or encounters relating to drug trafficking and, to a lesser extent, alien smuggling. One typical report, based on information acquired in July 2009 and published five months later, reads as follows:

> On 05 July 2009 at 1704 hours, Texas DPS officers stopped a 2007 three door Ford F-150, bearing identified Arizona license plates, for speeding eastbound on Interstate 40 at milepost 56 in Potter County. The driver and passenger were nervous and told conflicting stories regarding their travel. A search of the vehicle resulted in the seizure of 5.23 kilograms of methamphetamine. The methamphetamine was hidden in a false compartment built in to the floor of the vehicle behind the front seats. The occupants were reportedly traveling from Phoenix, Arizona to Oklahoma City, Oklahoma.
>
> The driver and the passenger of the load vehicle were identified U.S. persons (USPER1 and USPER2, respectively). (SOURCE COMMENT: USPER2 was previous[ly] convicted for attempting to smuggle 41.9pounds of marijuana into the United States from Mexico on 29 December 2003.)
>
> The Tucson HIDTA [High Intensity Drug Trafficking Area] has noted an increase in the number of methamphetamine seizures from Mexico over the last six months . . . .[176]

Additionally, the Subcommittee reviewed redacted, unclassified versions of the 39 classified HIRs published during the same the time period. About half appeared to contain no terrorism-related information. Those HIRs were published on average 142 days, or over four months, after the information was obtained by a DHS reporting official.

Though it may be relevant to broader departmental missions, the preponderance of non-terrorism related reporting raises concerns about DHS's fusion center involvement. If reporting on drug running and human smuggling are not top priorities in DHS's counterterrorism effort, it is unclear how the bulk of published reporting from fusion centers contributes to DHS's antiterrorism mission. Conversely, if the most useful fusion center contributions come in these areas, it is unclear why DHS does not describe fusion centers as essential to its counterdrug and anti-human-smuggling efforts, rather than to its counterterrorism mission.[177]

C. Terrorism-Related Reporting was Often Outdated, Duplicative, and Uninformative

Of the 386 unclassified HIRs published by DHS during the 13-month period reviewed by the Subcommittee, only 94 HIRs, or less than one-third, appeared to have a connection to a suspected terrorist or terrorist supporter, suspicious behavior that could indicate terrorist intent, or criminal activity that could indicate a potential terrorist plot, such as the theft of explosive material.

Those terrorism-related reports were published on average four months after they were first drafted. Some appeared to be based on previously published accounts. Some reports, which flagged activity by so-called "known or suspected terrorists," appeared to duplicate information already being shared by a faster, more efficient system managed by the FBI-led Terrorist Screening Center.

(1) Some Terrorism-Related Reports Were Based on Older Published Accounts

At times, it appears DHS reporting officials at fusion centers based their reporting not on sensitive intelligence and law enforcement information from state and local sources, but on previously-published accounts, including a press release and news articles.

Stolen Explosives. One particularly alarming HIR published in March 2010 described thefts in the Northwest of hundreds of pounds of explosives and explosive components, including 96 pounds of TNT; 27 pounds of deta-sheet, another type of explosive; 17 sticks of Dyno-Yello, yet another explosive; four 50-pound bags of "ammonium nitrate/fuel oil explosive"; 130 pounds of black powder; 14 bags of "rocket black powder"; 11 bags of KINEPAK, another explosive; 115 "small blasting cap boosters"; and hundreds of feet of detonation cord.[178]

The HIR had been drafted, however, in August 2009, seven months prior.[179] The author acquired the information about the thefts on August 13, according to the report.[180] The thefts occurred July 28, 2009, nearly two weeks before the report was apparently drafted.[181] And they were the subject of a press release at the time of the thefts: The U.S. Department of Justice's Bureau of Alcohol, Tobacco and Firearms (ATF), which led the joint investigation of the thefts, had issued a release to the media about the thefts on July 31, 2009, describing the missing materials in detail and asking the public for tips and leads.[182]

Blog Praising Fort Hood Shooting. In one HIR from November 2009, a DHS intelligence officer stationed at a California fusion center reported information relating to the Fort Hood shooting, which had taken place just days earlier in Texas. Anwar Nassar Al-Awlaki, the U.S.-born radical Muslim cleric, praised the shootings on his public blog, the intelligence officer reported in his draft HIR.[183]

On the same day the officer reported that news – November 9, 2009 – several news organizations, including the *Los Angeles Times*, ABC News and FOX News ran stories reporting the same information.[184] On November 13, 2009 – four days after the *Los Angeles Times* and others reported the same information – DHS officials circulated their HIR about Al-Awlaki's blog to colleagues at the NSA, the CIA, the Defense Intelligence Agency, the FBI, Special Operations Command (SOCOM), even the White House Situation Room.[185]

Surprisingly, a subsequent performance review for the HIR's author cited this report as a signature accomplishment. The performance review gave the author an evaluation of "Achieved Excellence," and recommended the official for a promotion to a leadership position "analyzing the most critical national security threats facing the Homeland."[186] "His outstanding analytical abilities would serve I&A well in any position," the appraisal stated.[187]

Terrorist Threat to Tourists in North Africa. In March 2010, DHS published an HIR by a fusion center DHS detailee in California on alleged terrorist threats to tourists in North Africa.[188] The HIR repeated verbatim six paragraphs of information from a bulletin published by the non-governmental Institute of Terrorism Research and Response (ITRR) 11 months earlier, in April 2009.[189] In the HIR version, the DHS reporter described "the veracity/reliability of the source and the information" as "unknown." The reporter did not note that the initial ITRR bulletin stated the "timeline" for the threat was "through 3 June 2009," indicating it was likely out of date by the time of its publication by DHS in March 2010.[190]

(2) Many Terrorism-Related HIRs from Fusion Centers Appeared to Duplicate a Faster, More Efficient Information-Sharing Process

Some of the published terrorism-related intelligence reports filed from fusion centers during the period reviewed by the Subcommittee appear to have duplicated a faster, more efficient information-sharing process already in place between local police and the FBI-led Terrorist Screening Center (TSC).

Of the 94 published terrorism-related intelligence reports from DHS officials at fusion centers, 27 of them relayed information about encounters between local law enforcement and individuals whose identities were listed in the Terrorist Identities Datamart Environment (TIDE), the federal government's central repository for information on who it considers a known or suspected terrorist entity. TIDE is maintained by the National Counter Terrorism Center (NCTC), an entity under the direction of the Office of the Director of National Intelligence (ODNI).[191]

These reports of so-called "TIDE matches" relayed information gathered in the course of routine law enforcement incidents, such as a traffic stop or a response to a 911 call, in which a state or local law enforcement officer came into contact with an individual whose identity was listed in the TIDE database, identifying him or her as a "known or suspected terrorist" according to the U.S. government.[192]

DHS officials whose responsibilities included reviewing these draft HIRs for release explained that in most cases, they published reports of TIDE matches not because the incident itself appeared to indicate planning or preparation for a terrorist attack, or even suggested an intent to do so, but because the report could contain new biographical data that could be used to update the subject's TIDE record.[193] Such reports were supported by DHS guidance contained in a June 2010 handbook on HIR production that DHS produced to the Subcommittee.[194]

As the DHS I&A Reporting Branch stated in its 2010 Standard Operating Procedures, "DHS TIDE based HIRs are written primarily to update the TIDE record, provide a more detailed background of the subject, indicate travel patterns or associations, and to highlight a recent incident while providing appropriate background context to a subject's importance for the IC. HIRs typically attempt to fill in the unkown backgrounds of some of these individuals or organization[s]."[195]

Such information could include a driver's license number, automobile registration information, information on the subject's origin or destination of travel, even what was in their pockets or in the car's backseat.[196] It could include any information lawfully collected by law enforcement during the encounter, officials from both DHS and the Department of Justice told the Subcommittee.[197]

DHS did not require that the subject of such a report be suspected of or charged with violating any law or ordinance to report his or her information. For example, the Subcommittee reviewed a report on a TIDE match who was a passenger in a car whose driver was cited for a moving violation, and two on TIDE matches who were crime victims.

The DHS reporting official at the local fusion center learned of a local police officer's interaction, possibly by reviewing an incident report.[198] The DHS official then prepared a draft HIR and filed it with DHS headquarters in Washington, D.C.[199]

At headquarters, such a draft HIR would go through the four-office review process described earlier. After weeks or months spent in the review queue, the HIR would be approved by the four offices involved in the process, and DHS would release the report to the intelligence community. DHS officials said they would flag these HIRs for NCTC, which maintains TIDE, suggesting it update its records on the entities named.

The result was that, several weeks or months after the incident with a possible TIDE match individual occurred, NCTC would receive a report from DHS with information to update its records.

However, as the Subcommittee learned from DHS's senior representative at NCTC, the very same data in those reports likely made it to the center within a day of the incident via an FBI-run process, possibly making DHS's reporting both untimely and duplicative.[200]

The FBI process occurs without the involvement of a fusion center or DHS: When a local police officer or state trooper encounters an individual in the field, for example in a traffic stop, he or she checks the person's identification electronically against the National Crime Information Center (NCIC) database, an online criminal information clearinghouse that has been run by the FBI since 1967.[201]

The NCIC database contains a "known and suspected terrorist" identities list.[202] It derives that list from the Terrorist Screening Database (TSDB), more commonly known as the Terrorist Watchlist.[203] The TSDB is maintained by the Terrorist Screening Center (TSC), an FBI-led organization. TSC obtains the identities for TSDB from the National Counterterrorism Center's TIDE database.[204]

When a local law enforcement officer checks an identity through NCIC, his or her computer will display a message if NCIC finds a possible match on its known or suspected terrorist list. The message instructs the officer to contact the TSC, which will rely on the officer's help to confirm whether the individual matches the identity on the watchlist.[205]

When that officer contacts TSC, TSC personnel will ask the officer "to get all the information you can," a Justice Department official told the Subcommittee. According to the procedure, the officer will gather the information, and share it with TSC personnel at the time of the stop.[206] TSC personnel immediately pass that information along to the NCTC, to update the individual's record, officials explained to the Subcommittee.[207]

According to Rick Kopel, DHS's senior representative to NCTC, that sharing of information typically occurs on the same day of the local law enforcement official's encounter. Mr. Kopel could think of no reason why TSC would fail to timely relay the information to NCTC, or which might justify DHS's maintaining a second pathway to share the same information. "There's no reason TSC would not report encounter data [to NCTC]," Mr. Kopel told the Subcommittee. "If that wasn't happening, that would be a problem."[208]

These facts indicate DHS may be using fusion center HIRs to report to NCTC information about an encounter days, weeks, even months after NCTC already received the same information, from the same local source, through TSC.[209]

Asked about this possible duplication, Undersecretary Wagner said if true, "it's probably not the most efficient use of resources. . . . I would say we should write [intelligence reports] that don't duplicate other reporting."[210]

D. DHS Intelligence Reporting Officials Who Repeatedly Violated Guidelines Faced No Sanction

The Subcommittee investigation found that a very small number of DHS reporting officials appeared to be responsible for many of the problematic HIRs that DHS reviewers later cancelled.[211] Just four reporting officials generated 108 of the 188 cancelled draft HIRs during the 13-month period reviewed by the Subcommittee, according to a tally of cancelled HIRs by the reporter codes which indicated authorship. Those reporters had higher cancellation rates than their peers, the tally showed. However, reporters' cancellation rates were not considered when managers assessed their performance, according to DHS officials.

"I don't recall noting poor reporting in an annual review. It never came up as a black mark against a guy," said Mikael Johnston, who oversaw IOs as head of the State and Local Program Office from October 2009 to March 2012. Jonathan Wilham, deputy director of the Reporting Branch, also said that when assessing ROs, "we don't use cancellation rates as a performance measure."[212] The Subcommittee also learned that those who repeatedly violated guidelines faced no apparent sanction for their transgressions.[213]

DHS detailees at fusion centers were not junior officials. Information provided by DHS indicates that detailees were typically GS-14s, near the highest end of the federal workforce pay scale.[214] During the period of reporting reviewed by the Subcommittee, salaries for GS-14 employees ranged from around $80,000 to over $100,000.[215] Additionally, the department distributed over $500,000 to the detailees in the form of bonuses, performance awards, and recruitment and relocation incentives in 2009 and 2010.[216]

One reporter had 26 of his 35 draft reports cancelled during the April 2009-April 2010 period. One former Senior Reports Officer said he knew the author and that he had a reputation as "a problem child" among Reporting Branch officials.[217]

"He didn't like to be told what he was doing was not in the realm of the program," the former official said, and stated he and others raised the officer's performance with higher-ups. "It was a well-known fact that information coming out of [the officer's area] was complete and utter crap."

"I cancelled a lot of them," said one Senior Reports Officer, when asked about that particular official's many nixed draft reports. Noting that his reporting often raised concerns about violating their subjects' civil liberties, she said, "I would say the person must not have understood what was reportable and what wasn't . . . . You could see this was a pattern."[218] The Subcommittee investigation reviewed the reporter's 26 cancelled drafts, and found that reviewers explicitly noted civil liberties concerns when canceling at least 12, because they improperly reported on Constitutionally-protected activity. That intelligence officer was responsible for more than a quarter of all draft HIRs rejected for potentially breaching DHS guidelines meant to keep reporters from violating Americans' privacy and civil liberties.

Another reporting official had 32 of his 84 reports – nearly 40 percent – cancelled by the Reporting Branch for various reasons. "That's a pretty high cancellation rate," said Mark Collier, a Senior Reports Officer and one-time reporting branch chief, when asked his reaction to that track record. "If that was my reporting officer, we would have real talks."[219]

Jonathan Wilham, a key DHS official overseeing the report review and release process, told the Subcommittee that reporters are not judged by how frequently their draft HIRs were cancelled. The reasons for cancellations were rarely similar, according to Mr. Wilham. "It was really case-by-case," he said.[220] Mr. Wilham cited three criteria by which he believed a reporters' products should be assessed; the reporter's rate of cancellation was not one of them.[221]

Reporters generating high rates of problematic reporting were a headache for the Reporting Branch. "You would have some guys, the information you'd see from them, you'd scratch your head and say, 'what planet are you from?'" one Senior Reports Officer recalled.

"Some individuals [were] producing 50 percent garbage. That would add to the queue."[222] Bad reporting was a concern, another former Senior Reports Officer recalled from the period. "We were heading down a path that wasn't in the best interests of the department," he told the Subcommittee.[223]

Mr. Vandover said he recalled as many as five cases in which he went to SLPO officials to complain about the quality of reporting by their intelligence officers. "The people who repeatedly did this kind of thing were reported," Mr. Vandover told the Subcommittee. "This went to Undersecretary levels, on these particular people."[224]

DHS officials interviewed could not identify a single official who faced significant consequences for shoddy reporting.[225] In a written response to the Subcommittee, DHS said that "a number of individuals involved in the [reporting] process . . . received informal counseling on the need to improve the quality of their [reports] and work with headquarters constructively to resolve any issues that arose from the clearance process."[226]

The problem of substandard reporting, according to former Deputy Undersecretary for I&A Jim Chaparro, was "systemic." In a January 2010 memo, Mr. Chaparro reported:

> [T]here have been cases where I&A state and local fusion center representatives have pushed ROs to submit reports which do not meet reporting criteria. Since most deployed ROs are contractors or junior personnel who are not in a position to speak authoritatively to the state and local representatives and as well, to avoid conflict, the CRD ROs have submitted reports which do not fall within the scope of these activities. This in turn creates a larger volume of reporting that goes into the review process only to be returned to the originator for failure to meet reporting criteria. It is important that a better understanding at the State and Local Fusion Center level be developed regarding what information is reportable under intelligence oversight standards.[227]

"I think that's in the past," said Undersecretary Wagner when asked about her officers' reporting information that potentially violated privacy and civil liberties protections. "The HIR Working Group [recommendations] are designed to ensure we report on information that met reporting criteria, and were respectful of privacy and civil liberties protections."[228]

E. DHS Did Not Sufficiently Train Its Fusion Center Detailees to Legally and Effectively Collect and Report Intelligence

Draft HIRs from IOs sometimes reported information that did not meet a DHS mission, improperly relayed information on Constitutionally-protected activity, or contained significant typographical errors, according to officials and internal documents. These problems were less likely to have occurred if reporting officials had received more extensive training and passed a rigorous certification process.

While the training process changed over time, the Subcommittee learned that DHS has never required more than five days of intelligence reporting training for DHS personnel assigned to fusion centers.[229] Moreover, DHS has not required its reporting officials to pass a test or exam, or demonstrate they met any formal standards before they went into the field to gather information, despite the fact that they often collect and report sensitive information on U.S. persons.

DHS intelligence reporting officials interviewed by the Subcommittee regarded their department's intelligence reporting training as inadequate. "You can barely teach people what the word ['intelligence'] means" in a week, said Harold "Skip" Vandover, who was chief of the reporting branch from December 2009 to December 2011.[230] "All the problems we saw – are all linked right straight back to training."[231]

"I knew we needed to rework training, I knew it was a problem," James Chaparro, I&A Deputy Under Secretary, told the Subcommittee in an interview.[232] Indeed, Mr. Chaparro had identified the need for more extensive training in a January 2010 memorandum to Bart Johnson, then acting Undersecretary of I&A.[233] Later in 2010, the HIR Working Group examined the issue and also noted weaknesses in intelligence reporter training and a lack of certification. In March 2011, I&A Undersecretary Caryn Wagner approved a recommendation to improve training and institute a certification process. As of September 2012, her office has conducted a pilot enhanced training course, but has yet to implement a new training program.[234]

The Five-Day Course. Until it was discontinued in 2012,[235] DHS's training for reports officers had been a five-day series of classes known as the DHS Reports Officers Basic Course (ROBC).

The 33-hour course spent one day on the background and basics of the job, including the history of DHS and the roles and responsibilities of a Reports Officer. One day was dedicated to intelligence requirements and thresholds; another day was spent on intelligence oversight issues, including privacy and civil liberties. The fourth day covered the HIR reporting format. The fifth day spent three hours on HIR writing practice, 90 minutes for review and questions, and a half-hour ceremony, at which participants received "graduation certificates" for their attendance at the training.[236]

Participants in that weeklong course received a total of two hours' training on civil liberties issues and two hours on privacy issues, according to Ayn Crawley, who has headed training for the DHS Office for Civil Rights and Civil Liberties since 2008.[237] Ms. Crawley told the Subcommittee she felt two hours was sufficient to train Intelligence Officers in what they needed to know to do their jobs while staying within the law and DHS guidelines. "I think it's doing the job it should do."[238]

Ms. Crawley confirmed that the trainers did not administer any final test or exam to the students, or assign a grade or score to their performance. Trainers did not even have the option of failing a student. Ms. Crawley said her belief in the adequacy of the training was based on first-hand observations by trainers. "I think what you're looking for is true transfer of knowledge," Ms. Crawley explained to the Subcommittee. "That interaction is a lot more powerful."[239]

Some officials who engaged in reporting from state and local fusion centers had little intelligence reporting experience of any kind prior to joining DHS.[240] For them, DHS's training was clearly insufficient to educate them on even the basics of intelligence, officials told the Subcommittee.

"The [reporting] process is not as simple as ending your sentences with periods," explained a former Senior Reports Officer at DHS who had spent nine years prior as an Army intelligence analyst. "There is a validation process, you fill intelligence gaps. I don't think that's something you can send someone to a weeklong training and expect them to understand it."[241]

The training program "probably wasn't adequate for most people," said another former DHS Senior Reports Officer (SRO). Before joining DHS, he had been an intelligence analyst in the Army, where he said he received six months of training, half of which was dedicated to report writing. The difference in depth and scope between his Army training and the DHS training, he said, was "night and day."[242]

Like these two former officials, some DHS reporters had prior intelligence experience, but virtually none of them had experience reporting on U.S. citizens and legal residents within the United States. "Privacy, [protections for] U.S. person data – it is extremely difficult to get them to understand . . . those nuances," Mr. Vandover said.[243]

"The reality is even if you came [to DHS] with extensive Intelligence Community experience, what we do is quite a bit different," said Mark Collier, a DHS Senior Reports Officer and one-time reporting branch chief. "You really need training."[244] Mr. Collier told the Subcommittee that the need to improve DHS's training of reports officers was "obvious."[245]

Internal documents between senior DHS officials show senior managers shared his view. In April 2009, an email from Barbara Alexander, then Director of I&A's Collections and Requirements Division, wrote to other I&A officials warning that DHS reporters at fusion centers were filing reports "on U.S. persons (USPER), without proper vetting[.]" She wrote that one of the main reasons for this was "a lack of training on proper collection and reporting procedures[.]"[246]

In a January 2010 memorandum, addressed to Bart Johnson, then the Acting Under Secretary for Intelligence and Analysis, former I&A Under Secretary for Operations James Chaparro stated that "the current quality of information in HIR reports is inconsistent," in part because reports officers "do not always apply sufficient scrutiny to the data which they are asked to turn into an HIR[.]" Mr. Chaparro prescribed "enhanced training of the ROs" to fix the problem.[247]

Despite that recommendation, the training regimen has not yet substantially changed. A year later, at the end of 2010, the HIR Working Group helmed by Ms. Kardell again pinpointed the Department's weak training of intelligence reporting officials as a serious problem.[248] In its final report, Ms. Kardell's group observed DHS had no standards or minimum qualifications that reporters had to meet before it sent them into the field to collect intelligence, largely information about U.S. persons. "Currently there are no formal [department-wide] standards or requirements for training or certification that must be met prior to an RO or SRO placement," the Working Group's final report stated. "The HIRWG unanimously felt that these standards and requirements should be established to ensure individuals engaged in HIR production, review, and control are trained and qualified in a uniform and satisfactory manner."[249] In March 2011, Undersecretary Wagner asked her office to act on the report's recommendations, including reform of the training program.[250]

Incomplete Training Overhaul. By August 2012, more than a year after Undersecretary Wagner approved the group's recommendation to develop and implement better training and requirements, no improvements have been institutionalized, although a new, longer training is being tested, according to documents and DHS officials.[251]

In August 2012, during the period of the Subcommittee's investigation, I&A suspended the five-day reporter training classes[252] Ms. Kardell's group and others had found so lacking for years prior, and began to reform and expand the Reports Officer Basic Course. But even the new training course may be inadequate. Mr. Vandover, who is a subject matter expert for DHS's effort, told the Subcommittee he recommended the course needed to be extended to six weeks.[253] He said he was told DHS could only afford a three-week course. Mr. Vandover told the Subcommittee he believed three weeks was insufficient time for proper training.[254]

When asked about the pilot training course, Undersecretary Wagner disagreed that financial concerns spurred the decision to limit the course length to three weeks. "I don't know about money [not being] available," she said. Instead, Ms. Wagner said the issue was that the course was not mandatory, and if it was too long then DHS components would not use it. "I think the likelihood of components sending people to a 6-week course was pretty slim," she told the Subcommittee. However if the course were to be voluntary, it would not fulfil the unanimous recommendation of the HIR Working Group, which stated: "Mandatory training will be required for all RO and SROs. . . . Components must require that their ROs and SROs receive this training prior to writing and releasing HIRs."[255]

F. "Two Different Chains of Command"

Another problem involved the differences between IOs and ROs assigned to fusion centers. As of May 2012, DHS has assigned 66 IOs and 18 ROs to centers across the country. IOs are overseen by the SLPO, while ROs are overseen by the Reporting Branch.

When Reporting Branch officials noticed an IO's intelligence reporting was subpar, inappropriate, or potentially illegal, there was little the Reporting Branch could do but notify SLPO officials, who oversaw those IOs but whose office had few rules or procedures for ensuring domestic intelligence collection activities were effective and appropriate. "You're talking two different chains of command, I didn't have control of those individuals," explained Mr. Vandover, the former Reporting Branch chief.[256] Thus the Reporting Branch, which was responsible for the reviewing draft HIRs and preparing them for publication, did not have the authority to oversee or manage the individuals preparing many of those reports.

G. Short-Staffing and Reliance on under qualified, Underperforming Contract Employees Hampered Reporting Efforts

Another problem with HIRs was that I&A was unable to hire sufficient numbers of sufficiently qualified personnel to staff its Reporting Branch, a problem that affected its efforts to receive and process intelligence originating at state and local fusion centers.

At times, Reporting Branch personnel were simply unable to handle the amount of reporting being drafted. In his January 2010 memo to Bart Johnson, Mr. Chaparro warned of staffing shortfalls affecting the reporting process from state and local fusion centers. "[T]here are too many HIRs being generated and not enough staff to review and edit the HIRs," wrote the Deputy Under Secretary. "There is little logic to drafting large numbers of HIRs [if] we lack the bandwidth to publish and disseminate them."[257]

As it did in other offices, DHS sometimes filled vacant spots in I&A's Reporting Branch with personnel provided under contract from private companies, including General Dynamics and Booz Allen Hamilton.[258]

DHS officials told the Subcommittee that contract employees were not always qualified or properly trained to do the work expected of them, and their productivity could be substandard.[259] When Mr. Vandover arrived as chief of the Reporting Branch in December 2009, he found a "lack of proficiency" among contract employees at the branch, who at the time outnumbered the federal employees under his direction, he recalled. "It's difficult to run a branch like this when you're so heavy on contractors," he said.[260]

Mr. Vandover recalled that he quickly identified four contract employees out of roughly a dozen who he believed were not doing their job. "What I mean by, 'not doing their job,' is – not doing their job," Mr. Vandover told the Subcommittee. He said he had them replaced.[261]

In his January 2010 memo, Mr. Chaparro explicitly noted concern about contractors drafting and reviewing intelligence reports. Mr. Chaparro stated he hoped to soon be "filling RO [reports officer] positions with government personnel versus contractors," which he believed would "help I&A to build and sustain a professional cadre of ROs."[262]

Still, the branch consisted mostly of contractors, and Mr. Vandover found himself managing his team not against the quality of their product but against contract deliverables. "If I have to tell you your deliverables, [I] have to be able to quantify. How many [reports] a day do you have to do?"[263] Instead of emphasizing the quality of the reporting, Mr. Vandover said, he had to emphasize minimum requirements of production.

The result was a quota system. Reports officers reviewing drafts "were tracked by the number [of reports] they produced, not by quality or evaluations they received," recounted a former Senior Reports Officer, who worked for Mr. Vandover. "If you wanted to stay employed, you produced reports."[264]

One former Senior Reports Officer described how part of his job was to track production by the Reports Officers under him. "How many reports did we produce this month?" he remembered being asked. "[P]roduction numbers were extremely important." The benchmark, he said, was producing more reports, not better reporting. "You had a good year if you put more reports out than the year before."[265] Those numbers were tracked on a regular basis via spreadsheets showing production for that time period versus the same period a year ago, according to Reporting Branch officials.[266]

Mr. Vandover confirmed that reporting quotas were a key measure of performance. He conceded it wasn't a system that would generate good intelligence. "We had to give them an average – a daily quota," Mr. Vandover said, "which is not the way you should do this."[267]

The reliance on contractors also appears to have derailed earlier efforts to improve the Reporting Branch training course. In 2009, Senior Reports Officer and one-time reporting branch chief Mark Collier worked to revamp the training program,[268] but he told the Subcommittee his superiors decided the new training could not go beyond a week in length, just like the old program. "I was told that if it was longer, the [reports officers] who were contractors couldn't [participate] because their company was paying for it," Mr. Collier explained. "The understanding was that contract employees were to come [to DHS] with the training they need, so other training shouldn't be necessary."[269]

H. Reporting Officials Aren't Evaluated on the Quality of Their Reporting

As of July 2012, DHS relied on 66 Intelligence Officers and nine regional directors to identify reportable intelligence from fusion centers,[270] while only 18 Reports Officers were in the field.[271] However, during the period of review, the State and Local Program Office, which oversees the IOs, did not evaluate IOs on the quality of their reporting.[272] The Reporting Branch did not have the authority or any mechanism to evaluate the performance of the IOs who draft HIRs at fusion centers. The Reporting Branch also did not evaluate the quality of the reporting filed by their own ROs, although materials provided by DHS suggest managers may take cancellation rates into account when reviewing RO performance.[273]

Jonathan Wilham, a longtime DHS Reporting Branch official and deputy chief of the branch, has overseen day-to-day operations at the branch since April 2009.[274] Mr. Wilham confirmed to the Subcommittee that his office does not have a method to evaluate reporting officials on the quality of their reporting. "We're still trying to figure out how we want to do it."[275]

In her interview with the Subcommittee, Undersecretary Wagner contradicted Mr. Wilham's statement. "Most ROs out there are evaluated by their reporting," she said. When informed of Mr. Wilham's statements, Ms. Wagner responded, "interesting."[276]

I. A Hastily-Implemented and Poorly Coordinated Review Process Delayed Reporting by Months

The enhanced review process required by DHS Deputy Secretary Lute began in May 2009. It was clearly necessary, given the poor quality of reporting. However, the new process had the foreseeable consequence of also slowing the dissemination of completed HIRs. For reports published in June 2009, officials took on average 104 days, more than three months, from generating a draft HIR to releasing it, according to a Subcommittee analysis.[277]

In the months that followed, the rate of publication came to almost a dead stop. From August to December 2009, DHS published only five or fewer HIRs per month that came from fusion centers, according to DHS records supplied to the Subcommittee.[278]

Meanwhile, DHS officials continued to portray fusion centers to the public as active and essential collaborators in the national counterterrorism intelligence effort. In a September 2009 hearing before the Senate Homeland Security and Governmental Affairs Committee, in the middle of the five-month period when intelligence reporting from fusion centers had all but ground to a halt, DHS Secretary Napolitano testified that state and local fusion centers were "key tools for stakeholders at all levels of government to share information related to threats," and "the primary way that DHS shares intelligence and analysis with our homeland security partners."[279] Delays in reporting from fusion centers were not mentioned at the hearing.

Although the new review process had clearly delayed DHS's ability to timely "connect the dots" by sharing raw intelligence among all levels of government – one of the reasons Congress and the White House created the Department – only one official interviewed by the Subcommittee could recall the Deputy Secretary's office inquiring about the problems the new policy had created, or what needed to be done to ensure it functioned more efficiently. Former Acting Under Secretary of I&A Bart Johnson said he remembered Deputy Secretary Lute asking how things were going. "Weeks, a month or so after the new guidance was issued, the Deputy Secretary asked basically, 'how's it going?'" Mr. Johnson told the Subcommittee. "I told her, it's creating some challenges, in terms of timelines."[280] The

Subcommittee invited a written response to these allegations from Ms. Lute's office, and documents supporting her response, but the Department provided neither.

DHS officials involved in the enhanced review process told the Subcommittee that the slowdown occurred in part because of problems at the Office of General Counsel (OGC).[281] An OGC representative told the Subcommittee that his office had workforce problems which "contributed" to the backlog. Specifically, he said that turnover at the junior attorney position responsible for reviewing HIRs "likely slow[ed] the process."[282]

When asked who within OGC was held accountable for the problems, Matthew Kronisch, DHS Associate General Counsel for Intelligence, answered, "By the end of December 2009, the attorney responsible for representing [OGC] in the review process during the period in which the backlog developed was no longer employed at DHS."[283]

At the Subcommittee's request, OGC identified the departed official. In an interview with the Subcommittee, the official stated that he was the primary OGC employee who reviewed the draft HIRs during 2009, and the volume of reporting meant the task of reviewing the drafts overwhelmed his other responsibilities.[284]

The official said he made his superiors at OGC aware of the situation, but they did not appear concerned. He indicated that they assigned no additional resources to assist him. "My understanding was HIRs were not an immediate priority – not to be ignored, but not first on anybody's list," he recalled for the Subcommittee.[285]

The official said he did not believe the task could be done by a single person. "It was a setup for failure," he said. He stated he was never reprimanded or counseled because of the delays in reviewing HIRs. He added that when he submitted his resignation, his superior, Mr. Kronisch, asked him to stay on another four months.[286] These OGC staffing problems were on top of inadequate staffing at the Reporting Branch, discussed earlier.

Another problem may have also contributed to the delays. DHS officials interviewed who had been involved in the review process for the Privacy Office and CRCL were unable to identify formal written guidance from their offices on how to review HIRs, what to look for, or what thresholds to apply in determining what was acceptable or unacceptable.[287]

J. Retaining Inappropriate Records is Contrary to DHS Policies and the Privacy Act

DHS personnel "are prohibited from collecting or maintaining information on U.S. persons solely for the purpose of monitoring activities protected by the U.S. Constitution, such as the First Amendment protected freedoms of religion, speech, press, and peaceful assembly and protest," as the department's Office of General Counsel reminded I&A employees in April 2008.[288]

This reminder appears to reflect the statutory prohibitions contained in the Privacy Act of 1974, which bars federal agencies from improperly collecting and storing information on U.S. citizens and lawfully admitted aliens based solely on First Amendment-protected activities without a valid reason to do so.[289]

The Subcommittee investigation reviewed 40 cancelled draft HIRs from the period of April 2009 through April 2010, each of which DHS officials had cancelled after raising privacy or civil liberties concerns about their content.[290]

As noted above, the Privacy Act prohibits agencies from storing information on U.S. persons' First Amendment-protected activities if they have no valid reason to do so. Additionally, DHS's own intelligence oversight procedures allow the department to retain information about U.S. persons for only 180 days, in order to determine if it can be properly retained. Once a determination is made that the document should not be retained, the "U.S. person identifying information is to be destroyed immediately."[291]

The Subcommittee investigation found, however, that DHS had retained the cancelled draft HIRs for a year or more after the date of their cancellation, and appeared to have no process to purge such inappropriate reporting from their systems. It was not clear why, if DHS had determined that the reports were improper to disseminate, the reports were proper to store indefinitely.

Asked why it was legal for the department to retain reports on U.S. persons that may improperly report on protected activities, DHS responded that "while a draft HIR or IIR may be cancelled based upon a determination that its publication would be outside the scope of I&A's mission, and, by extension, I&A's obligations under the Privacy Act, the cancelled document may be retained by I&A for administrative purposes such as audit and oversight."[292]

While auditing and oversight may qualify as legitimate "administrative purposes," several concerns arise regarding the Department's assertion that they form a reasonable basis for retaining the cancelled HIRs.

First, as noted by CRS counsel who examined the issue on behalf of the Subcommittee, the department's own requirement to destroy inappropriate records appears to contradict its justification for retaining them.[293] If the reports were considered inappropriate to disseminate due to civil liberties concerns, as the cancellation comments indicate, it is not clear how they are then appropriate to keep. "There also seems to be some inconsistency with the requirement for [DHS] document holders to destroy U.S. person information once he or she deems it to fall outside the guidelines; nothing in the guidelines explains how I&A personnel are to know which records are subject to audit rather than destruction or minimization, or what to do with records once it has been determined they should be held for audit."[294]

Second, the department's intelligence oversight guidelines include a list of documents it considers proper for retention as "administrative information." That list includes "personnel and training records, reference materials, contractor performance records, public and legislative affairs files, and correspondence files." It does not include intelligence reports, nor does it mention auditing as an administrative purpose.[295]

Third, DHS has no policy or practice of auditing its HIR reports. The internal November 2010 HIR Working Group (HIRWG) study concluded DHS had no formal auditing procedure for HIRs. "HIRWG found no record of any audits or studies of previous HIR releases, cancellations or tracking of substantive edits," the report stated. "The HIRWG recommends establishing a post-release audit process whereby HIRs could be systematically evaluated . . . to ensure proper adherence to the reporting thresholds, legal requirements, reporting quality and timeliness."[296]

As of July 2012, it still lacked such a process. "I want to say next fiscal year, we will start that process," Chuck Robinson, Deputy Director of I&A's Collection and Requirements Division, told the Subcommittee. "There is a draft plan. It has not been approved yet."[297] With no policy or practice for auditing its intelligence reporting, DHS's claim that it is retaining cancelled HIRs for auditing purposes is troubling.

In addition, when the Subcommittee requested copies of the cancelled draft HIRs as part of its oversight investigation, the Department initially sought to withhold the documents, explaining it was concerned about the effects of oversight on its reporting process:

> For drafts and cancelled HIRs, it would be helpful if you could articulate why the committee needs this information to further its oversight . . . . We believe it is important to protect the integrity of the process by which those reports are reviewed and subjected to internal editorial, analytic, legal, and operational scrutiny prior to publication decisions, so as not to impede officers in the field from reporting appropriately on topics of interest and importance to homeland and national security. Moreover, this could have a significant chilling effect on the quality of the reporting that ultimately is published and, as a result, the agency decisions it is intended to inform.[298]

These concerns are puzzling, given DHS's claim that the sole reason it is retaining the cancelled HIRs is for audit and oversight purposes. The apparent indefinite retention of cancelled intelligence reports that were determined to have raised privacy or civil liberties concerns appears contrary to DHS's own policies and the Privacy Act.

K. Problems with DHS Reporting Acknowledged, but Unresolved

Despite multiple memoranda and internal reviews which identified problems and made recommendations to fix DHS's intelligence reporting processes at fusion centers,[299] problems appear to remain. Some have been addressed.

For instance, DHS officials have stated they no longer suffer from understaffing within the Reporting Branch, which slowed the process.[300] In addition, the Department has shifted from using an ad hoc method involving Microsoft Word and unclassified email accounts to draft and share intelligence reports, to using a Department of Defense system and a secure network.

Other issues remain. For example, DHS officials who report intelligence from fusion centers still do not appear to be evaluated on the quality of their reporting, a problem flagged by Mr. Chaparro in January 2010.[301]

DHS also has not yet successfully instituted a more substantive training program or finalized a certification process for its reporting officials, an issue noted by Ms. Alexander in 2009, Mr. Chaparro in January 2010, and by Ms. Kardell's group in November 2010, although a pilot training program is being tested.

As of July 2012, more than 18 months after Ms. Kardell's HIR Working Group made its recommendations (and more than a year after Undersecretary Wagner approved them), some of the most important, including the recommendation to improve training, remain incomplete.

In addition, DHS has not yet finalized Standard Operating Procedures for the Reporting Branch to reflect procedures it currently follows, which Kardell's group recommended.[302] DHS has also failed to institute a process to review or audit its own intelligence reporting,[303] a problem which the HIR Working Group found "significantly complicates efforts to establish metrics for production, quality, cancellations, or reporting problems, and impedes the identification of best practices."[304]

V. DHS Does Not Adequately Oversee Its Financial Supportf or Fusion Centers

- DHS does not know how much it has spent to support fusion centers.
- DHS does not exercise effective oversight of grant funds intended for fusion centers.
- FEMA monitoring visits do not confirm grant funds are used appropriately.
- Federally required A-133 audits are not useful to monitor grant spending.
- DHS grant requirements do not ensure states spend fusion center funds effectively.
- DHS cannot say whether its spending has improved fusion centers' ability to participate meaningfully in the federal counterterrorism mission.

A. Overview

For most of its history, DHS has largely been unable to account for its spending in support of state and local fusion centers. Its recent efforts to fix the problem have fallen short.

DHS spending in support of fusion centers can be divided into two general categories: funds it spends on its own personnel and programs which interact with and provide operational support to fusion centers; and grant funds it awards to states and urban areas, with the intention that they will spend the money on their fusion centers.

This year, for the first time, DHS estimated what it spent on the first category – $17.2 million in 2011.[305] However, DHS remains unable to provide an accurate accounting of spending in the second category. DHS cannot say with accuracy how much grant funding it has awarded to support fusion centers, how that money was spent, or whether any of it improved fusion centers' ability to participate meaningfully in counterterrorism information-sharing with the federal government.

In a series of estimates it provided the Subcommittee, DHS said it has awarded between $289 million and $1.4 billion in grant funding to states and cities to support fusion centers and related efforts between 2003 and 2010.[306] These estimates differ by more than $1 billion, making them of questionable use. The Subcommittee investigation also found weaknesses in the grant award process, grant monitoring, and DHS's ability to assess the impact of those funds.

The Subcommittee investigation also reviewed expenditures by select state and local agencies on behalf of fusion centers around the country between 2006 and 2010. The review found that state and local agencies did not consistently spend federal grant dollars on items that would directly improve their ability to contribute to the federal counterterrorism effort. Instead, they spent DHS funds intended for fusion centers on vehicles, surveillance equipment, and even significant overhead costs like rent, which did little to improve their core intelligence analysis and sharing capabilities. Yet, all of those expenditures were allowable under the guidance which existed at the time, and would not have been questioned by DHS officials overseeing the grant program, officials told the Subcommittee.

In 2011 and 2012, DHS attempted to tighten its oversight of funding for fusion centers by requiring states to document how they intended to use FEMA preparedness grant funds to improve fusion centers' "must-have" information-sharing capabilities.[307] DHS officials said they expect that will help align its fusion center funding efforts, managed by FEMA, with its intelligence priorities for fusion centers, managed by its Office of Intelligence and Analysis (I&A). But as the Subcommittee investigation found, these new rules and processes do not fix the fundamental problems with how FEMA funds state and local fusion center efforts: they do not ensure states and cities spend the money wisely, nor do they significantly improve FEMA's ability to track the amount of federal funds actually spent on supporting fusion centers.

To assess the return on any program, one must know how much one has invested, how those funds were applied, and what goals the funding is intended to help achieve. However, DHS cannot identify how much it has spent intending to support fusion centers, nor has it examined how the bulk of that money has been used. As a result, DHS is unable to identify what value, if any, it has received from its outlays.

B. DHS Does Not Know How Much It Has Spent to Support Fusion Centers

FEMA officials told the Subcommittee that they do not have a mechanism to accurately and reliably identify the total amount of DHS grant funding spent on supporting fusion centers,[308] despite increasingly identifying fusion centers as a departmental priority.[309]

FEMA has not deemed fusion centers to be a separate mandatory category for tracking the expenditures of federal grant funds. Instead, it has required states to submit Biannual Strategy Implementation Reports (BSIR) which relay general updates of how the state is spending DHS funds, on fusion centers and other projects.

FEMA officials told the Subcommittee that the only way to estimate grant funding directed towards fusion centers was to perform a keyword search using project descriptions found in the BSIRs.[310] As FEMA officials noted in a briefing to the Subcommittee, such a search relies on data that are self-reported by those agencies (known by FEMA as "State Administrative Agencies," or SAAs), and changing the way in which search terms are applied can have a substantial impact on the results returned.[311]

Initially, FEMA officials conducted a broad search of the BSIR data, using terms like "fusion," "information sharing" and "data collection," that yielded an estimate $1.4 billion from 2003-2010, including $719 million in grant funding for fiscal years 2007-2009.[312] FEMA subsequently conducted a more narrow, revised search using only the term "fusion center" of the same data and yielded an estimate of $222 million for the 2007-2009 period.[313] The two estimates of federal funding of fusion centers from 2007 to 2009 differed by nearly half a billion dollars.

In addition to requesting data from FEMA, in 2010, the Subcommittee requested information from every state and local fusion center on the amount of federal funding, by source, each fusion center received for years 2007 through 2009.[314] Where possible, the Subcommittee compared the funding figures provided by fusion centers to those FEMA provided for the same centers. The Subcommittee found that the fusion centers' responses differed significantly from both sets of data provided by FEMA.[315] For instance, the Vermont Fusion Center indicated that it received no federal funding in 2007, 2008, or 2009, although data from FEMA identified between $1.2 and $1.6 million in funding for the same time period.[316] The Minnesota Joint Analytical Center reported receiving $4.3 million in federal funding, while FEMA reported between $2.3 and $7.3 million in funding.[317] These two examples show the FEMA figures could vary substantially from than the state estimates. The variability casts doubt on the accuracy and reliability of FEMA's data.

Because of a lack of specificity in FEMA's data or differences in the survey responses provided by the fusion centers, the Subcommittee investigation was able to compare FEMA's figures with those of only 29 fusion centers. It was unable to compare figures for fusion centers in states which had more than one center, since FEMA's BSIR data contains estimates of aggregate spending on fusion centers in a given state, and not spending on specific fusion centers. Thus the Subcommittee's analysis was limited to only those instances in which a state had only one recognized fusion center.

Of that group, only a small number of centers identified a total funding amount within 10% of FEMA's estimates for the 2007-2009 time period. The remaining 30 fusion centers identified funding amounts that differed, in some cases significantly, from FEMA's data.

FEMA officials acknowledged the limitations of the keyword-search approach used to identify fusion center funding, stating that it likely did not accurately capture all of the DHS funding supporting fusion centers. FEMA officials also acknowledged that grants for broader information-sharing efforts by states and localities may also assist fusion centers, although those items may not be identified in a keyword search, because they might not specifically contain "fusion center" or related terms in their descriptions.[318] FEMA officials stated that they were planning to implement a change in the BSIR reporting process by which SAA's will be asked to indicate with a "yes/no" response whether funding for a specific project is supporting a fusion center.[319] While such a change may reduce FEMA's reliance on performing a keyword search to identify grant funding to fusion centers, it remains dependent on self-reported information from the recipient agencies, which FEMA officials concede may not be accurate.[320]

C. DHS Does Not Exercise Effective Oversight of Grant Funds Intended for Fusion Centers

In 2010, DHS told auditors from the Government Accountability Office (GAO) it "had plans to assess the costs of the fusion center network," but it has yet to do such a comprehensive assessment.[321] Without an accurate tally of the amount of federal funds supporting each fusion center, FEMA, I&A and DHS not only fail to accurately track federal spending, but also remain unable to determine whether its investments are helping to meet the federal mission in a cost-effective manner.

While the Subcommittee investigation focused on grant funds intended to support state and local fusion centers, FEMA's inability to effectively monitor state and local grant spending affects its oversight of all preparedness grant funding it distributes.

The Department of Homeland Security's Inspector General stated flatly in a June 2012 report that, despite distributing over $800 million annually for state and local preparedness efforts: "FEMA did not have a system in place to determine the extent that Homeland Security Grant Program funds enhanced the states' capabilities to prevent, deter, respond to, and recover from terrorist attacks, major disasters, and other emergencies."[322]

Although FEMA did not determine whether states and localities had effectively spent the FEMA grant funds they received, that did not relieve the agency of the statutory obligation to continue to distribute DHS grant funds to the states under a mandatory formula specifying minimum state grants for preparedness.[323]

To oversee grant spending, including spending on fusion centers, FEMA relies on two mechanisms. First are FEMA grant monitoring reports, which are biennial reviews based on site visits by FEMA officials.[324] Second are grantee self-audits, known colloquially as "A-133s," after the Office of Management and Budget (OMB) circular requiring them. According to GAO, neither report is a sufficient tool for meaningful oversight.[325]

(1) FEMA Monitoring Reports

Currently, every two years, FEMA officials visit grant recipients and prepare monitoring reports based on those visits.[326] FEMA is required by law to conduct monitoring visits, but officials expressed a lack of faith in both the monitoring visits as well as the reports they produced. "I am not satisfied that our programmatic monitoring is as strong as it could be," said Elizabeth Harman, the FEMA Assistant Administrator in charge of its grants programs.[327] Until recently the monitoring visits were supposed to evaluate FEMA-funded projects against milestones the states promised to achieve with the money FEMA gave them. However, Matthew Bower, Branch Chief, Risk Analytics and Strategic Initiatives, FEMA/GPD/Preparedness Grants Division, noted that a FEMA monitoring visit likely would not involve the FEMA official physically confirming a state agency's claim that it had achieved any specific milestone.

Just because a FEMA official reports a milestone was achieved, "we are not viewing the capability" firsthand, Mr. Bowers said.[328] Even if a FEMA official rated a project milestone at 100 percent, indicating it was fully achieved, he might not base that on having personally verified the claim. "[That] may not mean we 'kicked the tires' on any of this stuff," Mr. Bower told the Subcommittee.[329] Despite that, Mr. Bower said the visits were important "to make sure projects are on track."[330]

Recently, the DHS Inspector General's Office examined FEMA's monitoring efforts. It reported that state officials told them FEMA's monitoring visits "do not include reviewing the state's progress in achieving annually identified investment project milestones."[331]

The Subcommittee investigation noted one particular case in which a FEMA monitoring official rated a fusion center project as having made no progress – zero percent – for certain milestones, yet FEMA continued to award grant funds for the project.[332] Mr. Bower told the Subcommittee that was possible because, among other reasons, FEMA had no "formal process" to review a recipient's monitoring reports as part of its grant award process. Mr. Bower said that it was "common" for FEMA to continue to award funding to projects which showed no progress on previous years' monitoring reports.[333] "Past performance does not affect future awards," Mr. Bower explained at one point.[334]

When asked how long a project must show no progress before FEMA questioned its funding, Bower said he would expect FEMA officials to raise questions if a project had received funding for three consecutive years and showed zero percent progress on any milestone for that three-year period.[335]

In its June 2012 report, the DHS IG criticized FEMA's monitoring program and the reports it generated for producing dated information of little value. "Our review of monitoring reports supported that the reports were not a source for tracking milestone progress," the IG stated. The IG said the visits were too rare, and reports filed too late, to be of any practical use. "With monitoring visits scheduled every two years, and the monitoring reports not being completed for several months following the visit, the results of the visits were not timely or current for reviewing project activity accomplishments when annual applications for grant awards were being reviewed."[336]

These findings echo what GAO found in 2008. "[FEMA] monitoring of grant expenditures does not provide a means to measure the achievement of desired program outcomes," GAO reported then.[337] Ms. Harman told the Subcommittee, four years after the GAO report, that her staff was currently researching how to improve the monitoring process for FEMA grants.[338] However, Ms. Harman noted, "As the federal government, it's not our job to micromanage these funds," she said. "We need to maintain a level of flexibility."[339]

Delaware Valley Intelligence Center (DVIC). The Subcommittee investigation, in addition to reviewing FEMA mechanisms for tracking federal grants funds spent on fusion centers generally, also examined FEMA monitoring reports for specific fusion centers. One that highlighted the weakness in the monitoring reports process involved a fusion center project in Philadelphia, known as the Delaware Valley Intelligence Center (DVIC) project.

The Southeastern Pennsylvania Regional Task Force (SEPARTF), the regional government coalition which manages the project, identified over $11 million in FEMA funding that has been committed to the DVIC project since 2006.[340] According to SEPARTF, the DVIC will employ over 130 personnel in a 24-hour-a-day, 7-days-a-week operation.[341]

In September 2009, a FEMA grant officer visited SEPARTF to conduct a grant monitoring site visit.[342] Despite FEMA's multi-million-dollar obligations to the center over a three-year period, the FEMA officer did not visit the actual location of the DVIC as part of the site visit. FEMA could not conduct a site visit of the fusion center itself, because despite years of grant funding, the center did not physically exist.

In 2009, the FEMA officer reviewed the promises the task force had made regarding the progress it would make on DVIC in 2008, when FEMA had awarded it $2.6 million.[343] The FEMA officer determined that no progress had been made on any of them – including what may have been the most fundamental: "Establish the DVIC facility and provide contractors and staff to operate the fusion center."[344] Three years and $11 million in obligations, yet the center did not exist.

"Milestones shows [sic] zero progress," the official noted in the 2009 monitoring report, but appeared to excuse the task force's inaction. "When the monitoring was conducted it was very early in the Grant cycle and the Grantees and Sub-recipients were in the process of ob[l]igating funds and initiating projects."[345] Despite finding no progress in 2009, FEMA continued to direct funding to the project in 2010 and 2011.[346]

In October 2011, a FEMA official conducted the next site visit to Philadelphia.[347] This monitoring visit took place five years after FEMA's initial grant to DVIC in 2006. By that time, the Commonwealth of Pennsylvania had frozen the FEMA grant funds it held that were intended for the center, because of concern that the local officials in charge of the project were planning to improperly spend millions in FEMA funding to refurbish and equip an old industrial building to house not only DVIC, but an even larger criminal intelligence center for the Philadelphia Police Department. FEMA grant guidance and federal law prohibit the use of grant funds for construction.[348] In addition, expenditures for non-fusion center needs would have gone against the task force's promises to use the funds exclusively for the fusion center.[349] State officials were so concerned they told SEPARTF that they would not reimburse any construction costs related to the DVIC until FEMA granted a waiver to do so.

FEMA officials were aware of these concerns at the time of the visit – indeed, according to state officials, FEMA shared their doubts.[350] Specifically, FEMA officials knew that project officials planned to use FEMA grant funds to pay for building renovations, which was explicitly barred by FEMA grant guidelines.[351] Just a few weeks earlier, local officials had written FEMA asking for an "immediate and favorable" decision to waive that restriction so that the project "may proceed along its current promised timeline."[352]

Despite local officials' efforts to get around FEMA spending restrictions and allocate millions of taxpayer dollars to disallowed construction and renovation costs, the FEMA monitoring report from the October 2011 visit contained no particular criticisms or sense of urgency regarding the fusion center. For instance, the report form asked: "During the course of the programmatic Site Visit, were there indicators of possible non-compliance with grant program requirements (e.g., unallowable expenditures) that should be brought to the financial analyst's attention?" The FEMA officer wrote, "No."[353]

As for progress, the official noted that work on the center was "not started," except for a segment of funds from a 2008 grant, which the official noted were "used for a temporary facility while the perm[a]n[e]nt DVIC is under construction." In that instance, the official recorded that "all investment activities" had been "completed."[354]

In February 2012, SEPARTF informed FEMA that it expected to use 2000 square feet of office space "for pre-operational activities related to establishment of the DVIC."[355] In August 2012, Pennsylvania officials told the Subcommittee they understand that SEPARTF had yet to hire any intelligence analysts.[356] To date, about $2.3 million of FEMA funds committed to the project have been spent.[357] The remainder of the grant funds has expired, been redirected to other projects, or remain unspent.[358] DHS continues to list DVIC as one of its officially recognized fusion centers in reports to Congress and public documents, even though after six years, the fusion center is not yet operational.[359]

FEMA's passivity in the face of years of questionable fusion center expenditures in Philadelphia is remarkable, but it is not exceptional. Fusion center grant recipients that have earned reputations among FEMA grant officials for poor spending practices typically face few consequences. FEMA officials told the Subcommittee that while they sometimes find instances of misspending, lax recordkeeping or other poor performance by grant recipients – on fusion centers and other projects – they almost never withhold funds.[360] In fact, FEMA officials could name only a few instances in which DHS withheld grant money from any grant recipient in any DHS program. In 2007, FEMA withheld grant funds from American Samoa in response to a major investigation into the misuse of millions in DHS grant funds for tsunami preparedness by the protectorate.[361] FEMA officials also indicated that they temporarily withheld funds from Pennsylvania and Texas that were to be used to support fusion center activities, because the states did not provide enough information in their applications about how the funds were going to be used.[362]

(2) A-133 Audits

The Office of Management and Budget (OMB) requires state, local and tribal governments who expend more than $500,000 in federal grant funds within a given fiscal year to audit their expenditure of those funds, as well as to conduct timely and effective oversight of any subgrantees' financial activities, through actions such as site visits.[363]

The process has long been problematic, as GAO and the President's Council on Integrity and Efficiency (PCIE) have reported.[364] The Subcommittee investigation reviewed A-133 audits of FEMA grant funds awarded to California, Arizona and Pennsylvania, and determined the audit reports did not follow a uniform reporting format, and often did not distinguish expenditures for fusion centers from other programs, rendering them useless for effective financial oversight of how state and local agencies spend federal grant dollars on fusion centers.

The difficulties experienced by the Subcommittee in using A-133 audit reports is consistent with broader concerns raised by earlier reviews of A-133s. In 2007, PCIE reported that nearly half of all A-133 audits were not adequate to meet the reporting requirements of the OMB circular – so much so that it considered them either wholly unacceptable or "limited in reliability." The council also pointed out that there has been no single federal entity responsible for monitoring compliance with the A-133 audit requirement, and agencies were not consistent in enforcing it.[365]

The A-133 audits conducted by California illustrate the problems. In 2009, the DHS Inspector General released its audit of the State of California's management of its State Homeland Security Program (SHSP) grants from 2004 to 2006. Among other findings, the DHS IG found that the state had failed to conduct any monitoring of the spending by its subgrantees until late 2005, and when it did, the review efforts were inadequate to provide "sufficient oversight" of the subgrantees' activities. Among other problems, nearly half of the subgrantees received no visits at all from state overseers, and the audits did not identify any procurement-related problems, although the IG's auditors found many. In fact, the IG found that "in an effort to improve operational efficiency," the state did not require subgrantees to give them any receipts, invoices or other documentation before disbursing federal grant funds to them.[366] Among its recommendations, the DHS IG informed California it should strengthen its site visits to subgrantees, and improve its financial oversight measures to ensure the subgrantees were spending federal grant funds "as intended." The state agreed to do so.[367]

In 2011, the DHS IG revisited the State of California's grant operations, this time to review its management of Urban Area Security Initiative (UASI) grants, another subset of FEMA's preparedness grants program. In its report, the IG noted the state was required by OMB Circular A-133 to monitor subgrantee spending through site visits and other means. It noted it had found an absence of meaningful financial oversight by California two years earlier. It noted the state of California had promised to improve its monitoring, including boosting its site visits, to comply with federal regulations.[368]

California officials told IG auditors they planned to initiate visits to subgrantees in three of the state's six urban areas receiving UASI funds from 2006 and 2007. The IG pointed out that left subgrantees in the other three areas unaffected, and held little promise of ensuring fiscal discipline, since nearly all of the 2006 and 2007 grant funds would have been spent and reimbursed by then.[369] The Subcommittee's review of Arizona and Pennsylvania A-133 audits were equally troubling, indicating these self-audits do not provide effective financial oversight of federal funds spent on fusion centers.

D. DHS Grant Requirements Do Not Ensure States Spend Fusion Center Funds Effectively

In administering its grant programs, DHS, through FEMA, outlines broad requirements for the types of activities that can be funded and equipment that can purchased. However, for several years DHS made no attempt at ensuring state expenditures on fusion centers addressed gaps in the centers' information-sharing capabilities. Recently, FEMA has made changes intended to make sure states and cities use FEMA grant dollars for fusion centers to improve these abilities, but those efforts still fall short of meaningful reform.

Before 2011, FEMA grant recipients faced few requirements on how they used grant funds for fusion center projects, beyond the general FEMA guidelines governing all preparedness grant projects. In 2011, FEMA and I&A instituted new procedures intended to better align FEMA grant funds with I&A priorities.[370]

To begin with, I&A initiated what are intended to be annual assessments of each fusion center, measuring each facility's key capabilities, a list of attributes which includes having an approved privacy policy, information-sharing policies, governance plans, analyst training, and more.[371]

In addition, beginning in 2011, FEMA required all states and cities to submit a project document known as an Investment Justification (IJ), in which they would describe how they planned to spend FEMA funds on their fusion centers.[372] FEMA asked recipients to use the IJ to show how they would use DHS grant money to address any weaknesses which had been noted by DHS assessments.[373]

When FEMA received the IJs from the states and cities, it shared them with officials at I&A.[374] I&A officials reviewed the IJs for each fusion center against their assessment of that center, to ensure that the recipient planned to use its grant funds to address the capability gaps I&A assessors had identified at the center.[375]

While this new procedure represents a significant improvement over past practice, the Subcommittee investigation identified three issues which weaken its effectiveness.

First, the new system does not ensure that federal funds are spent on federal priorities. While I&A reviews the submitted proposals to ensure FEMA recipients say they will use their funds to address identified weaknesses at each fusion center, DHS does not require that a significant portion of the federal grant funds it awards for fusion centers be directed towards eliminating those weaknesses. In a hypothetical situation, a state could indicate it was spending $300,000 to address a particular weakness, and another $2 million to buy unrelated equipment such as emergency response vehicles or wiretapping devices, or even to defray overhead costs, without demonstrating steps to achieve the "must-have" capabilities required by DHS.[376] Allowing fusion center expenditures for unrelated purposes significantly weakens FEMA's ability to ensure that federal funds for fusion centers are devoted to achieving federal priorities at those centers.[377]

Second, recipients of FEMA grant funds are under little obligation to follow through on commitments made in their Investment Justifications. FEMA gives preparedness grant recipients wide latitude to change their minds about spending priorities even after receiving grant funds. According to FEMA officials, recipients and their subgrantees are allowed to reprogram funds from one purpose to another without necessarily obtaining consent or notifying FEMA in advance.[378] This latitude makes it possible for states and cities to report intentions to shore up key weakness at a fusion center, but after receiving the funds, spend them on other purposes.

Third, no one at FEMA or I&A appears to be charged with ensuring that states and cities in fact, spend their fusion center funds on the commitments made in their IJs. When the Subcommittee asked FEMA officials who was in charge of checking to see if states were actually using funds as promised to address their identified weaknesses, FEMA said that the task fell to I&A.[379] When asked what role it played in overseeing states' and cities' spending federal dollars on fusion centers, I&A officials told the Subcommittee that they conducted no such oversight. "[I&A has] no role whatsoever in oversight," Joel Cohen, a senior I&A official, told Subcommittee. "It's true across the board .... We do not monitor [spending]. We do not provide oversight, we do not provide monitoring."[380] He indicated that was FEMA's responsibility, and added that FEMA coordinated its oversight efforts with I&A "all the time."[381]

To test the effectiveness of DHS and FEMA oversight practices, the Subcommittee reviewed spending by FEMA recipients and subgrantees at five fusion centers. At each, the Subcommittee investigation found significant instances in which state and local agencies spent federal dollars meant to improve fusion center capabilities on items that did little to achieve those improvements or were not used by the centers at all. Although all of the cases occurred before FEMA and I&A had implemented the new 2011 IJ review process for fusion centers, FEMA indicated all of the expenditures listed below appeared to be allowable under current rules.[382]

(1) Using Fusion Center Funds on Chevrolet Tahoes

In April 2008, the Arizona Department of Public Safety (AZDPS) bought a new Chevrolet Tahoe sport utility vehicle (SUV) using over $33,500 in DHS grant funds meant to enhance the capabilities of the Arizona Counter Terrorism Information Center (ACTIC), the state's fusion center. Specifically, the funds were intended to support Arizona's Terrorism Liaison Officers (TLO) Program, which is run by the ACTIC.[383] TLOs are specially trained law enforcement officers whose role is to, among other things, "relay terrorism related information and intelligence efficiently and appropriately between the ACTIC and field resources."[384]

For a law enforcement terrorism prevention grant FEMA awarded AZDPS in October 2007, the state indicated the funds would be used to purchase equipment, including a vehicle, for TLOs outside of the Phoenix area to respond to chemical, biological, radiological, nuclear, and explosive (CBRNE) incidents.[385] In accordance with the grant, a few months later, AZDPS provided the vehicle to the Flagstaff Fire Department for use by a city fire official designated as a TLO, under an agreement to "enhance domestic preparedness [CBRNE] response services concerning the activities of terrorism[.]"[386] DHS does not consider responding to CBRNE events, however, an essential fusion center capability.[387]

Moreover, according to Arizona records for the truck, the vehicle does not appear to qualify as a satisfactory CBRNE response vehicle: it is not equipped to respond to a zone affected by most types of CBRNE incidents, despite the award of an additional $9,400 in fusion center grant funds the state spent to install aftermarket equipment on the truck.[388] The state equipped the vehicle with lights, flashers, a siren and public address microphone, an anti-theft device, a notebook holder, computer mount, external cup holder, reinforced bumper, and a rear compartment partition, among other items.[389]

The only specialized equipment related to CBRNE accompanying the vehicle was a radiation-detecting dosimeter. The device can identify exposure to radiation, but offers no protection against it. The city official to whom the vehicle was assigned told the Subcommittee he keeps the truck at his house and uses it primarily to commute between his home and the Flagstaff Fire Department.[390]

A year later, in October 2009, Arizona purchased and outfitted a second Chevrolet Tahoe SUV with DHS funds that were likewise intended to support ACTIC, again claiming it to be a CBRNE response vehicle. The state used about $47,000 in Urban Area Security Initiative (UASI) funds, and gave the truck to the Arizona State University Police Department (ASUPD).[391] The vehicle was assigned to a K-9 officer who was designated as a TLO. The vehicle was outfitted to serve as a police K-9 unit vehicle, with a kennel, heat alarm system, lights and sirens, radios, a patrol rifle, chemical protective gear, a gas mask, a GPS unit, a ballistic helmet and vest, and training equipment for the dog.[392]

The dog is trained and equipped only to detect conventional explosives, according to his handler. The officer told the Subcommittee that he was trained and equipped to respond to several kinds of CBRNE incidents.[393] While enhancing CBRNE response is a legitimate use of FEMA grant funds, CBRNE response is not a baseline capability DHS expects of state and local fusion centers.

(2) Using Fusion Center Funds on Rent

From 2009 to 2011, Arizona used $1.98 million in FEMA grant funds to lease space for the ACTIC fusion center.[394] That amount covered the entire cost of ACTIC's lease from August 2009 to August 2011, which ran roughly $80,000 a month.[395] In interviews, FEMA stated that although its guidelines appear not to allow this use of DHS funds, it allowed the expenditures anyway. Such spending did little, if anything, to help the Arizona center address significant weaknesses in its ability to receive, analyze and share terrorism threat-related information with the federal government.

Before using FEMA funds to make payments on ACTIC's lease, an Arizona official queried FEMA about the allowability of the expenditure. The official's response indicates FEMA's guidelines are not rigidly enforced.

The Arizona official sent a February 2009 email to FEMA asking: "Can we reimburse rent for a fusion center?" A DHS official responded: "[A]llowable (M&A [Management and Administration]) costs can pay for the *leasing or renting* of space for newly hired personnel. And since new people will be hired during the period of this grant -you should have no problem with it."[396]

The Arizona official replied, noting that the expenses in question were not "M&A" expenses which are normally confined to costs for administering FEMA grants within the state. FEMA restricts grant recipients from using any but a very small portion of their funding on management and administration expenses, which might include overhead costs such as lease payments, office equipment, and administrative salaries.[397] "This would be under Organizational not M&A," the Arizona official wrote. "M&A is only allowable to 3% [of the grant] and these funds are used to support the direct administration of all grants (funds the AZDOHS office)."[398]

"Organizational, yes," the DHS official responded.[399]

Still apparently unsure, the Arizona official wrote again. "Thank you for your response, if I understand you correctly. AZDOHS [may] fund the fusion center rent with HSGP FY09 funds in the category of Organizational and not impact M&A funds?"[400]

"yes," the DHS official responded.[401]

FEMA grant guidance for the period indicates that rent or lease payments are allowed as organizational expenses, if it is "for leasing or renting of space for newly hired personnel during the period of performance of the grant program."[402] As such, rent or lease payments for space *not* intended for new personnel would not be allowed. However, that is how Arizona applied the funds: to pay for not only some percentage of ACTIC's lease to house new employees, but to cover ACTIC's entire lease, a cost of nearly $1 million a year.

Appearing to contradict their own guidelines, FEMA officials interviewed by the Subcommittee stated that they have approved using grant funds to cover fusion center lease payments several times. "There was a policy decision within our office, I know anecdotally we've allowed it many times in the past," FEMA's Matthew Bower told the Subcommittee.[403] FEMA provided the Subcommittee with a list of states it had allowed to use grant funds this way, but was unable to provide any documentation memorializing the policy decision to allow grant funds to reimburse lease costs, or informing other grant recipients of the change.[404]

When asked how and why FEMA allows federal grant funds to cover such a basic cost as rent for a fusion center, Elizabeth Harman, FEMA's grants chief, said she was "not well-versed on the rent issue." Ms. Harman noted that FEMA has "given [recipients] a lot of flexibility in how these grant dollars are spent."[405] Allowing fusion centers to use DHS funds to cover rental expenses, which are often substantial, necessarily reduces the funds available to develop baseline counterterrorism capabilities.

(3) Using Fusion Center Funds on Wiretap Room

In 2009, AZDOHS awarded the state's Department of Public Safety $105,112 under a DHS grant program for urban areas[406] to support IT infrastructure at ACTIC.[407] Officials from the fusion center told the Subcommittee and related documents indicate that roughly $64,000 of that total was used to purchase equipment for a surveillance monitoring room at the ACTIC fusion center.[408]

The money purchased software, a new laptop, two monitors and two 42" flat screen televisions.[409] Some of the funds were also used to send an employee to receive training related to surveillance technology, according to an Arizona official.[410] The monitoring room, which ACTIC officials referred to as "the wire room," is used for criminal investigations.[411]

As a state-run fusion center, it is the state of Arizona's prerogative to house criminal investigative resources within the fusion center. However, federal guidelines for fusion center key capabilities do not include covert or surreptitious intelligence gathering.[412] Indeed, fusion center capabilities used in DHS assessments relate to the ability to receive, analyze, and share information, not gather it. Nevertheless, FEMA approved the expenditures for ACTIC.

In all three of these cases, the state of Arizona acted in accordance with FEMA rules and guidelines. The use of DHS grant funds to purchase CBRNE response vehicles, surveillance equipment, and to cover rent costs are allowable under the grant program.

But DHS does not consider CBRNE response to be a baseline capability for fusion centers. Likewise, DHS does not consider surveillance to be a fusion center capability. Rental costs also do not address the counterterrorism baseline capabilities every fusion center is supposed to possess. The questioned purchases do not directly boost the center's needed capabilities; and no DHS rule or guideline currently encourages Arizona to focus its spending on those counterterrorism information-sharing priorities.

At the time these expenditures were made, ACTIC had a catalog of weaknesses inhibiting its participation in sharing terrorism threat information with the federal government. A 2010 assessment of the center on behalf of DHS concluded the center had no system for gathering, processing, collating and storing information; it had no analytic production plan; it had no training plan for analysts "that adheres to nationally-recommended standards;" it had no staffing plan or continuity of operations plan; and at the time, it had no privacy policy nor a way to be sure all personnel received privacy training.[413] In the most recent federal assessment of ACTIC in 2011, DHS found the center still lacked 14 out of 50 attributes needed to achieve minimal functionality as a fusion center contributing to federal counterterrorism efforts.[414]

(4) Using Fusion Centers Funds on Computers for County Medical Examiner

Another example of questionable fusion center spending involved the procurement of specialized computers. In Cleveland, Ohio, officials used $15,848 in 2007 FEMA grant funds for the Northeast Ohio Regional Fusion Center (NEORFC) to buy ruggedized Toughbook laptop computers.[415] In response to a Subcommittee inquiry, County officials reported the laptops were not located at the fusion center, but at the county medical examiner's office.[416]

When asked why laptops intended for the fusion center were located at the medical examiner's office, a Cuyahoga County official responded the that laptops were for processing human remains in the aftermath of a mass casualty event in the Cleveland area. The official stated his region had not experienced such an event.[417]

When asked how the purchase of the computers would benefit the fusion center and could be portrayed as a fusion center expenditure, the official said he assumed that in the aftermath of a mass casualty event, information about the human remains would have "intelligence value." He said he did not know whether the laptops were able to connect and securely transmit information to the fusion center.

In 2010, a capabilities assessment of NEORFC conducted on behalf of DHS concluded the center was all but completely incapable of functioning as a fusion center. "The center is lacking in its ability to process, collate, or disseminate information . . . . Based on [its] self-assessment, the Northeast Ohio Regional Fusion Center (NEORFC) appears to be struggling. [T]he center exhibits limited capability to support the intelligence cycle . . . . Limited personnel, few documented processes or plans . . . hinder the ability to achieve baseline capabilities . . . . [T]here is limited capability to process or disseminate information collected."[418]

When asked about the computer purchase, FEMA's Matthew Bower said, "[T]his would jump out to me as well. I can't give you a full answer." Mr. Bower noted that FEMA does not review purchases at the subgrantee level, rather relying on the state administrative agencies' to do so, so the agency was likely unaware of the purchase.[419]

(5) Using Fusion Center Funds for Surveillance Equipment, Computers, Televisions

In 2011, the San Diego area's fusion center, known as the Law Enforcement Coordination Center (SD-LECC), spent $25,000 on high-tech surveillance equipment, most of which was so sophisticated it eventually returned it for simpler devices.[420] This purchase was made, despite the fact that federal guidelines for fusion center key capabilities do not include covert or surreptitious intelligence gathering.[421]

SD-LECC used FEMA grant funds to make the following purchases:

- a covert, wireless audio/video recorder with a "shirt-button camera";
- an ultra-low-light "pinhole" VGA camera; and

- an ultra-low-light shirt-button camera "with interchangeable tops."[422]

In a document provided to the Subcommittee, SD-LECC officials stated that the center returned some of the equipment after it was deemed "simply too complicated for our customers to use."[423] In their place, the fusion center received other undercover surveillance devices, including a camera hidden in a hat and one disguised as a water bottle.[424] It is unclear how the San Diego fusion center's use of federal grant funds to buy surveillance equipment assisted the primary mission of DHS's fusion center effort. Nevertheless, the purchases were allowable under FEMA guidelines.

When asked if the surveillance equipment purchases, such as a shirt-button camera, raised concerns for him, Mr. Bower, head of FEMA's Risk Analytics and Strategic Initiatives Branch, told the Subcommittee he would "need to know the exact use of that equipment."[425] Mr. Bower noted that FEMA officials "don't review every piece of equipment that's purchased," but that was actually a strength of the agency's approach. "It's on purpose," Mr. Bower explained. "Asking for every single widget . . . isn't furthering the success of these grantees."[426]

The San Diego fusion center also spent nearly $200,000 on 116 computers, monitors, and related equipment.[427] Asked how 30 full-time employees used over 100 computers, SD-LECC officials told Subcommittee investigators that not all of the computers were for fusion center personnel; some were used by other law enforcement personnel to access the same network. The officials explained that some of the computers were not even located in the fusion center.[428] To justify the purchases, officials told Subcommittee staff that the computers could be used to share "case data" and "statistical data" with the fusion center.[429]

The San Diego center also spent nearly $75,000 on 55 flat-screen televisions. However, the intelligence training program they were meant to facilitate was never purchased.[430] When asked what the televisions were being used for, officials said they displayed calendars, and were used for "open-source monitoring." Asked to define "open-source monitoring," SD-LECC officials said they meant "watching the news."[431]

Officials responsible for the fusion center told the Subcommittee they now view the televisions as "a huge mistake," and stated the former fusion center director who authorized the purchase was "relieved of his duties."[432]

An October 2010 "baseline capabilities assessment" on behalf of DHS found a number of weaknesses at SD-LECC, ranking them below the national average in 9 of 12 capabilities.[433] Among other weaknesses, assessors noted the absence of memoranda of understanding and/or non-disclosure agreements with agencies who participate in the center; the absence of "a procedure manual that outlines privacy, physical security, and information security policies;" the absence of a list of "data sources and repositories necessary to conduct analysis;" and the absence of "a mechanism to receive stakeholder feedback."[434]

(6) Using Fusion Center Funds for Shifting Information Technology Needs

In some cases, state or regional grant recipients may substantially revise their stated intentions to spend funds requested on behalf of fusion centers. Consider, for example, the shifting descriptions and justifications associated with one project managed by the Washington, D.C. Homeland Security and Emergency Management Agency (HSEMA), which oversees the city's fusion center.

Early in 2008, the D.C. Metropolitan Police Department submitted an initial proposal to HSEMA requesting $725,000 for a project entitled, "Information Technology (Data Mining, Analytical Software)." The proposal provided no indication that the project was associated with a fusion center, nor did it identify any specific items that were to be purchased.[435]

Subsequently, HSEMA included this project in a broader application to FEMA for grant funding in 2008. In its application materials, HSEMA told FEMA it wanted to use $2.7 million Homeland Security grant funds on an effort that would enhance the capabilities of the police department as well as "the information and intelligence gathering and analysis capabilities of the D.C. Intelligence Fusion Center."[436] Specifically, the effort was to include an upgraded electronic records management system, data mining software, and an Automated License Plate Recognition system (LPR system). The city's description of how the data mining software was to be used noted that "installing improved analytical and data mining tools and training analysts to use them effectively will improve the quality of final intelligence products" and "will bolster the DC Intelligence Fusion Center analysts' ability to identify trends, track patterns, and generate quality analytical products."[437]

After receiving its allocation of grant funding from FEMA, D.C. HSEMA awarded a subgrant to the D.C. Metropolitan Police Department (MPD) in October 2008, worth $700,000 for the project, referred to in the grant document as "Analytical & Data Mining Software – Fusion Center."[438] In addition, the project as described in the award agreement documentation had changed. It included a records management system upgrade at a cost of $100,000, and "analytical software" at a cost of $90,000. The LPR system was dropped, though it may have been included in another DHS subgrant. The project also added for the first time sophisticated cell phone tracking devices, and "handheld citation issuance units and accessories." Those new items seem to be outside the scope of DHS-recognized key capabilities for a fusion center, yet their cost, $510,000, became the largest portion of the project.[439] Also of significance is that none of the $700,000 in funds was designated for the D.C. fusion center; instead, the sole named recipient was now the D.C. police department.

The grant award changes did not end there. In July 2010, the police department again altered the description, nearly two years after the subgrant was awarded. It updated the project plan to indicate that the records management system would now cost $376,070; the cell phone tracking tools and service would cost $266,000; and the remaining funds would now be used to purchase Closed Circuit television (CCTV) download kits for $12,250, and Liquid Crystal Display (LCD) "Status Boards" for $45,680. [440]

By the time the grant funds were actually spent in 2010, purchase orders and invoices reviewed by the Subcommittee indicate further changes to the cost of some items, and to what was purchased. It bought the records management system for $409,818, and the cell phone tracking and surveillance system for $260,935. Rather than purchase the CCTV download kits or LCD status boards, the police department spent $11,958 to purchase two Panasonic laptops; $5,552 to purchase six Dell computer towers; and $11,735 to pay fees to cellular providers.[441] Again, none of the equipment was destined for the D.C. fusion center.

HSEMA officials told the Subcommittee on multiple occasions that the funding associated with this subgrant was not used to support the D.C. fusion center, despite the original written justification HSEMA provided to FEMA to support the grant.[442] When asked about this series of events, Mr. Bower of FEMA noted that, as long as the equipment ultimately purchased using DHS grant funds is considered allowable under the grant guidelines, then states are allowed to purchase equipment that may differ from what is indicated in their initial Investment Justifications and may allocate it to an entity other than the one originally identified. Furthermore, states can exercise discretion in determining whether a proposed change merits requesting new approval from FEMA.[443]

When DHS and FEMA grant procedures allow grant recipients to change the identified subgrantee, the items to be purchased, the amounts to be spent, and the ultimate use of the purchased equipment, it is clearer why DHS and FEMA are unable to accurately track the taxpayer dollars actually awarded to or used by fusion centers. The loose rules render effective financial oversight of fusion center difficult, if not impossible.

VI. Fusion Centers Have been Unable to Meaningfully Contribute to Federal Counter Terrorism Efforts

- Two federal assessments found fusion centers lack basic counter terrorism capabilities.
- Despite promises, DHS has not assessed fusion center performance.
- Some DHS-recognized fusion centers do not exist.
- Many fusion centers do not prioritize counterterrorism efforts.
- DHS "Success Stories" do not demonstrate centers' value to counterterrorism efforts.
- Fusion centers may have hindered, not aided, some federal counterterrorism efforts.

A. Overview

The Department of Homeland Security has directed hundreds of millions of dollars to support and strengthen the capabilities of state and local fusion centers. DHS officials have spoken publicly about the centers' key role in assisting federal officials' fight against terrorism. Yet the centers themselves have fallen short of developing the capabilities necessary to meaningfully contribute to the federal counterterrorism mission.

"We have established programs that facilitate a strong, two-way flow of threat-related information, where SLTT [State, Local, Tribal and Territorial] officials communicate possible threat information to federal officials, and vice-versa," DHS Secretary Janet Napolitano said in testimony before the Senate Homeland Security and Governmental Affairs Committee in September 2010.[444] "[P]re-operational activity – such as target selection, reconnaissance, and dry runs – occur over a very short time period, or in open and crowded places.

Informing federal authorities . . . increase[es] the likelihood that an attack can be thwarted . . . . The nation's fusion centers have been a hub of these efforts, combined with other initiatives DHS has instituted to better partner with SLTT law enforcement."[445]

DHS has struggled to identify a clear example in which a fusion center provided intelligence which helped disrupt a terrorist plot, even as local and federal law enforcement have thwarted dozens of terrorist attacks on U.S. soil and against U.S. interests in the past decade.[446] In some cases, fusion centers' analytical efforts have instead caused frustration and embarrassment for themselves and DHS.

In four success stories that DHS identified, the Subcommittee investigation was unable to confirm that the fusion centers' contributions were as significant as DHS portrayed them;

were unique to the intelligence and analytical work expected of fusion centers; or would not have occurred absent a fusion center. In addition, two recent national assessments conducted by and for DHS found fusion centers often lacked one or more basic capabilities necessary to do the work expected of them, to share information which could help detect and disrupt terrorist plots against the United States. These assessments, conducted in 2010 and 2011, found weaknesses at most fusion centers they examined, from having insufficiently trained intelligence personnel, to having inadequate physical security, to an inability to distribute alert and warning information to state and local agencies, and an inability to effectively share appropriate information with the federal government or local partners.[447]

Each fusion center is different, and neither assessment indicated a sole reason the centers had not yet developed the necessary capabilities to contribute to the federal counterterrorism mission. However, neither assessment found a center which had developed all of the basic necessary capabilities to participate in federal counterterrorism intelligence efforts.[448]

As noted earlier, some fusion centers have gone years without a physical presence and without filing any intelligence reports. Others have operated for years without having DHS personnel on site to report counterterrorism information, effectively cutting the centers off from the larger DHS terrorism-related intelligence efforts.[449] Still other fusion centers have had DHS personnel on site, but have produced information of little value for federal counterterrorism intelligence efforts.[450] As well, many of the fusion centers have not made counterterrorism an explicit priority, and some have de-emphasized counterterrorism in favor of more traditional public safety and anti-crime work.

Despite these challenges, senior DHS officials have continued to claim that state and local fusion centers have made significant contributions to its counterterrorism efforts, and cited specific "success stories" which they claim demonstrate the centers' value. The Subcommittee examined four such cases in which DHS claimed fusion centers made important or "key" contributions to investigations of significant terrorist plots on U.S. soil.

The Subcommittee investigation found that the claims made by DHS did not always fit the facts, and in no case did a fusion center make a clear and unique intelligence contribution that helped apprehend a terrorist or disrupt a plot. Worse, three other incidents examined by the Subcommittee investigation raised significant concerns about the utility of the fusion centers, and raised the possibility that some centers have actually hindered or sidetracked federal counterterrorism efforts.

Federal officials have been well aware of these episodes, and the underlying weaknesses in fusion centers' capabilities that likely contributed to them. But they have chosen not to highlight the considerable shortcomings of fusion centers in public appearances or in briefings to Congress. Instead they have chosen to portray fusion centers as "linchpins" of the federal government's fight to prevent terrorism, making "vital" contributions to the federal government's efforts to keep the country safe from another terrorist attack. This portrayal is simply at odds with the actual counterterrorism records of the fusion centers.

B. Two Federal Assessments Found Fusion Centers Lack Basic Counterterrorism Capabilities

Two comprehensive assessments of fusion centers by or at the request of DHS, completed in 2010 and 2011, found widespread deficiencies in fusion centers' basic capabilities to properly collect, analyze, and share intelligence on homeland security threats.[451]

(1) 2010 Assessment

In 2010, seven years after DHS had begun funding state and local fusion centers, the Department's Office of Intelligence and Analysis (I&A) asked the Program Manager for the Information Sharing Environment (PM-ISE), a part of the Office of the Director of National Intelligence (ODNI), to lead an interagency team in conducting a nationwide assessment of state and local fusion centers.[452]

The assessment was carried out in two parts. First, PM-ISE asked fusion centers to complete a rigorous, 380-question self-assessment questionnaire. The questions were based on a set of eight "baseline capabilities" which had been identified by DHS, the Department of Justice, and a panel of fusion center experts. These eight baseline capabilities represented the "necessary capabilities required to support federal counterterrorism mission requirements."[453]

Second, teams of federal intelligence experts fanned out across the nation to visit fusion centers and validate whether each possessed the capabilities their officials claimed in their self-assessment responses. PM-ISE reported that although DHS publicly claimed to recognize 72 operational fusion centers at the time of the assessment, three were "not functional at a level to receive a visit," and one "was not operational" at all.[454] On-site visits were, thus, made to 68 fusion centers.

The "baseline capabilities" the assessors examined were precisely that: basic, minimum standards of functionality necessary to effective intelligence sharing. As the officials who identified the capabilities in 2008 wrote, "By achieving this baseline level of capability, a fusion center will have the necessary structures, processes, and tools in place to support the gathering, processing, analysis, and dissemination of terrorism, homeland security, and law enforcement information."[455]

The final 2010 assessment report was about 140 pages long. Supporting documents included an individual assessment of each of the 68 fusion centers then in operation. The final report found that a third of fusion centers had no defined procedures for sharing information gathered outside of their walls, one of the prime reasons for their existence. It found that more than half of all fusion centers lacked procedures for receiving and sharing with partner agencies information on threats received from DHS and other federal agencies. And "most" fusion centers told the assessors that their intelligence and analytical responsibilities were designed to assist with response and recovery efforts after a major event or attack,[456] not to prevent one, inverting the notion of what many perceive to be the primary purpose of the fusion centers.

The 2010 assessment concluded that most fusion centers not only lacked the minimum capabilities to function effectively, they also lacked plans showing how they would develop those capabilities. It also concluded that two-thirds of fusion centers had no way to assess the return on investment taxpayers received for funding their operations.[457]

Finally, the 2010 assessment criticized the federal government for failing to have adequately "defined and articulated" the capabilities it expected of the fusion centers in order to support federal missions, and for lacking a budget that detailed how it planned to fund fusion center efforts to "develop, deploy, and sustain these capabilities."[458]

DHS did not make any of these findings public or share them with Congress. Moreover, when the Subcommittee requested access to the findings of the 2010 assessment, DHS initially denied such a report existed. Then, after the assessment report was identified internally, DHS resisted turning it over to the Subcommittee. Some DHS officials contended that, although the Subcommittee had requested all fusion center analyses "produced within DHS," technically the assessment had been conducted at the request of DHS by another federal office, and therefore had not been literally "produced within DHS."[459]

In June 2011, during the course of an interview, a senior DHS intelligence official presented a copy of the national 2010 assessment to the Subcommittee, unaware that the Department had maintained to the Subcommittee no such document could be located.[460] DHS officials at the interview declined to leave that copy of the report with the Subcommittee, saying they needed time to resolve their concerns about agreements of confidentiality allegedly made with fusion centers. Those agreements, the officials stated, prohibited the Department from sharing the report with Congress.[461]

When the Subcommittee requested copies of those agreements, DHS responded that they were oral "assurances."[462] When the Subcommittee asked who made the agreements, DHS said they were made by PM-ISE officials.

PM-ISE officials interviewed by the Subcommittee said they did not recall any such agreements. Upon review of its records, PM-ISE determined that it may have made certain assurances in 2009 during a pilot study that preceded the baseline assessment. "[I]t appears that, in conducting the pilot study in 2009, PM-ISE made this point and stated that information would be treated as sensitive and not further disseminated without further consultation," PM-ISE stated. "It is not clear if similar assurances were given in 2010, but this appears likely as the same considerations . . . were present, and as a result, confidentiality was important to achieving the goals of the assessment."[463]

DHS eventually produced the "report cards" on individual fusion centers and the final 2010 assessment report to the Subcommittee after obtaining "consent" from a private, non-governmental organization, the National Fusion Center Association (NFCA), which supposedly had the authority to represent the 68 fusion centers subject to review. In a letter to the Subcommittee, NFCA explained it had "authorized" DHS to share the assessment information with Congress.[464]

NFCA, a private organization led by a former senior DHS grants official, advocates for increased federal funding for state and local fusion centers.[465] It is funded by corporations who seek to do business with fusion centers.[466] It is not a membership organization, but the group purports to represent all DHS-recognized fusion centers, and invites them to help elect its board of directors.[467]

In an interview with the Subcommittee, the group's director, W. Ross Ashley III, said he no longer stood by the language in his letter. "Maybe the term 'authorized release' wasn't appropriate," he said, calling his phrasing "a little boisterous on our part."[468]

(2) 2011 Assessment

In 2011, DHS did not request PM-ISE to repeat its fusion center baseline capability assessment. Instead, DHS itself assumed responsibility for conducting a nationwide fusion center assessment. Deeming the 2010 assessment "too exhaustive" and "almost irrelevant," DHS narrowed the assessment criteria to checking for 55 "attributes" which it believed composed the eight previously-defined capabilities, down from the 380 items examined in the 2010 assessment.[469]

Like the 2010 assessment, DHS asked fusion center directors to complete an online self-assessment, as well as provide data on staff, budget and operational costs.[470]

After that information was submitted, "validation teams" of personnel from DHS and other federal agencies reviewed the self-assessment data to "identify submission errors and inconsistencies and to minimize data discrepancies."[471] DHS noted later that the centers "provided inconsistent levels of detail in their responses on the 2011 assessment and in some cases provided incomplete responses."[472]

Unlike the 2010 assessment, the DHS teams did not visit the centers themselves to validate the answers were accurate, but instead conducted "structured telephone interviews" with fusion center officials.[473] During these calls DHS says the teams discussed the "identified issues" and gathered additional information.[474] After the data was "validated," DHS prepared individual reports for each fusion center, scoring each center on the basis of how many attributes it possessed.[475]

After DHS officials completed the scoring process, they realized that five of the minimum attributes they had defined related to having personnel who had attended trainings that DHS did not yet offer, including one training which was to be on a network portal that DHS had not yet created.[476] In other words, DHS's lack of training and technology offerings was itself responsible for fusion centers' inability to achieve five of the attributes DHS considered essential to have minimal operational capability.[477] To remedy the situation, DHS cut those five attributes from its list.[478]

Even with its more limited review, DHS still found weaknesses at state and local fusion centers. More than half lacked a strategic plan, and nearly as many lacked a communications plan. Nearly a third had no analytic production plan.[479] "For the National Network to fulfill its potential as a fully integrated participant in the National Information Sharing Environment . . . individual fusion centers must further develop and institutionalize their capabilities and facilitate interconnectivity," the report concluded.[480]

Due to the new design of the 2011 DHS assessment, its findings were largely non-comparable to the 2010 assessment conducted by PM-ISE. Therefore, it was generally not possible to measure progress made between the PM-ISE's 2010 findings and DHS's 2011 findings.[481] Nevertheless, DHS concluded its report by stating that "fusion centers made notable progress in developing their capabilities." However, it added, "significant work still remains."[482]

C. Despite Promises, DHS Has Not Assessed Fusion Center Performance

DHS has repeatedly committed itself to assessing not only fusion centers' capabilities, but also their performance. While the 2010 and 2011 assessments purported to examine what fusion centers were capable of, DHS committed to but has never attempted assessing fusion centers' actual contributions.

In a presentation to Congressional oversight staff in October 2011, DHS stated it had been working since September 2010 to develop "a fusion center performance management program, called the Fusion Center Performance Program (FCPP)."[483] That program, the presentation claimed, would use "a single, integrated, data-driven process" to measure the performance of fusion centers; the national network of fusion centers; and federal support for fusion centers. In February 2012, DHS I&A personnel went further, telling House and Senate staff that they were "implementing a Fusion Center Performance Program."[484]

When the Subcommittee sought detailed information about the FCPP, however, DHS admitted that no such program currently exists. In a July 2012 interview with Joel Cohen, the DHS official who oversaw the 2011 fusion center assessment process, he identified himself as the DHS official in charge of the FCPP.

In the interview, Mr. Cohen first described the FCPP as "a variety of projects and initiatives."[485] Asked to elaborate, Mr. Cohen stated that the assessment process was "the centerpiece."[486] There was also "an exercise component," he said, that would demonstrate whether fusion centers had the capabilities they claimed; and "all the survey stuff."[487] The department was also developing performance measures, Mr. Cohen said.[488]

The Subcommittee requested a document outlining the FCPP. Mr. Cohen stated such a document did not exist. "A document is being developed," Mr. Cohen told the Subcommittee. "We're building the plane as we're flying it," he said.[489]

When asked about the performance measures he was developing, Mr. Cohen said that performance measures are "tough."[490] When asked to elaborate on the exercise component, Mr. Cohen said, "There is no fully-developed exercise component."[491] Mr. Cohen also told the Subcommittee that for the two years his office has purported to be working on the program, he has not had sufficient staff to make progress.[492]

D. Some DHS-Recognized Fusion Centers Do Not Exist

One of the ongoing troubling features of DHS's fusion center efforts involves nonfunctional fusion centers whose very existence is a matter of dispute. In its October 2010 report, the PM-ISE identified four fusion centers out of the 72 DHS counted that were "not functional at a level to receive a visit," and one which "was not operational" at all.[493] Despite that finding, DHS officials continued to publicly allege it was engaged with 72 fusion centers around the country.

"Today, we have a national network of 72 recognized fusion centers – one in every state and 22 in major urban areas – and, with Department of Homeland Security support, they are being woven into the national and homeland security fabric of the United States," then-Undersecretary for Intelligence and Analysis Bart Johnson wrote on the DHS website, in an October 25, 2010, essay entitled, "How Fusion Centers Help Keep America Safe."[494]

"Today, there are 72 state-and locally-run fusion centers in operation across the nation," DHS Secretary Napolitano told the House Homeland Security Committee in her February 2011 testimony.[495]

"Today, 72 recognized fusion centers serve as focal points for the receipt, analysis, gathering, and sharing of threat-related information among the federal government and state, local, tribal, territorial and private sector partners," Secretary Napolitano stated in separate testimony in September 2011 before the Senate Homeland Security and Governmental Affairs Committee[496.]

Asked why Secretary Napolitano and other DHS officials claimed the existence of four fusion centers its own assessment could not demonstrate, Undersecretary Wagner said, "My understanding was that they operated as virtual fusion centers." When it was noted that PM-

ISE found that they literally were non-functional – PM-ISE said three were "not functional at a level to receive a visit" and one was "not operational," Ms. Wagner said, "There was no intent to obfuscate. It just took some of them [fusion centers] longer than others to get there."[497]

The Subcommittee examined two fusion centers which DHS has alleged to exist and has said it officially recognized, but whose existence was disputed by local officials or documentation.

(1) Wyoming

Since 2009, DHS has counted among its officially recognized fusion centers an entity in Wyoming it has referred to as the Wyoming Fusion Center.[498] In September 2009, DHS reported to Congress that such a fusion center existed, and it intended to detail an intelligence official there.[499]

But just prior to that, in August 2009, FEMA officials issued an assessment of the state's progress on meeting goals associated with establishing a fusion center at "zero," or no progress, on any aspect of the effort.[500]

According to Wyoming state officials, their state has no fusion center and never intended to create one. "It confuses me," said Kebin Haller, Deputy Director for the state's Division of Criminal Investigation (DCI). They have a criminal intelligence center, he said, but "we've chosen not to refer to it as a fusion center." Neither have state officials formally designated it as a fusion center for DHS to recognize; they have not accepted DHS grant funds for the center, or participated in any DHS assessment, he said.[501]

Asked about DHS's claim to have placed a detailee at the center, Mr. Haller said, "We did have a DHS detailee, interestingly enough." DHS hired away one of the center's senior criminal analysts, Mr. Haller explained, "but they didn't really have the office space" to house him. Mr. Haller said DHS asked if it could leave its new hire in his old office at the Wyoming DCI. "We said sure, as long as we don't need that office space," Mr. Haller recalled. He said his division eventually needed the desk back, and DHS moved their employee to another state. Wyoming has neither requested nor received another detailee, Mr. Haller said.[502]

(2) Philadelphia Fusion Center

DHS has also counted among its recognized fusion centers the Delaware Valley Information Center (DVIC), which it locates in Philadelphia, Pennsylvania.[503] The department has indicated plans to assign a detailee to the center; [504] and since 2006, DHS has awarded millions of dollars in grant funds in support of the project.[505]

In response to a 2010 survey from the Subcommittee, however, Philadelphia officials stated the center did not yet exist.[506] They stated DVIC was to begin operations in December 2010. Five months later, during a May 2011 interview, however, officials in charge of the DVIC project informed the Subcommittee the center had still not yet opened.[507] Since then, the State of Pennsylvania has frozen DHS funds associated with the project.[508]

As of August 2012, the center still did not physically exist. Yet, in its most recent capability assessment report on fusion centers, DHS again lists DVIC as a recognized fusion center.[509]

DHS's insistence on listing fusion centers with no physical presence is not only puzzling, but raises questions about its entire assessment process.

E. Many Fusion Centers Do Not Prioritize Counterterrorism Efforts

The White House, Congress and DHS itself have described fusion centers as key tools for gathering, analyzing, and sharing information to prevent terrorist attacks. Indeed, in 2007, Congress indicated DHS should consider any fusion center's commitment to doing counterterrorism work before detailing personnel to work there.[510] However, the Subcommittee investigation found some centers do not make terrorism a priority among their many efforts.

The 2010 Subcommittee survey found that 25 of 62 responsive fusion centers, or more than one-third, did not mention terrorism in their mission statements. And the trend appeared to be moving in that direction: at least five fusion centers reported recently revising their mission statements in ways that emphasized public safety and anti-crime efforts, and diminished or removed mentions of counterterrorism.[511]

In an interview, a DHS official who helps oversee the Department's support for and engagement with fusion centers acknowledged that some centers were not interested in focusing on counterterrorism. "We have trouble getting smaller, less mature fusion centers to pay attention to things like counterterrorism analysis," said Joel Cohen, head of policy and planning for the DHS State and Local Program Office (SLPO). "They are more concerned with day-to-day crime."[512]

But the trend away from prioritizing counterterrorism efforts does not appear isolated to smaller, "less mature" fusion centers. Indeed, statewide fusion centers and fusion centers in major cities indicate that they emphasize anti-crime efforts and "all-hazards" missions over an explicit focus on counterterrorism.

For instance, The Michigan Intelligence Operations Center (MIOC) changed its mission statement from the following:

> The State of Michigan's Intelligence Operations Center shall collect, evaluate, collate, and analyze information and intelligence and then, as appropriate, disseminate this information and intelligence to the proper public safety agencies so that any threat of terrorism or criminal activity will be successfully identified and addressed.[513]
>
> to:
>
> To promote public safety by operating in a public-private partnership that collects, evaluates, analyzes, and disseminates information and intelligence in a timely and secure manner while protecting the privacy rights of the public.[514]

Similarly, the Nevada Threat Analysis Center (NTAC) once defined its mission with a stated emphasis on preventing terror:

> NTAC embraces a team effort of local, state, federal and tribal law enforcement, fire, health, and private sector stakeholders, in cooperation with the citizens of the state of Nevada, for the timely receipt, analysis, and dissemination of terrorism and criminal activity information relating to Nevada while ensuring the safety of its citizens and critical infrastructure.[515]

But as of August 2012, their mission statement read:

> NTAC embraces a team effort of local, state, federal, and tribal law enforcement, fire, health, and private sector stakeholders, in cooperation with the citizens of Nevada, for the timely receipt, analysis, and dissemination of criminal information while ensuring the safety and privacy rights of our citizens and critical infrastructure.[516]

These revisions reflect a general shift towards a so-called "all-crimes, all-hazards" approach. That trend was noted in a 2008 Congressional Research Service report which found fusion centers were broadening their missions to encompass all crimes and all hazards as a way to encourage participation from local agencies, qualify for a wider array of grant programs, and because other centers were doing it.[517]

CRS noted that the "all-crimes" approach to counterterrorism was premised on an assumption that would-be terrorists would commit precursor crimes before attempting an attack. But CRS officials questioned whether that was a valid assumption, and whether the broad "all-crimes" approach diverted fusion center efforts towards working on criminal and other matters that bore no connection to terrorism.[518]

"[O]ne can reasonably question if sophisticated terrorists, those who have received formal terrorism training from established international groups and may be planning catastrophic attacks, engage in criminal activity prior to, and in support of, a terrorist attack. Will following all criminal leads and terrorism tips lead to the disruption of sophisticated terrorist plots?" CRS asked.[519]

In fact, some fusion center officials from major jurisdictions have championed a focus on traditional criminal activity over terrorist plots. "Our end state is to prevent terrorism, but in my own community, right across the bay from San Francisco where I work, the City of Oakland, they've had 740 shootings to date," stated Ronald Brooks, director of the Northern California Regional Intelligence Center (NCRIC) in San Francisco, in a hearing before the Senate Homeland Security and Governmental Affairs Committee (HSGAC) in October 2011. "That's a city of 400,000. That's terror right there in our own community. And that kind of terror is one that's experienced in big cities and small towns across the country."[520]

Like many other centers, Mr. Brooks' center in Oakland makes no mention of terrorism in its mission statement. His "all-crimes" fusion center aims to "coordinate the exchange of criminal intelligence, threats, and hazards and facilitate regional communication among Northern California Law Enforcement, First Responders, Government and Private Sector Partners."[521] An official with the Washington (D.C.) Regional Threat and Analysis Center (WRTAC), whose region includes some of the nation's most inviting terrorist targets, sounded a similar note in a Subcommittee interview. The D.C. fusion center was focused on "crime, crime, crime," the official said. "The last I checked, terrorism was still a crime."[522]

WRTAC's mission statement initially included a mention of terrorism, stating the center was "the focal point for collection, integration, assessment, analysis, and dissemination of intelligence relating to terrorism, criminal activity and catastrophic events[.]" A revised mission statement omits any specific mention of terrorism, and commits the center to enhancing its partner agencies' "ability to detect credible threats to the region from all hazards and all crimes."[523]

Indeed, the PM-ISE's 2010 Baseline Capabilities Assessment of fusion centers found that terrorism was a low priority for most of them. "Most [fusion] centers focus on the priority mission of the law enforcement agency that owns/manages them; primarily analytical case support to drug, gang, and violent crime investigations for the geographic area of responsibility," the report stated. "As a result many centers struggle to build the necessary capabilities required to support federal counterterrorism mission requirements, specifically in the areas of intelligence analysis and information sharing beyond their jurisdictions."[524]

F. DHS "Success Stories" Do Not Demonstrate Centers' Value to Counterterrorism Efforts

On its web site, DHS has devoted a page to fusion center "success stories."[525] On that page, DHS includes many events unrelated to terrorism in a long list of fusion center "successes." DHS praises, for example, fusion center efforts that have helped to reduce automobile thefts, apprehend a man suspected of kidnapping and rape, and bust up a drug ring.[526]

While those anticrime successes are notable, they do not advance the DHS counterterrorism mission; they do not fulfill the promise federal officials made to Congress and the public that the significant taxpayer support directed to fusion centers would aid in the fight against terror; and they do not meet the expectations set by legislative and executive mandates which make clear both branches expected fusion centers to perform as conduits of terrorism information-sharing to and from the federal government.

To evaluate fusion centers' contributions to federal counterterrorism efforts, the Subcommittee asked DHS to provide its best examples of how fusion centers have made such contributions. In response, DHS provided a handful of examples, although only a few related to actual terrorist plots. The Subcommittee examined four of them. It was unable to confirm that the fusion centers contributions were as significant as DHS portrayed them; were unique to the intelligence and analytical work expected of fusion centers; or would not have occurred absent a fusion center.

(1) Najibullah Zazi Case– CIAC

On its website and in presentations to Congress, DHS has cited the contributions of the Colorado Information Analysis Center (CIAC) to the investigation into Najibullah Zazi, an admitted terrorist. In 2009, the 25-year-old Afghan immigrant traveled from Colorado to New York City, where he has admitted that he planned to blow himself up on the subway around the anniversary of the 9/11 attacks. The FBI learned of his intention and arrested Mr. Zazi on September 19.[527]

"[I]n the Zazi plot to bomb the New York subway, it was a fusion center near Denver that played the key role in 'fusing' the information that came from the public with evidence that came in following the suspect's arrest by the FBI," DHS Secretary Janet Napolitano stated in a September 2010 speech.[528]

The DHS website is more circumspect. "The CIAC provided analytic support to the Denver FBI and the Department of Homeland Security regarding the suspicious activity reported to the CIAC through the public website and 1-800 number," DHS states on its site. "CIAC provided personnel to assist the Denver FBI in the investigation and support the field operations. CIAC analysts also assisted in the review and analysis of the evidence obtained during the execution of the search and arrest warrants." The department also notes that CIAC officials "addressed media inquiries" about the investigation and the threats it involved.[529]

When the Subcommittee asked CIAC itself for a more detailed explanation of its role in the Zazi case, the center provided a four-page summary.[530] CIAC did not claim to have "played the key role" in "fusing" evidence from the case with information from the public.[531] The center summarized its analytical contributions as "assisting in open source and law enforcement research" by checking databases. CIAC personnel also "assisted in the review of the information obtained through search warrants," the center's summary stated.[532] Additionally, the Subcommittee confirmed, the center responded to media inquiries.

In its summary, CIAC explained that most of its contributions to the case came from state troopers who were assigned to the center. Of the 605 hours CIAC states its personnel dedicated to assisting the FBI in the Zazi case between September 9 and September 16, 2009, only 60 of those hours came from its analysts. Troopers did the rest, including 145 hours of analytical work and 400 hours of operational work, including vehicle stops and augmenting the Colorado Governor's security detail.[533] The trooper who accounted for CIAC's largest contribution to the investigation – 120 hours in a one-week period – was a state trooper who was part of the troopers' "CIAC unit," but was also assigned to the FBI Joint Terrorism Task Force (JTTF), which was handling the investigation, the center's director explained to the Subcommittee.[534]

This examination does not diminish Colorado officials' support of the FBI investigation into Najibullah Zazi. But it does indicate that much of the contribution attributed to CIAC came from state troopers, and could have – hopefully, would have – occurred absent a fusion center.

(2) Faisal Shahzad Case–NYSIC

On May 1, 2010, Faisal Shahzad attempted to detonate a car bomb in New York City's Times Square. Mr. Shahzad's attempt was foiled by alert street vendors, who noticed smoke coming from a parked vehicle and notified authorities. DHS Customs and Border Patrol agents apprehended Mr. Shahzad two days later on May 3, after he successfully boarded a commercial flight bound for Dubai, UAE. He eventually pled guilty to charges arising from the attempted attack.[535]

On its web site, DHS cites as a fusion center success the contributions made by the New York State Intelligence Center (NYSIC) in Latham, New York, to the FBI's Shahzad case.[536] The department's description omits a small detail, however, which has the effect of potentially mischaracterizing the value of the center's contribution.

"In New York, an alert AAA employee filed a SAR [Suspicious Activity Report] with the New York State Intelligence Center [(NYSIC)] regarding a call on May 2, 2010 – when Shahzad called for assistance because he had locked his keys inside the vehicle," DHS states on its web site.[537] While that information may have been useful in building the case against the would-be bomber, it neither helped disrupt his plans nor hastened his capture. According to NYSIC, it received the information from AAA on May 4, the day after Mr. Shahzad's dramatic airport arrest. The Department does not disclose that later date, allowing a reader to believe the information was shared by the fusion center on the same day as the call. NYSIC included the later date in a narrative it provided to the Subcommittee.[538]

NYSIC also noted that it assisted the FBI investigation by conducting database searches for vehicle identification numbers and Department of Motor Vehicles (DMV) photographs.[539] The fusion center was uniquely able to provide DMV photographs because it is currently the only other entity with which the New York State Department of Motor Vehicles shares the pictures, according to a NYSIC official.[540] "New York is one of the few states that doesn't make DMV photos readily available to law enforcement," Mr. Timothy Parry of the New York State Police told the Subcommittee.[541]

In its recounting, NYSIC also noted it "sent out teletype messages nationwide on the National Crime Information Center (NCIC) network requesting all agencies to conduct [License Plate Reader] checks through their systems," and send positive hits to NYSIC. However, the NCIC system is a Department of Justice network that predates fusion centers, and even DHS itself, and a NYSIC official told the Subcommittee the FBI may have been able to utilize NCIC on its own. "Could they do it? Yes. Is it as easily and quickly done? No. [We are] trying to make it more streamlined and efficient," he said.[542]

(3) Faisal Shahzad Case–Florida Fusion Center

In addition to the work performed by NYSIC, DHS cites on its webpage of fusion center successes efforts by the Florida Fusion Center (FFC) in the Shahzad case. DHS does not characterize the FFC's work as making a significant contribution to the case, and the facts it cites are corroborated by the State of Florida's own comments provided to the Subcommittee. Following the May 3 arrest of Faisal Shahzad, FFC personnel "immediately began to query state databases seeking any association with Shahzad," according to FFC Director Robert LeFiles.[543] The center identified two individuals having possible associations with Mr. Shahzad, and passed the information to the FBI JTTF pursuing the case. The information was used in a finished intelligence product, but nothing further was reported by either FFC or DHS about the leads.[544] The information does not appear to have played any key role in the Shahzad case.

(4) Francis "Schaeffer" Cox Case–AKIAC

DHS also pointed to work by the Alaska Information Analysis Center (AKIAC) regarding Francis "Schaeffer" Cox, an Alaskan militia leader who was arrested in March 2011,[545] and convicted in June 2012 on charges stemming from a murder plot against federal officials.[546]

In September 2012, the Department asserted the Alaska center had played an important role in disrupting Mr. Cox's plans. "From December 2010 through February 2011, the Alaska Information Analysis Center (AKIAC) provided consequential information that assisted an FBI Anchorage Field Office investigation that culminated in the arrest and conviction of a Sovereign Citizen/Militia Leader and two associates," DHS told the Subcommittee.

Alaska officials may have provided useful information to the federal investigation of Mr. Cox. In a September 2012 interview with the Subcommittee, Lt. Rex Leath, an Alaska State Trooper, said that in late 2010, state law enforcement officials collected information about Mr. Cox and his associates from several local law enforcement agencies around Alaska, and shared it all with the bureau. They learned Mr. Cox had been arrested for domestic assault, that he may have been booby-trapping his house in case law enforcement visited, that Mr. Cox's associates were conducting surveillance of off-duty police officers, and that Mr. Cox had stationed armed guards around his house.[547] "This dynamic started to develop, we would keep tabs on local law enforcement [information], and we would pass it on to the [FBI's] JTTF [Joint Terrorism Task Force]," Lt. Leath said. Some of that information was later cited in testimony by an FBI agent at Mr. Cox's trial.[548]

However, in his interview with the Subcommittee, Lt. Leath explained that that information-sharing was done not by officials at the fusion center, but by those at the state troopers' criminal intelligence unit, in conjunction with local law enforcement and the local JTTF. The trooper criminal intelligence unit had the lead on the case, Lt. Leath said.

Lt. Leath, who is the AKIAC director, told the Subcommittee that his fusion center put out a request for information from other states on Mr. Cox in early 2011, "around January."[549] Lt. Leath said the center learned of ties between Mr. Cox and other states, including Alabama, Michigan and Montana – ties Lt. Leath said indicated "funding, training, and verbal encouragement."[550]

The fusion center compiled the information into an intelligence report,[551] and shared it with the FBI in Anchorage that January, Lt. Leath said. "As soon as we got that information, it got the attention of the local FBI office," Lt. Leath said. "[T]hat's when the FBI got involved."

However, the FBI had been actively investigating Mr. Cox for months prior, according to news accounts. The bureau's Anchorage office reportedly began a preliminary investigation into Mr. Cox in February 2010.[552] Agents utilized two confidential informants against Mr. Cox,[553] one of whom was responsible for more than 100 hours of surreptitious recordings, including one of an "initiation ceremony" into Mr. Cox's militia in August 2010.[554]

In an October 2012 letter to the Subcommittee, Lt. Leath stated that AKIAC itself had been gathering and documenting information about Mr. Cox for almost a year before it compiled its January 2011 intelligence report. "[T]he AKIAC learned of these acts [by Mr. Cox] and began documenting them in early 2010," Lt. Leath wrote.[555]

In this case, local, state and federal officials appear to have engaged in useful information-sharing. Mr. Cox and his associates were arrested and convicted, and lives were possibly saved. However, it is not clear the role the state fusion center played in the process, or if it was as important or influential as DHS has alleged.[556]

G. Fusion Centers May Have Hindered, Not Aided, Federal Counterterrorism Efforts

Fusion centers have also made significant intelligence errors, with embarrassing results for themselves and the Department. Three examples of these errors – involving both faulty intelligence analysis and reporting – have led DHS to misinform decision-makers and prompt clarifications and apologies from fusion center officials.

(1) Russian "Cyberattack" in Illinois

On November 10, 2011, the Illinois Statewide Terrorism & Intelligence Center (STIC) published a report alerting officials that a hacker in Russia had stolen an unknown number of usernames and passwords to sensitive utility control systems, and used that information to hack into a local water district's computerized control system. Once inside the system, the fusion center report alleged, the hacker sent commands which caused a water pump to burn out.[557]

"An information technology services and computer repair company . . . determined the system had been remotely hacked into from an Internet Provider (IP) address located in

Russia," the fusion center's report stated. "It is believed the hackers had acquired unauthorized access to the software company's database and retrieved the usernames and passwords of various [control] systems, including the water district's system."[558]

Although it may sound like a minor prank, the intrusion would have represented a significant and troubling event, had it been real. Earlier that year, U.S. Department of Defense officials stated that the United States could treat such cyberattacks, if they caused widespread casualties, as acts of war.[559] The Illinois attack, which purportedly involved exercising remote control over a U.S. water system, would have been the first known attack of its kind on a U.S. facility, and was considered for a time to be "a major new development in cybersecurity."[560]

In truth, there was no intrusion, and DHS investigators eventually concluded as much.[561] The so-called "intrusion" from Russia was actually an incident of legitimate remote computer access by a U.S. network technician who was working while on a family vacation.[562] Making the intrusion allegations all the more perplexing, the contractor had logged on from Russia in June, five months before the pump broke; and although the access had been under his username and password, no one from the fusion center, the water utility or DHS had contacted him to find out if he had logged on from Russia.

"A quick and simple phone call to me right away would have defused the whole thing immediately," the contractor told a reporter after the report had been discredited. "All I did was I logged on."[563]

In addition to the fusion center report, DHS intelligence officials issued their own intelligence report on the alleged hacking incident, publishing it five days after the Illinois fusion center published its own, on November 10, 2011.[564] Like the fusion center report, DHS stated the allegations as fact, not as theory, claim or hunch – none of which are reportable under DHS reporting guidelines. The author, a DHS Senior Reports Officer with I&A's Reporting Branch, drafted the bulletin.[565] He wrote that his report was based on "first and secondhand knowledge of information . . . deemed reliable," and used no language indicating the "attack" was a mixture of allegation and conjecture.[566]

"[T]he Springfield, Illinois Curran-Gardner Public Water District's Supervisory Control and Data Acquisition (SCADA) system experienced a network intrusion from a Russian IP address," the briefing slide stated. "The perpetrator used an authorized user account of an employee from an identified US business that developed and installed the SCADA system. System controls were manipulated resulting in a pump burnout."[567]

Apparently aware of how important such an event could have been, had it been real, DHS intelligence officials included the false allegations – stated as fact – in a daily intelligence briefing that went to Congress and the intelligence community.[568]

After receiving the Illinois center's November 10 report, the FBI opened an investigation into the allegations. A week later, after receiving DHS's own intelligence report on the hacking claims, the Department's Cyber Emergency Response Team (CERT)[569] also began investigating the incident. On November 23, 2011, CERT issued its own report with this finding: "After detailed analysis of all available data, ICS-CERT and the FBI found no evidence of a cyber intrusion into the SCADA system of the Curran-Gardner Public Water District in Springfield, Illinois."[570]

"In addition," CERT's report continued, "there is no evidence to support claims made in the initial Illinois STIC report – which was based on raw, unconfirmed data and subsequently leaked to the media – that any credentials were stolen, or that the vendor was involved in any malicious activity that led to a pump failure at the water plant. In addition, DHS and the FBI have concluded that there was no malicious or unauthorized traffic from Russia or any foreign entities, as previously reported."[571]

Almost no part of the initial reports of the incident had been accurate – not the fusion center report, or DHS's own intelligence report, or its intelligence briefing. The only fact they got right was that a water pump in a small Illinois water district had burned out.

DHS I&A did not subsequently issue a correction or notification of its erroneous reporting. In an interview with the Subcommittee, DHS officials responsible for the reporting incident said they believed there was no need to issue a correction for the faulty report or briefing slide, because "they are not finished intelligence."[572] They agreed that the report did not include caveats for its reporting, and that it was "not typical" for such reports to state uncorroborated claims and hypotheses as fact. But "there is a premium for getting IIRs out," one official explained. "Analytical judgements are saved." Despite its inaccuracies and sloppy phrasing, DHS officials characterized the IIR as a success. "[It did] exactly what it's supposed to do --generate interest."[573]

(2) Shooting of Representative Giffords and 18 Others

A second recent example of flawed information issued by a fusion center involves the Arizona Counter Terrorism Information Center (ACTIC) about a high-profile shooting. This example showed how a center's weak analysis could actually hinder anti-terrorism and law enforcement efforts.

In January 2011, Jared Loughner opened fire at a public event in Tucson, Arizona. He shot and killed six people and wounded 13 others, including Arizona Representative Gabrielle Giffords.[574] Fox News reported that an ACTIC document indicated that the center's analysts had a "strong suspicion" that Mr. Loughner was connected to American Renaissance, which the document termed an anti-Semitic, anti-government group.[575] The memo stated then-Representative Giffords was "the first Jewish female elected to such a high position in the US government," suggesting that was a possible reason Mr. Loughner had targeted her.[576]

Closer scrutiny of the ACTIC document's claims revealed that many were false. Ms. Giffords was not the first Jewish female elected to Congress; the alleged anti-government, anti-Semitic, white supremacist group, American Renaissance, says it is neither anti-Semitic nor anti-government, nor even a membership organization. American Renaissance was instead a newsletter, and its publishers quickly confirmed Mr. Loughner did not subscribe.[577]

In the wake of reports debunking the analysts' assertions, the ACTIC director backed away from the document, characterizing it as a "quick summary" that "was never intended for public dissemination."[578]

ACTIC "just didn't have its facts straight," concluded one news analysis, which went on to question why the fusion center was attempting to participate in a criminal investigation. "Presumably, law enforcement authorities in Tucson and from the FBI were on the case when the memo was written," the analysis reasoned. "One wonders why the fusion center was involved at all, but clearly, it was operating out of its league."[579]

(3) Missouri MIAC Militia Report

A third example of fusion center missteps took place in February 2009 when a problematic analysis issued by the Missouri Information Analysis Center (MIAC) provoked public outrage. Deemed a "strategic report," "The Modern Militia Movement" attempted to provide a summary analysis of the recent history of violent militia organizations in the United

States.[580] The report was poorly researched and written.[581] It attempted to show connections between certain Constitutionally protected, non-violent political activity and a tendency towards violent extremism. For instance, the report alleged that "militia members most commonly associate with 3rd party political groups," including the Libertarian Party. It stated that "these [militia] members are usually supporters of . . . Ron Paul, Chuck Baldwin, and Bob Barr." Further, it claimed militia members might display signs, cartoons or bumper stickers featuring "anti-government rhetoric," as well as "anti-immigration, and anti-abortion" material. Most surprising to some, it identified as "the most common symbol displayed by militia members" the so-called "Gadsden Flag," featuring a coiled snake and the words, "Don't Tread on Me."[582] As the report properly noted, the flag was designed by a U.S. General, Christopher Gadsden, and first gained notice in the 1700s. And while it may hold significance to members of the militia movement, it is considered by many to be a symbol of American patriotism, and a popular symbol at Tea Party rallies. The report, which became public in March 2009, caused an avalanche of criticism of MIAC, as well as the Missouri Department of Public Safety, which oversaw the center. One former state government official said the report "looks like a Missouri State University fraternity brother wrote something and put it on state letterhead and sent it out."[583] The department's chief issued public apologies to Mr. Paul, Mr. Baldwin and Mr. Barr, stating in letters to the men, "I regret that those comments were ultimately included in the final report[.]"[584] These three examples of poor quality intelligence reports by fusion centers suggest some centers do not qualify as the counterterrorism successes portrayed by DHS. Fusion centers are controlled by state and local agencies, and staffed largely by state and local personnel. It should be no surprise, nor should it necessarily be a cause for concern, that they are primarily concerned with addressing state and local needs. The federal government has also repeatedly stated, however, its expectation that fusion centers be capable of contributing to the federal counterterrorism mission. It is that expectation that has been used to justify the federal government's strong and growing support for fusion centers, from providing hundreds of millions of dollars in federal grant funds and dispatching federal personnel, to installing data connectivity, and supplying secure equipment and facilities capable of handling classified information. Unfortunately, despite a significant investment of resources and time, fusion centers today appear to be largely ineffective participants in the federal counterterrorism mission. Much of the blame lies with DHS, which has failed to adequately implement a fusion center program that would produce the results it promised. But significant responsibility for these failures also lies with Congress, which has repeatedly chosen to support and praise fusion center efforts, without providing the oversight and direction necessary to make sure those efforts were cost effective and useful.

VII. Recommendations

- **Congress should clarify the purpose of providing federal monetary and other support for DHS' fusion center efforts.** The Subcommittee's investigation could not verify that the statutory basis for DHS' involvement in fusion centers – to strengthen federal counterterrorism efforts – was reflected in the department's efforts. Congress should require DHS to conform its efforts to match its counterterrorism statutory purpose, or redefine DHS' fusion center mission.

- **DHS should reform its intelligence reporting efforts at state and local fusion centers to eliminate duplication.** DHS reporting from fusion centers duplicates – often poorly –better intelligence-sharing processes undertaken by other agencies. The Joint Terrorism Task Forces receive threat-related information; the National SAR Initiative shares suspicious activity reports from state and locals; and the Terrorist Screening Center gathers information on state and local officials' interactions with individuals in the National Counter Terrorism Center's TIDE database.
- **DHS should improve its training of intelligence reporters.** DHS must ensure that any DHS personnel engaged in reporting intelligence information from within the United States be adequately trained and certified to prevent violations of U.S. law or DHS guidelines, policy or regulations.
- **DHS should strictly align fusion center grant funding to meet federal needs.** When FEMA gives states and cities grant funds for a fusion center, it should not allow those dollars to be spent on items that do not directly contribute to improving the fusion center's abilities to contribute to its federal mission of counterterrorism.
- **DHS should track how much money it gives to each fusion center.** FEMA should identify how much money it grants to states and urban areas for direct or indirect support of each individual fusion center, and report those amounts annually to Congress.
- **PM-ISE should evaluate fusion center capabilities and performance.** At the request of DHS, the Program Manager for the Information Sharing Environment (PM-ISE) in the Office of the Director of National Intelligence conducted a national assessment of fusion center capabilities that produced useful findings, and PM-ISE should use that model to conduct future evaluations. In addition, it should begin to evaluate fusion centers' performance as participants in federal counterterrorism information-sharing efforts.
- **DHS should link funding of each fusion center to its value and performance.** Granting funds for state and local fusion center efforts year after year, without expecting or even examining the results received from previous grants, provides no mechanism to ensure federal taxpayers receive a return on their investments.
- **DHS should timely disclose to Congress significant problems within its operations.** Serious issues plagued DHS fusion center efforts for years, yet officials were reluctant to share them with Congress. Even when asked about these problems, DHS avoided acknowledging the problems, initially withheld documents, and repeatedly resisted Subcommittee requests, which unnecessarily prolonged the Subcommittee investigation.
- **DHS should align its practices and guidelines to protect civil liberties, so they adhere to the Constitution, federal law, and its statutory mission.** DHS should strengthen its protections to prevent DHS personnel from improperly collecting and retaining intelligence on Constitutionally protected activity. It should not retain inappropriate and illegal reporting. It should strictly enforce policies, and hold all of its employees to the highest standards, including by promptly barring poorly performing personnel from issuing domestic intelligence reports involving Americans.

APPENDIX A. EXCERPT FROM DEPARTMENT OF JUSTICE, GLOBAL JUSTICE INFORMATION SHARING INITIATIVE, *BASELINE CAPABILITIES FOR STATE AND MAJOR URBAN AREA FUSION CENTERS, SEPTEMBER 2008*

Fusion Center Capability Areas

I. Fusion Process Capabilities

> *"Adhere to the National Criminal Intelligence Sharing Plan (NCISP) and other sector-specific information sharing plans, and perform all steps of the intelligence and fusion processes." — Guideline 1, Fusion Center Guidelines.*

The Fusion Process capabilities identify those capabilities and standards necessary to perform the steps of the Intelligence Process within a fusion center, including the gathering, analysis, and dissemination of information and intelligence. Though the steps and actions of the Fusion Process do not comprehensively mirror the steps of the Intelligence Process, the Intelligence Process provides the foundation to carry out the Fusion Process and assist in the identification of the capabilities needed to successfully complete the Fusion Process.

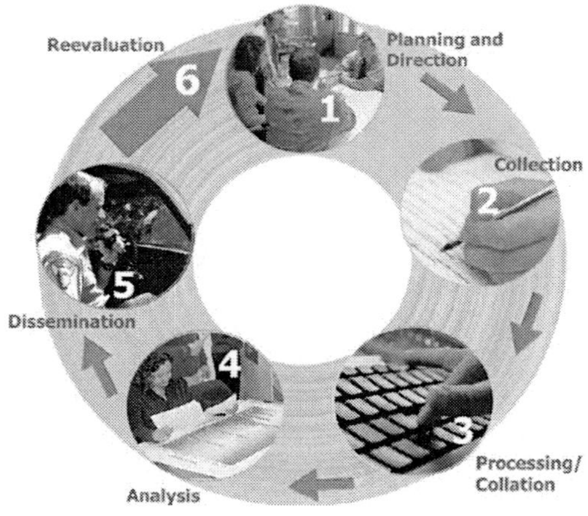

The Intelligence Process.

The Intelligence Process is defined in the NCISP and incorporated into Guideline 1 of the *Fusion Center Guidelines*. For purposes of baseline capabilities, the Fusion Process capability areas are modified to be:

- Planning and Requirements Development
- Information Gathering/Collection and Recognition of Indicators and Warnings
- Processing and Collation of Information
- Intelligence Analysis and Production
- Intelligence/Information Dissemination
- Reevaluation

The following capabilities address the plans and their associated policies, standards, processes, and procedures (collectively "procedures") needed to perform various aspects of the Fusion Process: the gathering, processing, analyzing, and disseminating of terrorism, homeland security, and law enforcement information. For these capabilities to be considered achieved or accomplished, the plans and procedures should be documented and provided to appropriate center personnel and partners. Though the types of plans and procedures are broken down by topic, they are in practice integrated aspects of the Fusion Process; therefore, many of these plans should be developed concurrently to the extent possible. In many cases, the resulting plans and procedures may not be separate documents but may be individual components of a larger document, such as a center's Concept of Operations, Standard Operating Procedures, or Policies and Procedures Manual.

The following capabilities do not include capabilities that are otherwise addressed in Section II. Management and Administrative Capabilities (e.g., Information Privacy Protections, Security, Information Technology).

A. Planning and Requirements Development

The Planning and Requirements Development stage "lays the foundation for the types of information that will be collected."— Guideline 1, Fusion Center Guidelines, p. 21.

1. **Intrastate Coordination—In developing and implementing all Fusion Process-related plans and procedures, the center shall coordinate with other fusion centers (the designated state fusion center and/or any UASI fusion center(s)) within its state to identify the roles and responsibilities of each center in carrying out the Fusion Process (gathering, processing, analyzing, and disseminating of terrorism, homeland security, and law enforcement information) on a statewide basis.**
   a. Identify and incorporate local and tribal law enforcement, homeland security, or other discipline analytic centers that do not meet the definition of a fusion center but are within the fusion center's geographic area of responsibility, and develop and maintain coordination procedures and communication methodologies.
   b. The plan should address the further dissemination of federally generated alert, warning, and notification messages, bulletins, and situational reports, including

the identification and establishment of a communications platform to support the timely dissemination of these products.

c. The plan should clearly identify who is responsible for disseminating what types of products and to whom (which local, tribal, and federal authorities; the private sector; and the general public, as appropriate), in order to reduce duplicative dissemination to the extent possible.

2. **Risk Assessment—Fusion centers shall conduct or contribute to a statewide and/or regional risk assessment that identifies and prioritizes threats, vulnerabilities, and consequences at regular intervals.**
   a. Use available national and statewide risk assessments and other relevant products that identify patterns and trends reflective of emerging threats in the development of statewide and regional risk assessments.
   b. Develop site-specific and topical risk assessments as appropriate.
   c. Provide the risk assessment or a summary and/or briefings on the risk assessment to law enforcement and homeland security officials with planning, resource allocation, and budgeting responsibilities, including appropriate elected officials from the executive and legislative branches.
   d. Maintain mechanisms to contribute information of value to other state, multistate, and national-level risk assessments.
3. **Information Requirements—The information requirements for the fusion center shall be defined, documented, updated regularly, and consistent with the center's goals and objectives as defined by the governance structure and reflect the risks identified in the statewide and/or regional risk assessment.**
   a. Use the risk assessment to identify and prioritize the information requirements in order to address the risks (threats, vulnerabilities, and consequences) posed in the center's geographic area of responsibility.
   b. Create a formal process to define, communicate, and modify intelligence requirements and intelligence gathering.
   c. Establish goals and objectives for collecting, producing, and sharing information.
   d. Review and consider including relevant requirements from the national intelligence requirements as provided by DHS and the Federal Bureau of Investigation (FBI).
   e. Coordinate with the state and major urban area homeland security advisors and the DHS Protective Security Advisor(s) to ensure coordination and support of the *National Infrastructure Protection Plan* (NIPP).
   f. Coordinate information requirements with other interested agencies (local FBI Field Intelligence Group [FIG], Joint Terrorism Task Forces [JTTF], High Intensity Drug Trafficking Areas [HIDTA], etc.) as appropriate.
4. **Suspicious Activity Reporting (SAR)— Fusion centers shall develop, implement, and maintain a plan to support the establishment of a suspicious activity and incident reporting process for their geographic area of responsibility, in a manner consistent with the *Findings and Recommendations of the Suspicious Activity Report (SAR) Support and Implementation Project.*[585] Specifically, centers shall have the ability to receive, process, document, analyze, and share SARs in a manner that complies with the ISE-SAR Functional Standard.[586]**

a. Adhere to the state and local responsibilities for SARs outlined in Appendix 1 of the *National Strategy for Information Sharing* (page A1-6).
b. The fusion center's SAR process should complement and support the SAR processes established or being established by state or local law enforcement agencies within the fusion center's geographic area of responsibility.
c. In cooperation with state or local law enforcement agencies within the fusion center's geographic area of responsibility that have developed or are developing a SAR process, the fusion center shall support:
   i. Defining and documenting the process to be used by the originating agency to ensure that suspicious activity reporting is made available to fusion centers and local JTTFs in a timely manner.
   ii. Developing outreach material for first responders, public safety, and private sector partners and the public to educate them on recognizing and reporting behaviors and incidents indicative of criminal activity associated with international and domestic terrorism.
d. The fusion center, in the absence of a specified threat or risk, should utilize SARs to analyze data trends and identify any potential terrorism linkage or activity (including precursor activity) and disseminate to the JTTF and other appropriate federal, state, and/or local entities.
e. The designated statewide fusion center shall coordinate an effort or support existing efforts to identify system requirements for the state's designated shared space[587] that will support statewide reporting, tracking, and accessing of SARs in a manner that ensures consistent use of data elements and collection procedures. (Refer to Section II.E. Information Technology/Communications Infrastructure, Systems, Equipment, Facility, and Physical Infrastructure; the ISE-SAR Functional Standard; and the *Findings and Recommendations of the Suspicious Activity Report (SAR) Support and Implementation Project.*)
f. Fusion centers should support or develop training for law enforcement and nontraditional partners to identify and appropriately report suspicious activities, indicators, and warnings.

5. **Alerts, Warnings, and Notifications—Fusion centers shall ensure that alerts, warnings, and notifications are disseminated, as appropriate, to state, local, and tribal authorities; the private sector; and the general public.**
   a. Fusion centers shall develop and implement a written policy outlining standard operating procedures to govern the receipt of further dissemination of federally generated alert, warning, and notification messages, consistent with the intrastate coordination plan called for by Section I.A.1.
   b. In response to federally generated alert, warning, and notification messages and/or significant events, the fusion center shall support or facilitate the identification of actions that were taken by state, local, and tribal authorities and the private sector and report those back to the appropriate federal agency.
   c. Adhere to the state and local responsibilities for alerts, warnings, and notifications outlined in Appendix 1 of the *National Strategy for Information Sharing* (page A1-8).
6. **Situational Awareness Reporting— Fusion centers shall develop processes to manage the reporting to key officials and the public of information regarding**

significant events (local, regional, national, and international) that may influence state or local security conditions.

a. Fusion centers shall develop and implement a written policy outlining standard operating procedures to govern the receipt and further dissemination of federally generated information bulletins and other situational awareness messages, consistent with the intrastate coordination plan called for by Section I.A.1.

b. Adhere to the state and local responsibilities for situational awareness reporting outlined in Appendix 1 of the National Strategy for Information Sharing (page A1-9).

7. **Data Sources—Fusion centers shall identify and document data sources and repositories needed to conduct analysis based on the mission of the center, the findings of the Risk Assessment, and the center's defined Information Requirements.**

    a. Refer to Section II.E. Information Technology/ Communications Infrastructure, Systems, Equipment, Facility, and Physical Infrastructure to further develop plans for access to data sources based on the fusion center's defined mission and core business processes.

8. **Coordination With Response and Recovery Officials—Fusion centers shall identify and coordinate with emergency managers and appropriate response and recovery personnel and operations centers to develop, implement, and maintain a plan and procedures to ensure a common understanding of roles and responsibilities and to ensure that intelligence and analysis capabilities can be leveraged to support emergency management operation activities, as appropriate, when events require such a response.**

    a. Ensure that the center has identified its intelligence and analytical roles and responsibilities in accordance with the National Incident Management System (NIMS) and Incident Command System (ICS).

    b. The plan should identify roles, responsibilities, and protocols to govern the timely reporting of significant events occurring within state or local jurisdictions to federal authorities and, when appropriate, other states, localities, or regional entities.

    c. Ensure that the plan addresses the contingency and continuity-of-operations (COOP) planning during an emergency. (See Section II.E.)

9. **Coordination With Private Sector and Critical Infrastructure and Key Resources (CIKR) Information Sharing—Fusion centers, in partnership with locally based federal authorities, shall develop, implement, and maintain a plan and procedures for sharing information with owners of CIKR and, in general, the private sector, in a coordinated manner.**

    a. All centers shall include in the plan the procedures to disseminate alerts, warnings, and notifications and other relevant analytic reports to critical infrastructure sectors and/or private sector entities that are affected by the threat.

    b. The plan should document the decision of the center's governance structure—based on the center's mission, risk assessment, and information requirements—whether the center will establish a CIKR capability to integrate and analyze threat, vulnerability, and consequence data and enable and support state, local, and private sector decision making and activities to protect CIKR.

Note: At a minimum, the baseline capabilities require fusion centers to have the capability to receive information from the private sector and disseminate critical information to members of the private sector. Beyond those baseline capabilities, some fusion centers are encouraged, but not required, to incorporate the needs of the CIKR protection activities into their Fusion Process. This option should be considered by the governance structure as a part of the mission development process. (See Section II.A.)

References: For those centers interested in incorporating the support of CIKR into their Fusion Process, an appendix to this document is being developed that will outline the fusion center capabilities for supporting CIKR protection activities.

10. **Exercises—Fusion centers should conduct or participate in another agency's scenario-based tabletop and live training exercises to regularly assess their capabilities.**
    a. Exercises should include simulations, games, tabletops, functional exercises, and full-scale field exercises.
    b. Exercises should involve all relevant center personnel and constituents and should contribute to understanding the value of the statewide Fusion Process, the center's collection plan, the SAR process, analytical products, the center's role in the Information Sharing Environment, and the center's role in response and recovery activities in accordance with NIMS and ICS.
    c. Centers should use the exercises to validate center operations, policies and procedures, and training activities and develop action plans to mitigate any identified gaps.

B. Information Gathering/Collection and Recognition of Indicators and Warnings

"The stage in which the planning and requirements development stage becomes operational...information is collected from various sources, including law enforcement agencies, public safety agencies, and the private sector. This stage is essential for fusion centers to be effective."—Guideline 1, Fusion Center Guidelines, p. 21.

1. **Information-Gathering and -Reporting Strategy—Fusion centers shall develop, implement, and maintain an information-gathering and -reporting strategy that leverages existing capabilities and shall identify methods for communicating information requirements and the overall information-gathering strategy to partners, to include any applicable fusion liaison officers.**

a. Clearly outline the collection process, including how the collectors of information are identified and tasked—or if the center lacks the authority to task, identify how such requests are made to partners.
b. Leverage and/or coordinate with the JTTF and other federal, state, local, tribal and private sector information sharing and counterterrorism efforts.
c. Clearly outline the processes that partner organizations—including law enforcement, public safety, private organizations, and the public—use to report information to the fusion center.
d. The strategy and associated processes shall be consistent with the governance structure's defined, agreed-upon, and auditable privacy policy. (Reference Section II.B.)

2. **Feedback Mechanism—Fusion centers shall define and implement a feedback mechanism that:**
   a. Provides the reporting entity an acknowledgement of the receipt of its information and, to the extent possible, provides feedback on the value of the information and actions taken with the information.
   b. Allows collectors to make suggestions to improve the strategy, plans, or processes, as well as seek clarification on information requirements.
   c. Allows recipients of information or products to make suggestions to improve products.
3. **Collection and Storage of Information— Fusion centers shall define the policies and processes and establish a mechanism for receiving, cataloging, and retaining information provided to the center.**
   a. Ensure that policies, processes, and mechanisms comply with the center's privacy policy— particularly regarding data retention, purging, and redress. (Reference Section II.B.)
   b. Fusion centers should reference the Commission on Accreditation for Law Enforcement Agencies (CALEA) Standard 51.1.1 regarding intelligence collection and the types of information to collect, methods for purging out-of-date or incorrect information, and procedures for the utilization of intelligence personnel and techniques.[588]
   c. Adhere to the Law Enforcement Intelligence Unit (LEIU) *Criminal Intelligence File Guidelines*[589] and the LEIU *Audit Checklist for the Criminal Intelligence Function*[590] for the maintenance of criminal intelligence files.
   d. Adhere to the collection, storage, and retention requirements of 28 CFR Part 23.
   e. Establish processes to routinely identify progress achieved against individual information requirements and the overall information-gathering strategy, and provide summary assessments to fusion center partners, management, and the governance body on a routine basis.
   f. The mechanism used to catalog and retain information shall enable timely retrieval by the center's analysts.
   g. Develop protocols to ensure the archiving of all appropriate data, information, and intelligence to support future efforts.
   h. To the extent the processes and mechanisms are automated, adhere to the Information Technology/ Communications Infrastructure, Systems, Equipment, Facility, and Physical Infrastructure capabilities. (Section II.E.)

C. Processing and Collation of Information

"Processing and collation involves evaluating the information's validity and reliability. Collation entails sorting, combining, categorizing, and arranging the data collected so relationships can be determined."—Guideline 1, Fusion Center Guidelines, p. 20.

1. **Information Collation—Fusion center analysts shall use the necessary and available tools to process and collate information and intelligence to assist with accurate and timely analysis.**
   a. Fusion center analysts should consider utilizing the appropriate tools identified in Global's *Analyst Toolbox* to assist in the collation of information.
   b. Fusion center analysts should reference IALEIA and Global's *Law Enforcement Analytic Standards* when developing the processes for collating information.
   c. Fusion centers should consider the development or utilization of an intelligence collection system that allows for the collection, processing, collation, and storage of information related to the mission of the center.
2. **Levels of Confidence—Fusion centers shall liaise with partners to ensure that information collected is relevant, valid, and reliable.**
   a. Fusion center personnel should consider regular meetings with information providers to discuss information collection requirements.
   b. Fusion center personnel should ensure that partners are aware of the various levels of confidence of information provided to the center.
      i. 28 CFR Part 23 states, "Information shall be labeled to indicate levels of sensitivity, levels of confidence, and the identity of submitting agencies and officers."
      ii. Levels of confidence relate to reliability, validity, and relevancy.

D. Intelligence Analysis and Production

> *"Analysis transforms the raw data into products that are useful...the goal is to develop a report that connects information in a logical and meaningful manner to produce an intelligence report that contains valid judgments based on analyzed information. ...One of the goals of the fusion center during this stage is to identify trends or information that will prevent a terrorist attack or other criminal activity."*
>
> *— Guideline 1, Fusion Center Guidelines, pp. 20–21.*

1. **Analytic Products—Fusion centers shall develop, implement, and maintain a production plan that describes the types of analysis and products they intend to provide for their customers and partners (which, at a minimum, include Risk Assessments; Suspicious Activity Reporting; Alerts, Warnings, and Notifications; and Situational Awareness Reporting [see Sections I.A.2, 4, 5, and 6 for further details on these product types]), how often or in what circumstances the product will be produced, and how each product type will be disseminated.**
   a. Adhere to the tenets in IALEIA and Global's *Law Enforcement Analytic Standards* booklet,[591] particularly Standards 17, 20, and 21, which address Analytic Product Content, Report, and Format standards.
   b. The production plan shall be prioritized based on the center's mission, information requirements, and priority functions.
   c. Identify stakeholders and customer base for specific product lines and request feedback from customers to guide future products.
   d. Ensure the production of value-added intelligence products that support the development of performance-driven, risk-based prevention, protection, response, and consequence management programs.
2. **Fusion Process Management—An intelligence commander/ manager should be designated to oversee the management of the Fusion Process (including the collection, collation, analytic function, dissemination, and reevaluation of information and intelligence) within the center.**
   a. The commander/manager should address the day-to-day intelligence management functions of the center.
   b. The commander/manager should prioritize critical intelligence products and ensure that the critical outputs of the fusion center are accomplished.
   c. The commander/manager should have the necessary skill sets to oversee the production of intelligence products that are effective, efficient, and permissible under state and federal laws and regulations.
   d. The commander/manager should have previous experience and management training.
      i. Training should include the intelligence cycle, analytical training, intelligence management, the role of the fusion center, and legal issues.
3. **Enhancing Analyst Skills—The fusion center should develop and implement a Training and Professional Development Plan to enhance analysts' critical thinking, research, writing, presentation, and reporting skills.**

a. The supervisor of the analytic function should work with each analyst to draft a Training and Professional Development Plan. Components of the plan should include training and mentoring opportunities for learning new subject matter/areas of expertise and exposure to new analytic techniques and technologies.
   i. The initial training goal should be the completion of the Foundations of Intelligence Analysis Training program or its training equivalent and the certification of analysts.
   ii. Adhere to the tenets in IALEIA and Global's *Law Enforcement Analytic Standards* booklet,[592] particularly Standards 1–7 for analysts.
   iii. Utilize IALEIA and Global's *Law Enforcement Analytic Standards* and the *National Criminal Intelligence Sharing Plan* in the development of the training plan.

b. Analysts should be provided routine opportunities to present their analytic findings and receive feedback on the quality of their written reports and oral presentations.

c. Performance evaluations should be conducted at least annually, and the Training and Professional Development Plan updated accordingly.

4. **Information Linking—Fusion centers shall ensure that analysts are able to understand and identify the links between terrorism-related intelligence and information related to traditional criminal activity so they can identify activities that are indicative of precursor behaviors, terrorist activities, and threats. (Guidelines 12, 13, 14, *Fusion Center Guidelines*)**
   a. Training regarding precursor activities of terrorists should be provided to analysts and relevant fusion center personnel following the standards outlined in the *Minimum Criminal Intelligence Training Standards for Law Enforcement and Other Criminal Justice Agencies in the United States*.[593]
   b. Ensure that analysts receive training on the analytic process, analytical writing and briefing skills, and reporting skills.

5. **Strategic Analysis Services—Fusion centers shall develop the capability to provide strategic analysis services for the jurisdiction served. (Guideline 14, *Fusion Center Guidelines*.)**

6. **Open Source Analysis Capability— Fusion centers shall establish an open source analysis capability utilizing the free training and tools provided by the federal government.**

7. **Analyst Specialization—Fusion centers should assign "accounts" or "specialties" to analysts based on the priorities of the fusion center, to allow the development of analytic depth.**

8. **Analytical Tools—Fusion centers shall provide the necessary tools to analysts for the analysis of information and data. (Guidelines 11 and 14, *Fusion Center Guidelines*)**
   a. Fusion centers should provide all tools outlined in Global's *Analyst Toolbox* document.
   b. Training should be provided for the identified analytic tools so that relevant personnel are proficient in their use.
   c. Analysts shall be provided with routine mechanisms to communicate with other fusion center analysts within the state or region. (Examples include "chat rooms"

available via Homeland Security State and Local Intelligence Community of Interest [HS SLIC] or other collaborative networks or regular phone calls.)

d. Analysts shall have access to and understanding of where to find information sources and available expertise to support the information priorities of the fusion center.

E. Intelligence/Information Dissemination

"The process of effectively distributing analyzed intelligence utilizing certain protocols in the most appropriate format to those in need of the information to facilitate their accomplishment of organizational goals"— Definition of Dissemination, Criminal Intelligence Glossary.

1. **Dissemination Plan—Fusion centers shall develop a high-level dissemination plan that documents the procedures and communication mechanisms for the timely dissemination of the center's various products to the core and ad hoc customers.**
   a. The plan should be consistent with the intrastate coordination plan. (See Section I.A.1.)
   b. Consider a variety of methods to distribute information, including Web site; e-mail; secure portal; regional and national information sharing systems such as Regional Information Sharing Systems® (RISS), Homeland Security Information Network (HSIN), Law Enforcement Online (LEO), and HS SLIC; pager; fax; telephone; video teleconferencing system; and personal contact. (Reference Guideline 6, *Fusion Center Guidelines*, for further suggestions.)
2. **Reporting of Information to Other Centers—Fusion centers shall develop the processes and protocols for ensuring that relevant and vetted priority information is reported to fusion centers in other states and localities to support regional trends analysis. (Guideline 7, *Fusion Center Guidelines*)**
3. **Reporting of Information to Federal Partners—Fusion centers shall develop the processes and protocols, in coordination with the FBI and DHS Office of Intelligence and Analysis (I&A), for ensuring that relevant and vetted priority information is reported to the JTTF and other appropriate federal agencies to support its inclusion into national patterns and trends analysis.**
   a. In addition to the priority information processes (SAR; Alerts, Warnings, and Notifications; and Situational Awareness Reporting), share information to address national security and criminal investigations.
   b. Ensure that information provided to the federal government is shared according to the fusion center's privacy policy. (See Section II.B.)

c. Utilize the protocols established in the SAR report, National Information Exchange Model (NIEM), and Information Exchange Package Documents for information exchange.

F. Reevaluation

"Reevaluation assesses current and new information, assists in developing an awareness of possible weak areas as well as potential threats, and strives to eliminate previously identified weaknesses that have been hardened as a result of the Fusion Process. Overall, this step provides an opportunity to review the performance or effectiveness of the fusion center's intelligence function."— Guideline 1, Fusion Center Guidelines, p. 20.

1. **Performance Evaluation—Fusion centers shall develop and implement a plan to reevaluate the center's performance of the intelligence cycle on a regular basis.**
   a. Develop mechanisms to receive stakeholder feedback on all parts of the intelligence cycle.
   b. Incorporate feedback from training and exercises.
   c. Update plans and procedures as appropriate.
2. **Fusion Center Processes Review—Fusion centers shall establish a process to review and, as appropriate, update the center's information requirements, collection plan, and analytic production strategy on a regular basis and any time one of the following is received:**
   a. New threat or vulnerability information;
   b. New federal or state standing or ad hoc information requirements;
   c. Federal or state alerts, warnings, or notifications or situational awareness bulletins; and/or
   d. Updated risk assessment.

II. Management and Administrative Capabilities

A. Management/Governance

"Fusion centers will have many demands placed on them, and it is important to have clear priorities."— Guideline 2, Fusion Center Guidelines, p. 23.

"Establishing a governance structure creates a supported environment that frames the ability for the center to function and operate, assign tasks, allocate and manage resources, and develop and enforce policy."— Guideline 3, Fusion Center Guidelines, p. 25.

"Examples of how to include the private sector in the governance structure:

- *Including representatives from the Sector Coordinating Councils (SCC), the Information Sharing and Analysis Centers (ISACs), or InfraGard.*
- *Coordinating with an existing critical infrastructure or private sector advisory council that provides advice to the state or major urban area homeland security advisor, emergency manager, or law enforcement agency.*
- *Leveraging the expertise of local sector associations or coalitions."*

1. **Governance Structure—Fusion centers shall have a governance structure that provides appropriate representation for the jurisdictions and disciplines in the center's area of responsibility. (Guidelines 3, 4, and 5, *Fusion Center Guidelines*)**
   a. Ensure that stakeholders have the opportunity to provide input into the establishment of the governance structure. (See Section II.A.3. regarding identifying stakeholders.)
   b. The center's governance body should include representatives from the state and local law enforcement and public safety disciplines.
      i. If the mission of the center is primarily law enforcement-focused, the center should include representation from the public safety discipline in at least an advisory capacity. This will enhance the center's ability to perform key baseline capabilities, including:
         a) Receiving tips from and disseminating alerts, warnings, notifications, and relevant analytic products to public safety organizations; and
         b) Supporting emergency management, response, and recovery planning activities based on likely threat scenarios and at-risk targets.
   c. The center's governance body should include representatives from the federal government in at least an advisory capacity.
      i. Include local representatives from the FBI (i.e., the JTTF and FIG) and appropriate components of DHS (i.e., Protective Security Advisor, U.S. Coast Guard, Federal Emergency Management Agency [FEMA], U.S.

Immigration and Customs Enforcement [ICE], United States Secret Service [USSS], etc.).

ii. Also consider including or coordinating with the following efforts as appropriate to the center's mission and location: HIDTAs and the U.S. Attorney's Office's Anti-Terrorism Advisory Council (ATAC).

d. Consideration should be given to include the perspectives of the private sector, where appropriate, in at least an advisory capacity.

e. Ensure that the governance body is composed of officials with decision-making authority, capable of committing resources and personnel to the center.

f. Ensure that bylaws for the operations of the governance structure are developed and adopted by the governance body.

g. The governance body shall clearly define the management and command structure of the center.

h. The governance body should develop and approve key fusion center policies, including the center's privacy and security policies. (See Sections II.B. and C. for more information on Information Privacy Protections and Security capabilities).

i. The governance body shall receive at least annual reports on the center's compliance with the defined privacy and security policies.

j. Develop communication mechanisms to provide the governance body with feedback from center management and personnel, stakeholders, and recipients of information within the state or region.

k. The governance body should include representation from and ensure that the fusion center management coordinates with other fusion centers within the state (the designated state fusion center and/or any UASI fusion center(s)), in order to identify the roles and responsibilities of each center in carrying out the Fusion Process (gathering, processing, analyzing, and disseminating of terrorism, homeland security, and law enforcement information) on a statewide basis.

l. Review the governance structure and membership at regular intervals to determine whether additional organizations or disciplines should be included based on the current risk assessment and the fusion center's mission.

2. Mission Statement—Fusion centers shall have a defined mission statement that is clear and concise and conveys the purpose, priority, and roles of the center. (Guideline 2, *Fusion Center Guidelines*)

a. The governance body shall develop and adopt the mission statement, unless it has been predefined by law or executive order.

b. In defining the mission statement, consideration should be given to the risks identified in the center's geographic area of responsibility.

c. In defining the mission statement, the governance body should consider using an all-crimes approach and/or an all-hazards approach (see Glossary for definition of these terms), recognizing that precursor crimes or incidents may have national security implications.

i. If the governance body determines that the center will incorporate certain public safety disciplines into the fusion center's mission and/or determines the center will use an all-hazards approach, centers shall adhere to the forthcoming appendices to this document, which will outline the baseline capabilities for incorporating the following disciplines into the center:

a) Fire Service
b) Public Health
c) Critical Infrastructure and Key Resources

ii. If the fusion center utilizes an all-crimes approach, the center should liaise with applicable agency and multijurisdictional task forces and intelligence units, including:

a) Gang task forces and intelligence units, as well as the National Gang Intelligence Center (NGIC)[594]
b) Narcotic-related task forces and intelligence units, as well as the National Drug Intelligence Center (NDIC)
c) Violent crime/fugitive task forces and intelligence units
d) Economic crime task forces and intelligence units

d. The governance body shall provide oversight to ensure that the mission statement, the most recent risk assessment, and the identified customer needs inform the Planning and Requirements Development process. (See Section I.A., particularly the prioritizing of fusion center functions and tasks.)

3. **Collaborative Environment—Fusion centers shall identify the organizations that represent their core (permanent) and ad hoc stakeholders and the roles and responsibilities of each stakeholder and develop mechanisms and processes to facilitate a collaborative environment with these stakeholders. (Guidelines 4 and 5, *Fusion Center Guidelines*)**

a. Review the most recent risk assessment, if available, and identify relevant stakeholders that should be included to address the highest identified risks.

b. Include the identification of entities and individuals responsible for planning, developing, and implementing prevention, protection, response, and consequence-management efforts at the state, local, and tribal levels.

c. When identifying the roles and responsibilities of core and ad hoc stakeholders, identify their needs as a customer of the center, as well as their contributions to the center (for example: providing resources such as funding, personnel, and access to expertise or providing access to information or databases).

d. After a governance structure has been established and a mission statement approved, review the identified stakeholders and their roles and responsibilities to determine whether any additional organizations should be included or whether roles and responsibilities need to be revised based on the center's defined mission.

e. Develop standard processes and mechanisms to facilitate communication between the stakeholders and center personnel, to include in-person meetings and briefings on operational and administrative matters, as needed.

f. Develop and implement a Memorandum of Understanding (MOU) or Agreement (MOA) and, if needed, nondisclosure agreements (NDA) between the center and each stakeholder who intends to participate in or partner with the fusion center. (Review Guideline 5 for further details.)

g. Ensure that appropriate legal authorities review the agreements before signature.

h. Identify the organizations with executive and legislative oversight and funding responsibilities, and provide routine briefings on the establishment and operations of the center.

RECOMMENDED RESOURCES

- *Refer to Appendix C: Functional Categories, Fusion Center Guidelines, for a list of organizations, disciplines, and functions to consider including as stakeholders.*
- *See Guidelines 4 and 5, Fusion Center Guidelines, for issues to consider when developing MOUs, MOAs, and NDAs.*

4. **Policies and Procedures Manual—Fusion databases to statistically capture, store, and report centers shall develop a policies and procedures manual for center operations. f. Publicize performance to the public, policymakers, (Guideline 15, *Fusion Center Guidelines*)**
   a. Include the center's mission, goals, policies, 6.procedures, rules, and regulations.
   b. Include the center's privacy policy and its physical and information security policies within the manual, which should include guidance on the use of information specifically for criminal investigations and compliance with local and state confidentiality laws and how to safeguard information.
   c. Outline the roles and responsibilities of all entities involved in the center and their function.
   d. Outline the day-to-day management and command structure of the center.
   e. Include in the manual the relevant processes developed in accordance with the Planning and Requirements Development capabilities (Section I.A.), to include outlining how and from whom intelligence requirements are developed.
   f. Implement an annual review of center directives, and purge or revise outdated policies and procedures.
5. **Center Performance—Fusion centers shall define expectations, measure performance, and determine effectiveness of their operations. (Guideline 16, *Fusion Center Guidelines*)**
   a. Develop outputs and outcomes that measure expected performance of identified mission, goals, and objectives.
   b. Coordinate the development and review of measures and performance with participating agencies.
   c. Create internal measures pertaining to administrative matters and external measures to evaluate the performance of the intelligence cycle. (See Section I.F., Reevaluation.)
   d. Utilize participation in a regular cycle of exercises to evaluate capabilities and assess performance. (See Section I.A.10.)
   e. To the extent possible, leverage systems and databases to statistically capture, store, and report performance.
   f. Publicize performance to the public, policymakers, and customers.
6. **Outreach—Fusion centers shall establish a policy to govern official outreach and communications with leaders and policymakers, the public sector, the**

private sector, the media, and citizens and develop a plan to enhance awareness of the fusion center's purpose, mission, and functions. (Guidelines 12 and 13, *Fusion Center Guidelines*)

a. Outreach efforts should include information about the center's privacy policy, the Fusion Process, and the types of information that should be reported to law enforcement or the fusion center and how to do so.
b. If there is more than one fusion center operating within the state, the centers should jointly determine how to communicate the value, roles, and responsibilities of each of the centers, consistent with the plan required by Section I.A.1.
c. Develop a process to liaise with and educate elected officials and community leadership to promote awareness of center operations.
d. Train personnel on communications policy.

B. Information Privacy Protections[595]

"Develop, publish, and adhere to a privacy and civil liberties policy."—Guideline 8, Fusion Center Guidelines.

"Protecting the rights of Americans is a core facet of our information sharing efforts. While we must zealously protect our Nation from the real and continuing threat of terrorist attacks, we must just as zealously protect the information privacy rights and other legal rights of Americans. With proper planning we can have both enhanced privacy protections and increased information sharing—and in fact, we must achieve this balance at all levels of government, in order to maintain the trust of the American people."—National Strategy for Information Sharing, p. 27.

1. **Privacy Official—Fusion centers shall designate an individual to serve as the privacy official and/or establish a privacy committee to be responsible for coordinating the development, implementation, maintenance, and oversight of the privacy protection policies and procedures. (ISE Privacy Guidelines—Section 12)**
   a. If the privacy official is not an attorney, the fusion center shall have access to legal counsel to help clarify laws, rules, regulations, and statutes governing the collection, maintenance, and dissemination of information and assist with the development of policies, procedures, guidelines, and operation manuals.
   b. The privacy official or committee should review all other fusion center policies and procedures to ensure consistency with the privacy policy.

c. The privacy official or committee shall coordinate with the center's designated security officer to ensure that security measures provide the proper protection to information in compliance with all applicable laws and the center's privacy policy protection policies.

d. Identify stakeholders to include nongovernment organizations, advocates, the media, and others that are essential to the development and implementation of the privacy policy.

   i. To the extent possible, fusion centers should use existing outreach mechanisms, such as a state or local government's privacy advisory committee, or outreach conducted by the state or local law enforcement or homeland security organizations to facilitate engagement with the community and privacy advocacy groups.

2. Privacy Policy Development—In developing the privacy policy, fusion centers shall:

a. Develop guidance statements that include the vision, mission, values statements, goals, and objectives for the creation of the privacy policy. (ISE Privacy Guidelines—Section 3)

b. Develop a project charter that will include an introduction, background, membership, and the previously drafted guidance statements.

c. Analyze the flow of information and the legal environment for the protection of privacy to identify what gaps exist between existing technological and legal requirements.

   i. Information flow analysis helps determine what personally identifiable information the agency collects, uses, maintains, and disseminates. (ISE Privacy Guidelines—Section 4)

      a) Identify the fusion center's data holdings and establish mechanisms to ensure their review before protected information is shared through the ISE.

      b) Establish mechanisms to identify the nature of protected information so it can be handled in accordance with applicable legal requirements.

   ii. All policies and procedures are compliant with the U.S. Constitution, the state's constitution, applicable laws, and executive orders. (ISE Privacy Guidelines—Section 2)

      a) Conduct a rules assessment and adopt policies and procedures requiring the fusion center to seek, receive, or retain only the protected information which it is legally permitted to seek, receive, or retain and which was lawfully obtained.

      b) Establish a process to allow for the ongoing identification and assessment of new and/or revised laws, court decisions, and policies that impact issues related to privacy, civil rights, and civil liberties.

      c) If an issue posing a significant risk to privacy is identified, develop policy and procedural protections.

d. Perform a gap analysis to identify legal and technological gaps.

e. Vet the privacy protection policy internally and externally during its development by soliciting commentary and buy-in from stakeholders and agency constituents prior to finalizing the policy.

f. Formally adopt a privacy protection policy to guide the collection, use, maintenance, and dissemination of personal information. (ISE Privacy Guidelines—Section 12.d.)
   i. Obtain formal adoption of the policy by the project team, privacy and civil liberties officer, the fusion center's governance structure and, if applicable, any legislative body.

3. **Privacy Protections—Fusion centers shall develop and implement a privacy protection policy that ensures that the center's activities (collection/gathering, analysis, dissemination, storage, and use of information) are conducted in a manner that protects the privacy, civil liberties, and other legal rights of individuals protected by applicable law, while ensuring the security of the information shared. The policy shall cover all center activities and shall be at least as comprehensive as the requirements set forth in the Information Sharing Environment Privacy Guidelines and consistent with 28 CFR Part 23 and DOJ's Global *Privacy and Civil Liberties Policy Development Guide and Implementation Templates.***
   a. The privacy protection policy shall include procedures to ensure data quality. (ISE Privacy Guidelines—Section 5)
      i. Establish accuracy procedures to ensure that information is accurate, and prevent, identify, and correct errors regarding (1) protected information and (2) any erroneous sharing of information in the ISE.
      ii. Establish and implement a process to provide written error notice of any potential error or deficiency to the privacy official of the source agency when it is determined that the protected information received may be erroneous, includes incorrectly merged information, or lacks adequate context such that the rights of the individual may be affected.
      iii. Adopt and implement the ISE policies and procedures for merger of information, investigation, and correction/ deletion/nonuse of erroneous or deficient information, and retain only information that is relevant and timely for its appropriate use.
   b. Establish criteria for types of information that partners can submit to the center.
   c. Include provisions for the use of privately held data systems information and commercially obtained data.
   d. Review the center's security policies and ensure that they are sufficient for providing appropriate physical, technical, and administrative measures to safeguard protected information. (See Section II.C. and ISE Privacy Guidelines—Section 6.)
      i. Ensure that the center's privacy and civil liberties policy articulates a process for responding to and addressing security breaches, in coordination with the center's designated security officer. (See Section II.C.2.)
   e. The privacy protection policy shall include documentation on how the policies and procedures meet the following ISE Privacy Guidelines requirements (ISE Privacy Guidelines— Section 12):
      i. Fusion centers shall adopt policies and procedures limiting the sharing of information through the ISE to terrorism, homeland security, and law

enforcement (terrorism-related) information, as defined for the ISE (see Glossary) and ensure that access to and use of protected information[596] are consistent with the authorized purpose of the ISE.[597] (ISE Privacy Guidelines—Section 3)

ii. Fusion centers shall identify protected information to be shared through the ISE.

4. **Privacy Policy Outreach—Fusion centers shall implement necessary outreach and training for the execution, training, and technology aspects of the privacy protection policy. (ISE Privacy Guidelines—Section 9)**
   a. Ensure that privacy protections are implemented through training, business process changes, and system designs.
   b. Provide ongoing training to center personnel and any other liaison partners on the fusion center's privacy policies and procedures. Training should be tailored to the audience (management, analysts, collectors, consumers of center products, etc.) but, at a minimum, should include:
      i. An overview of the policies and procedures for collection, use, disclosure of protected information, data quality, accountability, enforcement, auditing, and redress.
      ii. How to report violations of the privacy policy.
      iii. An overview of sanctions or enforcement mechanisms for failure to comply with the privacy policy.
   c. Consider and implement appropriate privacy-enhancing technologies.
   d. Fusion centers shall facilitate public awareness of their privacy protection policy by making it available to the public or otherwise facilitating appropriate public awareness. (ISE Privacy Guidelines—Section 10)
5. **Privacy Policy Accountability—Fusion centers shall ensure accountability with regard to the privacy protection policy and identify evaluation methods for auditing and monitoring the implementation of the privacy policy and processes to permit individual redress and incorporate revisions and updates identified through the evaluation and monitoring as well as redress processes. (ISE Privacy Guidelines—Section 7)**
   a. Fusion centers shall develop or modify policies, procedures, and mechanisms for accountability, enforcement, and auditing of the center's privacy protection. (ISE Privacy Guidelines—Section 7)

      i. Require reporting, investigating, and
      ii. responding to violations of the center's privacy protection policy. Encourage cooperation with audits and reviews.
      iii. Provide for receipt of error reports by the agency privacy official or committee. (See Section B.2., above.)
      iv. Implement adequate review and audit mechanisms to verify the center's compliance with its privacy protection policy.
      v. Incorporate the core elements of the ISE Privacy Guidelines' Accountability, Enforcement, and Audit guidance into the fusion center ISE privacy policy.
   b. Fusion centers shall develop internal procedures for redress—particularly to address complaints from protected persons regarding personally identifiable

information about them under fusion center control. (ISE Privacy Guidelines—Section 8)

i. Incorporate the core elements of the ISE Privacy Guidelines Redress guidance into the fusion center ISE privacy protection policy.

c. Fusion centers should utilize the LEIU *Audit Checklist for the Criminal Intelligence Function* when reviewing their "criminal intelligence function to demonstrate their commitment to protecting the constitutional rights and the privacy of individuals, while ensuring the operational effectiveness of their criminal intelligence function."[598]

C. Security

"Ensure appropriate security measures are in place for the facility, data, and personnel." —Guideline 9, Fusion Center Guidelines.

1. **Security Measures—Fusion centers shall establish appropriate security measures, policies, and procedures for the center's facility (physical security), information, systems, and personnel and visitors and document them in a security plan consistent with the NCISP, the *Fusion Center Guidelines*, Global's *Applying Security Practices to Justice Information Sharing* document, and 28 CFR Part 23. (Guidelines 8, 9, and 10, *Fusion Center Guidelines*)**
2. **Security Officer—Fusion centers shall designate an individual to serve as the security officer responsible for coordinating the development, implementation, maintenance, and oversight of the security plan. (Guideline 9, *Fusion Center Guidelines*)**
   a. For fusion centers colocated with other organizations (e.g., HIDTA, FBI), the fusion center can opt to use the other organization's security officer, provided that the officer is willing to perform the capabilities required of the fusion center security officer. If a colocated organization's security officer cannot or will not perform all of the functions, the fusion center should designate an individual to partner with the other organization's security officer to ensure that each of the baseline capabilities for security is met.
   b. Ensure that the designated security officer has at least some exposure to or experience with physical, information, systems, and/or personnel security.
   c. Ensure that the security officer receives routine training in the areas of physical, information, systems, and personnel security, to include the relevant DHS- or FBI-required training if the fusion center intends to establish and maintain a certified storage environment at the Secret level.

d. The security officer should:
   i. Conduct security training and awareness on the center's overall security plan and the center's security measures, policies, and procedures.
   ii. Provide regular updates to the center's management and the governance body on compliance with the security plan.
   iii. Coordinate with federal security officials to the extent needed for facilitating federal security clearances for personnel, facility security certifications, and access to federal information systems. (Reference Section II.E. regarding security clearances for personnel.)
   iv. Establish and coordinate the processes used to conduct background checks on all center personnel prior to commencement of duties. (Reference Section II.D.2.)
   v. Receive, document, and investigate reports of security violations according to the center's security policies.

3. **Securing Information—Fusion centers' security policies shall address the ability to collect, store, and share classified, controlled unclassified, and unclassified information to address homeland security and criminal investigations. (Guidelines 7 and 14, *Fusion Center Guidelines*)**
   a. In coordination with the appropriate federal security official, develop a process to receive, handle, store, and disseminate Secret-level information, to include establishing and maintaining a certified storage environment[599] if one is not readily available.[600]
   b. Fusion centers shall follow the regulations and processes for security management of the certified storage environment, as required by the federal security manager (i.e , DHS or FBI), to include, but not limited to:
      i. Certification of computers and other electronic devices for classified information.
      ii. Storage of both paper and electronic media containing classified information.
      iii. Level of security clearance required to access the facility without escort.
      iv. Processes for certifying the security clearances of individuals assigned to or visiting the facility.
      v. Rules for access with escort for individuals not holding the requisite level of security clearance.
      vi. Processes for derivative classification and marking of classified information created within the facility
      vii. Processes for dealing with any security incidents or violations that may take place.
   c. In coordination with the appropriate federal agencies, establish a policy to receive, handle, store, and disseminate federal information that is provided under the Controlled Unclassified Information Framework. (See Glossary.)
   d. Ensure that security policies allow for timely distribution of the center's intelligence products to the center's constituency base, which may include daily, weekly, and monthly analysis reports and assessments; advisories; alerts; warnings; executive reports; briefings; etc.

e. If a fusion center has chosen to incorporate the CIKR discipline, it shall have the ability to collect, store, and share Chemical-terrorism Vulnerability Information (CVI) (in accordance with 6 CFR Part 27), Safeguards Information (SGI), Sensitive Security Information (SSI) (in accordance with 49 CFR Part 1520), and Protected Critical Infrastructure Information (PCII) in accordance with the PCII Final Rule.
f. Consider whether a state law for security and confidentiality of public and private sector data is needed.
g. Adopt established, accredited models for secure horizontal and vertical information and intelligence sharing (e.g., RISS, LEO, HSIN, OneDOJ).
h. Ensure that controls and safeguards for data access to all appropriate systems are in place.

D. Personnel and Training

"Achieve a diversified representation of personnel based on the needs and functions of the center."—Guideline 11, Fusion Center Guidelines.

1. **Staffing Plan—Fusion center managers should develop a staffing plan based on the center's mission and goals and update as needed based on the current information requirements, collection strategy, and analytic production plan. (Guideline 11, Fusion Center Guidelines)**
   a. Managers should determine which positions require access to classified national security information based on the roles and responsibilities of the position and, through the center's security officer, make the request for national security clearances to the federal security manager.[601]
   b. Where appropriate, make clear when employment is contingent upon the applicant's ability to meet the requirements necessary for receiving national security clearances.
   c. Adhere to the education and hiring standards for analysts in IALEIA and Global's *Law Enforcement Analytic Standards* booklet.[602]
   d. The staffing plan should address the following support of functions: administration, information technology, communications, graphics, designated security officer (Section II.C.), and designated privacy official (Section II.B.).
   e. The staffing plan should address the center's requirements to access legal counsel to help clarify laws, rules, regulations, and statutes governing the collection, maintenance, and dissemination of information and liaison with the

development of policies, procedures, guidelines, and operation manuals. (Also required by Section II.B.2.a.)

2. **Background Checks—Ensure that background checks are conducted on center personnel (whether private or public) prior to the commencement of duties. (NCISP Recommendation 27 and Guideline 9, *Fusion Center Guidelines*)**
3. **Training Plan—Fusion centers shall develop and document a training plan to ensure that personnel and partners understand the intelligence process and the fusion center's mission, functions, plans, and procedures. The plan shall identify the basic training needs of all center personnel and identify specialized training needed to address the center's mission and current information requirements. (Guidelines 12 and 13, *Fusion Center Guidelines*)**
   a. Reference each capability grouping for further details on minimum training requirements for particular capabilities (e.g., Analysis and Production, Management and Governance, Information Privacy Protections, and Security).
   b. At a minimum, all center personnel should be trained on:
      i. The intelligence process and types of intelligence, crime-specific training, and how these factors contribute to implementation of the center's collection plan, through the use of the NCISP training objectives and the *Minimum Criminal Intelligence Training Standards for Law Enforcement and Other Criminal Justice Agencies in the United States*.
      ii. Roles and responsibilities of intelligence and analytical functions in accordance with NIMS and ICS.
      iii. The center's privacy and security policies and protocols.
   c. Training should be provided to all fusion center personnel upon assignment to the center and include regular retraining.
      i. All fusion center personnel—including analysts, intelligence officers, and non-law enforcement personnel assigned to the center (corrections, fire services, public health, private sector, and others)—assigned both full-time, part-time, and on an "as needed" basis should be included in the training plan.

   d. See Guidelines 12 and 13, *Fusion Center Guidelines*, for additional information.

E. Information Technology/Communications Infrastructure, Systems, Equipment, Facility, and Physical Infrastructure

"Integrate technology, systems, and people." —Guideline 10, Fusion Center Guidelines.

1. **Business Processes Relating to Information Technology—Fusion centers shall identify and define their business processes prior to purchasing or developing information technology, communications infrastructure, systems, or equipment to handle those processes.**
   a. Utilize the methodology and templates for analyzing the fusion center's business architecture provided by the Global document *Fusion Center Business Architecture*.
2. **Information Exchange within the Center—Fusion centers shall establish an environment in which center personnel and partners can seamlessly communicate—effectively and efficiently exchanging information in a manner consistent with the business processes and policies of the fusion center. (Guidelines 6, 7, and 10, *Fusion Center Guidelines*)**
   a. Ensure that appropriate personnel are colocated and/or virtually integrated within the center.
   b. Leverage databases, systems, and networks available from participating entities to maximize information sharing, and plan for future connectivity to other federal, state, local, and tribal systems under development.
   c. Utilize the latest version of NIEM for information exchange.
   d. Maintain a repository of information to be made available to the Information Sharing Environment, which will be a component of ISE Shared Spaces.[603]
3. **Communications Plan—Fusion centers shall have a plan to ensure safe, secure, and reliable communications, including policies and audit capabilities. (Guideline 18, *Fusion Center Guidelines*)**
   a. Identify how fusion center partners will communicate during an incident or emergency. Ensure that existing communications capabilities are interoperable.
   b. Incorporate current communications plans utilized by law enforcement and emergency services.
   c. Ensure that redundancy is incorporated into the plan.
   d. Test the communications plan on a routine basis to ensure operability and maintenance of current contact information for fusion center participants.
   e. See Guideline 18 for recommended aspects of the communications plan.
4. **Contingency and Continuity-of-Operations Plans—Fusion centers shall have contingency and continuity-of-operations plans to ensure sustained execution of mission-critical processes and information technology systems during an event that causes these systems to fail and, if necessary, to ensure performance of essential functions at an alternate location during an emergency. (Guidelines 9, 10, and 18, *Fusion Center Guidelines*)**
   a. Conduct a threat/vulnerability assessment to determine risk to the facility, data, and personnel.
   b. Develop the plans in coordination with emergency managers and other appropriate response and recovery officials. (See Section I.A.8.)

c. Clearly define personnel roles and responsibilities during emergency situations.
d. Ensure that contact information for the constituency is up to date.
e. Ensure redundancy of infrastructure, resources, personnel, communications, and systems.
f. Establish an emergency power source.
g. Conduct continuity-of-operations exercises to ensure the operational resiliency of the center.
h. Reference Guidelines 9, 10, and 18 for recommended aspects for developing contingency and continuity-of-operations plans.

F. Funding

"Establish and maintain the center based on funding availability and sustainability." —Guideline 17, Fusion Center Guidelines.

1. **Investment Strategy—Fusion centers shall develop an investment strategy to achieve and sustain baseline capabilities for the center's operations, including a delineation of current and recommended future federal versus nonfederal costs. (Guideline 17, *Fusion Center Guidelines*)**
   a. Base funding on center priorities identified by center leadership.
   b. Identify capability gaps and develop an investment strategy and resource plan to achieve the baseline capabilities.
   c. Establish an operational budget.
   d. Leverage existing resources/funding from participating entities and identify supplemental funding sources.
   e. Ensure that resource commitment of participating entities is addressed in the MOU.
   f. Identify return on investment for fusion center partners.
   g. Engage executive and legislative officials who have oversight and funding responsibilities, and provide routine briefings on the establishment, operations, and budgetary needs of the center.
   h. Ensure that the investment strategy is communicated to and coordinated with the state homeland security advisor (HSA) and State Administrative Agency (SAA) to ensure coordination and support of the state's homeland security strategy and any respective state and/or urban area grant program investment justifications.

Appendix B. Excerpt from Department of Homeland Security, 2011 National Network of Fusion Centers, Final Report, May 2012

Appendix 1. 2011 Assessment Attributes and Scoring

Individual fusion center scores are calculated using the validated Assessment data from 50 attributes aligned to the four Critical Operational Capabilities (COC) and four Enabling Capabilities (EC). Each COC is worth 20 points, and the ECs combined are worth 20 points (i.e., 5 points each) for a total of 100 points.

COC 1: Receive	**5 Attributes**
Fusion Center Attributes	
1. Fusion center has approved plans, policies, or standard operating procedures (SOP) for the receipt of federally generated threat information	
2. Fusion center has a plan, policy, or SOP that addresses the receipt and handling of National Terrorism Advisory System (NTAS) alerts	
3. Fusion center staff with a need to access classified information are cleared to at least the Secret level	
4. Fusion center has access to sensitive but unclassified information systems (e.g., Homeland Security Information Network [HSIN], Law Enforcement Online [LEO], Homeland Security State and Local Community of Interest [HS SLIC])	
5. Fusion center has access to the Homeland Secure Data Network (HSDN) and/or the Federal Bureau of Investigation Network (FBINet) (i.e., within fusion center or on-site)	

COC 2: Analyze	**11 Attributes**
Fusion Center Attributes	
1. Fusion center has approved plans, policies, or SOPs for assessing the local implications of time-sensitive and emerging threat information	
2. Fusion center has a documented analytic production plan	
3. Fusion center has access to multidisciplinary subject matter experts (SME) within its area of responsibility (AOR) to inform analytic production	
4. Fusion center has access to multidisciplinary SMEs outside of its state to inform analytic production, as required	
5. Fusion center has a process to provide the U.S. Department of Homeland Security (DHS) with information and/or intelligence that offers a local context to threat information in the event of an NTAS-related alert	
6. Fusion center conducts threat assessments within its AOR	
7. Fusion center contributes to or conducts a statewide risk assessment (threat, vulnerability, and consequence analysis)	
8. Fusion center contributes to national-level risk assessments	
9. Fusion center has a customer satisfaction mechanism for its analytic products	
10. Fusion center evaluates the effectiveness of the customer feedback mechanism on an annual basis	
11. All fusion center analysts have received at least 20 hours of issue-specific training in the past 12 months	

COC 3: Disseminate	**6 Attributes**
Fusion Center Attributes	
1. Fusion center has approved plans, policies, or SOPs governing the procedures for the timely dissemination of products to customers within its AOR	
2. Fusion center has a dissemination matrix	
3. Fusion center has a primary sensitive but unclassified mechanism to disseminate time-sensitive information and products	
4. Fusion center has a plan, policy, or SOP that addresses dissemination of NTAS alerts to stakeholders within its AOR	
5. Fusion center has a mechanism to disseminate NTAS alerts	
6. Fusion center has a process for verifying the delivery of products to intended customers	

COC 4: Gather	**8 Attributes**
Fusion Center Attributes	
1. Fusion center has an approved Nationwide Suspicious Activity Reporting (SAR) Initiative (NSI) site plan or an approved plan, policy, or SOP governing the gathering of locally generated information	
2. Fusion center has a tips and leads process	
3. Fusion center has a process for identifying and managing information needs	
4. Fusion center has a process for managing the gathering of locally generated information to satisfy the fusion center's information needs	
5. Fusion center has approved Standing Information Needs (SIN)	
6. Fusion center has an annual process to review and refresh SINs	
7. Fusion center has a request for information (RFI) management process	
8. Fusion center has a process to inform DHS of protective measures implemented within its AOR in response to an NTAS alert	
EC 1: Privacy, Civil Rights, and Civil Liberties (P/CRCL) Protections	**6 Attributes**
Fusion Center Attributes	
1. Fusion center has a privacy policy determined by DHS to be at least as comprehensive as the *Information Sharing Environment (ISE) Privacy Guidelines*	
2. Fusion center provides formal and standardized training to all personnel on the fusion center's privacy policy annually	
3. Fusion center's policies, processes, and mechanisms for receiving, cataloging, and retaining information (provided to the center) comply with 28 CFR Part 23	
4. Fusion center trains all personnel who access criminal intelligence systems in 28 CFR Part 23	
5. Fusion center has identified a P/CRCL Officer for the center	
6. Fusion center has a privacy policy outreach plan	
EC 2: Sustainment Strategy	**5 Attributes**
Fusion Center Attributes	
1. Fusion center has an approved strategic plan	
2. Fusion center conducts an annual financial audit	
3. Fusion center completes an annual operational cost assessment	
4. Fusion center participates in an exercise at least once a year	
5. Fusion center measures its performance and determines the effectiveness of its operations relative to expectations it or its governing entity has defined	

EC 3: Communications and Outreach	3 Attributes
Fusion Center Attributes	
1. Fusion center has a designated Public Information Officer or Public Affairs Officer	
2. Fusion center has an approved communications plan	
3. Fusion center has a process for capturing success stories	

EC 4: Security	6 Attributes
Fusion Center Attributes	
1. Fusion center has an approved security plan that addresses personnel, physical, and information security	
2. Fusion center trains all personnel on the fusion center's security plan	
3. Fusion center has a designated Security Liaison	
4. Fusion center's Security Liaison (or other organization's Security Liaison) completes annual training	
5. Fusion center has access to the Central Verification System (CVS)	
6. Fusion center's Security Liaison (or other organization's Security Liaison) is trained on how to use CVS	

Since attributes are not equally distributed across the COCs and ECs, the value of each attribute between capabilities varies. Each attribute is worth a specific value, and an individual fusion center is credited the value once it has successfully achieved an attribute. Out of 50 attributes, 30 attributes are aligned to the COCs, and 20 attributes are aligned to the ECs. Below is a list of attributes organized according to COCs and ECs.

End Notes

[1] Congress has defined fusion centers as "a collaborative effort of 2 or more Federal, State, local, or tribal government agencies that combines resources, expertise, or information with the goal of maximizing the ability of such agencies to detect, prevent, investigate, apprehend, and respond to criminal or terrorist activity."

[2] Remarks by DHS Secretary Janet Napolitano, National Fusion Center Conference, Denver, Colorado (3/15/2011).

[3] Testimony of Caryn Wagner, "Homeland Security Department Intelligence Programs and State and Local Fusion Centers," before the House Subcommittee on Homeland Security of the Committee on Appropriations (3/4/2010).

[4] Subcommittee interview of former DHS Senior Reports Officer (3/21/2012).

[5] Subcommittee interview of Harold "Skip" Vandover (3/22/2012).

[6] Implementing Recommendations of the 9/11 Commission Act of 2007, P.L. 110-53, § 511, 121 Stat. 317, 318-24(2007). http://www.gpo.gov/fdsys/pkg/PLAW-110publ53/pdf/PLAW-110publ53.pdf.

[7] "2011 Fusion Center Federal Cost Survey: Results," DHS (6/2012). The Department of Justice also provides support to some fusion centers.

[8] See "9/11 Commission Report," National Commission on Terrorist Attacks Upon the United States (7/22/2004), at 400, http://govinfo.library.unt.edu/911/report/911Report.pdf.

[9] Implementing Recommendations of the 9/11 Commission Act of 2007, P.L. 110-53, § 511, 121 Stat. 317, 318-24(2007). http://www.gpo.gov/fdsys/pkg/PLAW-110publ53/pdf/PLAW-110 publ53.pdf.

[10] 8/31/2012 Mike Blasky, "Fusion center helps police with school violence prevention," *Las Vegas Review-Journal*, http://www.lvrj.com/news/police-finalists-for-award-for-school-violence-prevention168226076.html.

[11] "Preventing Terrorism Results," DHS website, http://www.dhs.gov/topic/preventing-terrorism-results, accessed 9/19/2012. In 2010, a federal assessment could confirm at best 68 in existence. "2010 Fusion Center Baseline Capabilities Assessment," PM-ISE, (10/2010) at 8, DHS-HSGAC-FC-007231.

[12] "Standard Operating Procedure for Homeland Intelligence Report Production," DHS I&A Reporting Branch (6/25/2010), at 4, DHS-HSGAC-FC-056471. Other branches of I&A prepare analytic reports for distribution

to fusion centers, as well as joint analytical products in conjunction with fusion center personnel. Other DHS components also assign representatives to fusion centers.

[13] Memorandum from Charles E. Allen to Michael Chertoff, "SUBJECT: State and Local Fusion Center Implementation Plan" (3/16/2006), DHS-HSGAC-FC-004031.

[14] Memorandum from Charles E. Allen to Michael Chertoff, "SUBJECT: State and Local Fusion Center Implementation Plan" (3/16/2006), at 6, 10, DHS-HSGAC-FC-004031.

[15] Id. at 3, DHS-HSGAC-FC-004035. For a fuller discussion of DHS' analysis, *see* CRS, "Fusion Centers: Issues and Options for Congress," updated January 18, 2008, at 3-6.

[16] Department of Justice, Global Justice Information Sharing Initiative, "Baseline Capabilities for State and Major Urban Area Fusion Centers," September 2008, http://www.it.ojp.gov/ documents/baselinecapabilitiesa.pdf.

[17] This year DHS reported what it believes it has spent on fusion centers directly, which totals $17.2 million, but that figure does not include DHS funds granted to state and local governments intended to support fusion centers, which is believed to be a significant portion of federal spending on fusion centers. "2011 Fusion Center Federal Cost Survey: Results," DHS (6/2012).

[18] Congress has repeatedly pressed DHS for detailed reporting on its fusion center efforts. In 2006, appropriators began requesting quarterly reports from DHS on its fusion center efforts. See H. Rept 109-699, H. Rept 110-181, S. Rept. 110-84, P.L. 110-329. However, that failed to yield consistently prompt and accurate responses from the department. In 2010, appropriators noted DHS "has failed to submit the quarterly reports on this activity." H. Rept 111-157. They criticized DHS for creating "an unacceptable lack of visibility into DHS's intelligence programs," and "disregard[ing] Congress' explicit direction to provide timely information." H. Rept. 111-298.

[19] These failures have not gone unnoticed by Congress. In 2010, Senate appropriators explicitly stated their expectation "that performance metrics will be developed to judge the success of I&A's SLFC [State and Local Fusion Center] program. S. Rept. 111-222. The following year, House appropriators directed DHS "to develop robust programmatic justification to better identify and quantify the Federal benefit and return on investment from the State and Local Fusion Center (SLFC) program," and present it by February 2012. A DHS official told the Subcommittee in April 2012 they were still working on such an evaluation. Subcommittee interview of Joel Cohen (4/22/2012).

[20] Remarks by DHS Secretary Janet Napolitano, National Fusion Center Conference (3/15/2011).

[21] Testimony of Caryn Wagner before the House Counterterrorism and Intelligence Subcommittee of the Committee on Homeland Security (5/12/2010).

[22] "2011 National Network of Fusion Centers, Final Report, May 2012," DHS-HSGAC-FC-057027, pp. v-vi.

[23] Figures are based on separate estimates DHS provided to the Subcommittee. "Fusion Center Funding Report," Spreadsheet, 6/22/2012, DHS HSGAC FC 058336, and "Fusion Keyword Search Solution Area Funding Report," Spreadsheet, 2/24/2010, DHS HSGAC FC 057017, at 2.

[24] "Preventing Terrorism Results," DHS.gov, http://www.dhs.gov/topic/preventing-terrorism-results, accessed September 16, 2012. A 2010 assessment performed for DHS, however, documented only 68 functional fusion centers. "2010 Baseline Capabilities Asssessment," PM-ISE, (10/2010), DHS-HSGAC-FC-007031.

[25] January 18, 2008, Rollins, John, "Fusion Centers: Issues and Options for Congress," Congressional Research Service, RL34070, at 15.

[26] Homeland Security Act of 2002, P.L. 107-296 (11/25/2002).

[27] DHS website, "Creation of the Department of Homeland Security," http://www.dhs.gov/creation-department-homeland-security, accessed 9/16/2012.

[28] "The Terrorist Threat Integration Center," FBI.gov, http://www.fbi.gov/news/stories/2004/april/threat_043004, accessed 9/24/2012.

[29] "New Terrorist Screening Center Established" (9/13/2003), FBI publication, http://www.fbi.gov/news/stories/ 2003/september/tsc091603.

[30] "DHS Performance and Accountability Report, Fiscal Year 2003" (2/13/2004), http://www.dhs.gov/xlibrary/ assets/PerformanceAccountabilityReportFY03.pdf, at 37.

[31] July 2004, "The 9/11 Commission Report," Chapter 13, the National Commission on Terrorist Attacks Upon the United States, http://govinfo.library.unt.edu/911/report/911Report_Ch13. pdf.

[32] As just one example, DHS pointed to the landmark document in its 2011 publication, "Implementing 9/11Commission Recommendations, Progress Report." In it DHS called fusion centers a "critical feature" of the United States' "strengthened homeland security enterprise" that "align with – and respond to" the 9/11 Commission's recommendation of "expanding information sharing." "Implementing 9/11 Commission Recommendations, Progress Report," DHS, at, http://www.dhs.gov/xlibrary/assets/implementing-9-11-commission-report-progress-2011.pdf.

[33] See Executive Order No. 13,356, 69 Fed. Reg. 53599 (9/1/ 2004); "Intelligence Reform and Terrorism Prevention Act of 2004," P.L. 108-458, 118 Stat. 3638 (2004).

[34] Id.

[35] See 2005 Responses to Questions for the Record submitted by DHS, for the 3/4/2004 hearing, "Department of Homeland Security's Information Analysis and Infrastructure Protection Budget Proposal for Fiscal Year 2005," House Committee on Homeland Security, http:// ftp.resource.org/gpo.gov/hearings/108h/22589.txt.

[36] Memorandum from Charles E. Allen, "State and Local Fusion Center Implementation Plan" (3/16/2006), at 2, DHS-HSGAC-FC-004031.

[37] Id. at 9.

[38] Id.

[39] Id..

[40] Subcommittee interview of Robert Riegle (6/1/2012).

[41] Id.

[42] Id.

[43] Subcommittee survey of fusion centers (2010).

[44] Implementing Recommendations of the 9/11 Commission Act of 2007, P.L. 110-53, § 511, 121 Stat. 317, 318-24 (2007). http://www.gpo.gov/fdsys/pkg/PLAW-110publ53/pdf/PLAW-110publ53.pdf.

[45] Conference Report to Accompany H.R. 1 (7/25/2007), http://www.gpo.gov/fdsys/pkg/CRPT-110hrpt259/pdf/ CRPT-110hrpt259.pdf, at 304.

[46] Implementing Recommendations of the 9/11 Commission Act of 2007, P.L. 110-53, § 511, 121 Stat. 317, 318-24 (2007). http://www.gpo.gov/fdsys/pkg/PLAW-110publ53/pdf/PLAW-110publ53.pdf.

[47] Id. at 318-24.

[48] Conference Report to Accompany H.R. 1 (7/25/2007), http://www.gpo.gov/fdsys/pkg/CRPT-110hrpt259/pdf/ CRPT-110hrpt259.pdf, at 304.

[49] Implementing Recommendations of the 9/11 Commission Act of 2007, P.L. 110-53, § 511, 121 Stat. 317, 318-24(2007). http://www.gpo.gov/fdsys/pkg/PLAW-110publ53/pdf/PLAW-110publ53.pdf.

[50] October 2007 "The National Strategy for Information Sharing," White House, available at http://georgewbush-whitehouse.archives.gov/nsc/infosharing/index.html.

[51] September 2008, "Baseline Capabilities for State and Major Urban Area Fusion Centers," Department of Justice, Global Justice Information Sharing Initiative, http://www.it.ojp.gov/ documents/baselinecapabilitiesa.pdf. For the full list of baseline capabilities, please see Appendix A of this Subcommittee report.

[52] September 2008, "Baseline Capabilities for State and Major Urban Area Fusion Centers," Department of Justice, Global Justice Information Sharing Initiative, http://www.it.ojp.gov/ documents/baselinecapabilitiesa.pdf. Two subsequent DHS assessments, each with different methodologies but both purportedly based to some degree on the2008 list of baseline capabilities, have found most fusion centers continue to lack necessary minimum capabilities to support the federal counterterrorism mission. "2010 Baseline Capabilities Assessment," PM-ISE, DHS-HSGAC-FC-007231; "2011 National Network of Fusion Centers, Final Report, May 2012," DHS-HSGAC-FC-057027.

[53] 1/18/2008 CRS Report, "Fusion Centers: Issues and Options for Congress," John Rollins, at 44, http://www.fas.org/sgp/crs/intel/RL34070.pdf. Derived from CRS transcription of Secretary Chertoff's Keynote Address to the first annual National Fusion Center Conference (3/6/2007), Footnote 135.

[54] 1/18/2008 CRS Report, "Fusion Centers: Issues and Options for Congress," John Rollins, at 44, http://www.fas.org/sgp/crs/intel/RL34070.pdf. Derived from CRS transcription of Secretary Chertoff's Keynote Address to the first annual National Fusion Center Conference (3/6/2007), Footnote 135.

[55] Memorandum from Bart R. Johnson to Secretary Janet Napolitano, "Subject: DHS State and Local Fusion Center Initiative" (7/20/2009), at DHS-HSGAC-FC-058964.

[56] Id.

[57] Remarks by Secretary Napolitano at the Council on Foreign Relations (7/29/2009), DHS.gov, http://www.dhs.gov/news/2009/07/29/secretary-napolitanos-remarks-council-foreign-relations.

[58] "2010 National Security Strategy," White House, http://www.whitehouse.gov/sites/default/files/rss_viewer/ national_security_strategy.pdf.

[59] Remarks by Janet Napolitano before the National Fusion Center Conference (3/11/2009), DHS.gov, http://www.dhs.gov/news/2009/03/13/napolitanos-remarks-national-fusion-center-conference.

[60] Remarks by Janet Napolitano before the National Fusion Center Conference (3/11/2009), DHS.gov, http://www.dhs.gov/news/2009/03/13/napolitanos-remarks-national-fusion-center-conference.

[61] Testimony of DHS Secretary Janet Napolitano before the Senate Homeland Security and Governmental Affairs Committee, "Eight Years After 9/11: Confronting the Terrorist Threat to the Homeland" (9/30/2009).

[62] Remarks by DHS Secretary Janet Napolitano, National Fusion Center Conference, Denver, Colorado (3/15/2011).

[63] Testimony of DHS Secretary Janet Napolitano before the Senate Homeland Security and Governmental Affairs Committee, "President Obama's Fiscal 2013 Budget Proposal for the Homeland Security Department" (3/21/2012).

[64] I&A also oversees the intelligence activities of the department's component divisions. Its chief is an Under Secretary who reports directly to the Secretary of the Department. She is also the Department's Chief Intelligence Officer, and in that capacity is responsible to the Director of National Intelligence. I&A is not

responsible for the department's funding of fusion centers, which is handled through the grants division of the Federal Emergency Management Agency (FEMA).

[65] 11/2011 "DHS' Efforts to Coordinate and Enhance Its Support and Information Sharing With Fusion Centers,OIG-12-10" DHS Office of Inspector General, at 16-17.

[66] I&A publishes both "raw" intelligence reporting and "finished" analytical products. Raw intelligence is produced by the Reporting Branch, which receives the information from DHS personnel mostly outside the directorate, from personnel at component agencies, or from detailees in state and local fusion centers. The Reporting Branch also receives, reviews and publishes raw intelligence from DHS components.

[67] In October 2011, DHS changed its terminology to "Intelligence Information Reports," or IIRs, but the format was largely unchanged. For simplicity, this report uses the term HIRs throughout.

[68] "Standard Operating Procedure for Homeland Intelligence Report Production, v. 1.1" (6/25/2010), DHS-HSGAC-FC-056471

[69] Testimony of Caryn Wagner before the House Counterterrorism and Intelligence Subcommittee of the Committee on Homeland Security, "The DHS Intelligence Enterprise-Past, Present, and Future" (6/1/2011). Recently, DHS has partnered with DOJ on a "National SAR (Suspicious Activity Reporting) Initiative," which encourages fusion centers to file reports on "suspicious activity," which the departments define as "observed behavior reasonably indicative of preoperational planning related to terrorism or other criminal activity." Those reports can be written by state and local personnel, and are shared through a DOJ-managed process. "About NSI," Nationwide SAR Initiative, http://nsi.ncirc.gov/ about_nsi.aspx.

[70] Attachment 2: Homeland Intelligence Report Threshold, HIRWG Phase 1 Report and Recommendations, DHS-HSGAC-FC-056566.

[71] 6/25/2010 "Standard Operating Procedure for Homeland Intelligence Report Production, v. 1.1," DHS-HSGAC-FC-056471, at 056498; "Reports Officer Basic Course, Student Guide, Rev 0511," DHS-HSGAC-FC-057118, at 11.

[72] "'For Official Use Only' (FOUO) is the term used within DHS to identify unclassified information of a sensitive nature that is not otherwise categorized by statute or regulation." 3/14/2011 "DHS Sensitive Systems Policy Directive 4300A," DHS.gov, https://www.dhs. gov/xlibrary/assets/foia/mgmt_directive_4300a_policy_v8.pdf. In the 13 months' worth of reports the Subcommittee reviewed, 36 HIRs were classified, 574 were unclassified.

[73] "Since DHS I&A's adoption of the DIA IIR formatting, dissemination and security standards in 2004, any association of an assigned FRN with the name of the corresponding DHS reporter has been considered classified information at its inception." Email from DHS to the Subcommittee (7/15/2011), "Subject: Fusion Centers." PSI-DHS-72-000002.

[74] DHS explained that its reporters' identities were a national security secret, because terrorists or criminals could seek retribution for being subjects of their reporting. "[R]eleasing the identities of Reports Officers would expose those Officers to retribution from or exploitation by the adversaries that are the subjects of those Officers' reporting, causing serious damage to national security." Response from DHS to the Subcommittee (8/1/2012), DHS-HSGAC-FC-059275. When asked about the purpose of classifying reporters' identities, DHS I&A Under Secretary Caryn Wagner stated, "I don't think we're talking about personal danger, just, why would you need to know?" Subcommittee interview of Caryn Wagner (9/16/2012).

[75] Subcommittee interviews of former Senior Reports Officer (3/30/2012) and Mark Collier (3/8/2012).

[76] Subcommittee interview of Keith Jones (4/2/2012).

[77] DHS response to Subcommittee inquiry (9/21/2012), DHS-HSGAC-FC-059982.

[78] DHS response to Subcommittee inquiry (8/1/2012), DHS-HSGAC-FC-059275.

[79] Subcommittee interview of Robert Riegle (6/1/2012). The first DHS detailee at a fusion center was placed in January 2006, to the Los Angeles Joint Regional Intelligence Center, before Allen's plan, which contained a strategy for detailing personnel, was approved. Subcommittee interview of Joel Cohen (4/16/2012).

[80] "Position Description, Intelligence Operations Specialist," DHS-HSGAC-FC-058978.

[81] At first the Reporting Branch deployed contract employees provided by federal contractors; they eventually replaced them with federal employee Reports Officers. Subcommittee interview of Jonathan Wilham (3/6/2012).

[82] DHS Support to Fusion Centers, as of 5/3/12, PSI-DHS-56-0021.

[83] Executive Order 12333, as amended, http://www.fas.org/irp/offdocs/eo/eo-12333-2008.pdf.

[84] DHS written response to Subcommittee inquiry (8/24/2012) DHS-HSGAC-FC-059584. The Department stated it generally follows the definition of "overt collection" from the CIA's Glossary of Intelligence Terms and Definitions (June 1989): "The acquisition of intelligence information from public media, observation, government-to-government dialogue, elicitation, and from the sharing of data openly acquired; the process may be classified or unclassified; the target and host governments as well as the sources involved normally are aware of the general collection activity, although the specific acquisition, sites, and processes may be successfully concealed."

[85] Subcommittee interviews of Harold "Skip" Vandover (8/22/2012) and DHS Office of General Counsel (8/12/2012); DHS written response, DHS-HSGAC-FC-059275; Memorandum from Charles E. Allen and

Matthew L. Kronisch to All Employees, Detailees, and Contractors Supporting the Office of Intelligence and Analysis, "SUBJECT: Interim Intelligence Oversight Procedures for the Office of Intelligence & Analysis," (4/3/2008) DHS-HSGAC-FC-047637.

86 Subcommittee interview of Harold "Skip" Vandover (3/22/2012).

87 DHS Support to Fusion Centers (5/3/2012), PSI-DHS-56-0021.

88 Subcommittee interview of Harold "Skip" Vandover (3/22/2012).

89 DHS now calls HIRs Intelligence Information Reports (IIR). In this report, the terms are used interchangeably, however HIR primarily refers to reporting during the review period. During the period reviewed by the Subcommittee, IOs drafted HIRs. In July 2011, DHS refined the roles of ROs and IOs, stating that ROs primarily draft IIRs, and IOs should pass tips and leads to ROs for drafting into a report. Memorandum from Christopher Button and Michael Potts, "Subject: Management of I&A Personnel at State and Major Urban Area Fusion Centers" (7/29/2011), DHS-HSGAC-FC-059289.

90 Subcommittee interview of Keith Jones (4/12/2012).

91 Subcommittee interview of Charles Robinson (7/18/2012); DHS response to Subcommittee inquiry (8/30/2012), PSI-DHS-67-0001; "Standard Operating Procedure for Homeland Intelligence Report Production, v. 1.1," DHS, (6/25/2010) DHS-HSGAC-FC-056477. In the uncommon case of a draft HIR that was classified, it was transmitted via the Homeland Security Data Network (HSDN), a Secret-level classified network. Email from DHS to the Subcommittee (8/30/2012), PSI-DHS-67-0001. Because DHS classifies its reporters' identities, its procedure requiring reporters to email draft reports via unsecure networks may represent improper handling of classified information.

92 6/25/2010 "Standard Operating Procedure for Homeland Intelligence Report Production, v. 1.1," DHS, at DHS-HSGAC-FC-056478.

93 Subcommittee interviews of Senior Reports Officer (3/1/2012), Senior Reports Officer (3/20/2012), and Keith Jones (4/2/2012).

94 Both entities are oversight offices located outside of I&A.

95 "Rightwing Extremism: Current Economic and Political Climate Fueling Resurgence in Radicalization and Recruitment" (4/7/2009), DHS-HSGAC-FC-059277.

96 See, e.g., "Soon, We'll All Be Radicals," ACLU, http://www.aclu.org/blog/national-security-technology-and-liberty/soon-well-all-be-radicals (4/16/2009); Transcript of "Hannity," segment "Joe the Plumber at Atlanta Tea Party," http://www.foxnews.com/story/ 0,2933,516835,00.html (4/15/2009).

97 Email from MGMTExecSec, "Subject: Management Action Directive: Coordination of Intelligence Products" (4/17/2009), DHS-HSGAC-FC-047649.

98 Email from Jonathan Wilham to Timothy Bailey, Ole Broughton, et al, "Subject: Vetting of DHS HIRs" (5/5/2009), DHS-HSGAC-FC-047651.

99 Id.

100 Subcommittee interview of James Chaparro (6/28/2012).

101 Subcommittee interview of Ken Hunt (2/27/2012).

102 HIRs from fusion centers published in June 2009 were published on average nearly three months after the information contained therein had been acquired, the Subcommittee investigation found. The delay persisted through April 2010, the end of the period of reporting the Subcommittee reviewed.

A March 9, 2011 memorandum suggests that in late 2010 DHS cut the publication lag to an average of 14 days, but by the date of the memorandum a second backlog had developed. The backlog likely included – and impacted – reporting from DHS components, as well. Memorandum from Harold "Skip" Vandover to Mike Potts, "SUBJECT: Reporting Backlog" (3/9/2011), DHS-HSGAC-FC-059705.

Documents indicate the backlog persisted through most of 2011. Email from Harold "Skip" Vandover to Donald Torrence, "Subject: RE: UPDATED HIR Triage Definitions" (5/3/2011), DHS-HSGAC-FC-050748 ("I intend to monitor the backlog to see how it is coming down before I take more drastic measures"). Email from Harold "Skip" Vandover to Jonathan Wilham, et al, "Subject: S&L HIR "Surge" (8/24/2011), DHS-HSGAC-FC-050741 ("As it stands right now, there are over 500 HIRs waiting to be reviewed and published . . . we are continuing to slip further behind.")

A November 2011 document indicates a significant backlog was still present at that time – 307 draft reports were waiting for publication, 267 of which were more than 10 days old. "DHS Reporting Branch Weekly Passdown" (11/10/11), DHS-HSGAC-FC-056589.

103 DHS website, "Fiscal Year (FY) 2012 Homeland Security Grant Program (HSGP) Frequently Asked Questions (FAQs)," http://www.fema.gov/pdf/government/grant/AFG.pdf. Before 2008, DHS also funded fusion centers through its Law Enforcement Terrorism Prevention Program (LETPP), which no longer exists as a separate program.

104 FEMA Preparedness Grants Authorized Equipment List, https://www.rkb.us/mel.cfm? subtypeid=549, accessed 9/24/2012.

105 FEMA Homeland Security Grant Program, Program Guidance and Application Kits, 2007-2011.

106 Id.

107 Implementing Recommendations of the 9/11 Commission Act of 2007, P. L. No. 110-53, § 2004 (e) (2007), codified at 6 U.S.C. § 605 (e).

108 DHS, Homeland Security Grant Program, Program Guidance and Application Kit, Fiscal Years 2007-2009.

109 Remarks by Secretary Napolitano at the Council on Foreign Relations (7/29/2009), http://www.dhs.gov/ynews/speeches/sp_1248891649195.shtm.

110 Testimony of Caryn Wagner before the House Subcommittee on Homeland Security of the Committee on Appropriations, "Homeland Security Department Intelligence Programs and State and Local Fusion Centers," (3/4/2010).

111 Memorandum from Charles E. Allen, "State and Local Fusion Center Plan" (3/16/2006), at 2, DHS-HSGAC-FC-004031.

112 Subcommittee interview of Harold "Skip" Vandover (3/22/2012).

113 Subcommittee interview of former Senior Reports Officer (3/21/2012).

114 Id. Others also noted the frequency of substandard reporting. "It's quite apparent when you look at some of the reporting that the HUMINT [human intelligence] skills aren't there," said one former Senior Reports Officer, who reviewed and edited HIRs from fusion centers. Subcommittee interview of Senior Reports Officer (3/1/2012).

115 Email correspondence from MGMTExecSec (4/17/2009), DHS-HSGAC-FC-047649; Email correspondence from Jonathan Wilham, "Subj: Vetting of DHS HIRs" (5/5/2009), DHS-HSGAC-FC-047651.

116 See 3/2011 Homeland Intelligence Report Working Group (HIRWG) Phase 1 Report and Recommendations, November 2010, DHS-HSGAC-FC-050770.

117 Some DHS officials told the Subcommittee that from 2006 to as recently as 2010, DHS allowed state and local officials to file reports; in fact, DHS officials trained them to do so, and accepted reporting from them. For more on this topic, see the Background section.

118 "State and Local Fusion Center Program: Quarterly Report, Fiscal Year 2009 Report to Congress, First Quarter," (8/4/2009), at 2.

119 Subcommittee interview of Caryn Wagner (9/16/2012).

120 DHS Support to Fusion Centers (5/3/2012), PSI-DHS-56-0021.

121 Memorandum from James Chaparro to Bart Johnson, "Homeland Intelligence Reports," (1/7/2010), DHS-HSGAC-FC-050742.

122 Id.

123 Id.

124 Mr. Chaparro left I&A on February 13, 2010. Subcommittee interview of James Chaparro (6/28/2012). The Senate confirmed Ms. Wagner to Undersecretary for I&A on February 11, 2010. Biography of Caryn Wagner, DHS web site, http://www.dhs.gov/caryn-wagner, accessed 9/18/2012.

125 Subcommittee interview of Caryn Wagner (9/16/2012). Ms. Wagner said she was not only concerned with the quality of reporting DHS received from fusion centers, but the quality of reporting DHS pushed out to the centers. "We had to improve the information flowing out," she said. "We weren't providing very good products to the fusion centers, either." Subcommittee interview of Caryn Wagner (9/16/2012). In 2010, the DHS Inspector General found that DHS reporting to fusion centers was often months old. "As a result, the information contained in the HIRs may no longer be relevant by the time it reaches the fusion centers," the IG reported. DHS Office of Inspector General, Report, "Information Sharing With Fusion Centers Has Improved, but Information System Challenges Remain," Report 11-04, http://www.oig.dhs.gov/assets/Mgmt/OIG_11-04_Oct10.pdf).

It is unclear how much the process has improved since then. GAO reported in September 2012 that fusion centers said DHS reporting "was not always timely," and that "sometimes . . . I&A information is already available through media outlets and other information sources." Government Accountability Office, Report, "INFORMATION SHARING: DHS Has Demonstrated Leadership and Progress, but Additional Actions Could Help Sustain and Strengthen Efforts," Report GAO-12-809, http://www.gao.gov/assets/650/648475.pdf).

126 Subcommittee interview of Amy Kardell (6/5/2012).

127 Subcommittee interviews of Amy Kardell (6/5/2012) and Caryn Wagner (9/16/2012).

128 Subcommittee interview of Amy Kardell (6/5/2012).

129 Poor reporting training and its consequences had been flagged in an email conversation between I&A officials in April 2009, several months before Mr. Chaparro's memorandum. Email from Barbara Alexander to James Chaparro, et al., "Subject: Open Source Requirements," DHS-HSGAC-FC-059585.

130 "Terms of Reference for HSIC HIR Working Group," (11/2010) DHS-HSGAC-FC-056566.

131 Subcommittee interview of Amy Kardell (6/5/2012).

132 Id.

133 The Reporting Branch assembled a document of Standard Operating Procedures in June 2010, during the period of the HIRWG review. It does not appear to reflect current practices.

134 "Homeland Intelligence Report Working Group (HIRWG) Phase 1 Report and Recommendations," (11/2010) DHS-HSGAC-FC-050770.

[135] Id.

[136] While Undersecretary Wagner made reference to the study and its recommendations in public testimony, she said her office did not share the report with Congress until the Subcommittee requested a copy as part of its investigation. Subcommittee interview of Caryn Wagner (9/16/2012).

[137] Subcommittee interview of Caryn Wagner (9/16/2012); DHS response to Subcommittee inquiry, DHS-HSGAC-FC-059968.

[138] Of those, 574 were unclassified, 36 were classified.

[139] DHS disseminated HIRs to other fusion centers, although I&A personnel understood their primary consumers to be the federal intelligence community – other DHS components, intelligence agencies, even the White House Situation Room. See, "Standard Operating Procedure for Homeland Intelligence Report Production, v. 1.1," (6/2010) at 6, DHS-HSGAC-FC-056483. ("[I]nformation. . . may be drafted and published as an HIR if it contains information of intelligence value to members of the IC.")

[140] This imbalance in reporting did not go unnoticed within the DHS Reporting Branch. Keith Jones, who headed the branch for part of 2009 and 2010, estimated that most reporting from fusion centers during his time came from a half dozen DHS officers. "In a couple cases there was a lot going on," he told the Subcommittee. "In a couple of others they were looking for stuff [to report] so they could wave their flag." Subcommittee interview of Keith Jones (4/2/2012).

[141] Undersecretary Wagner said she believed "[HIRs] are not the premier process of reporting counterterrorism from fusion centers." Asked what was, Ms. Wagner said, "daily ongoing collaborations," which she defined as "phone calls" and "secure video teleconferences." Subcommittee interview of Caryn Wagner (9/16/2012).

[142] "Human smuggling vehicle concealment method," draft HIR report, cancelled 7/6/09, DHS-HSGAC-FC-17078.

[143] Id.

[144] "Narcotics and Currency Smuggler Arrested . . . " draft HIR report, cancelled 4/30/2010, DHS-HSGAC-FC-16967; "Police Discover Meth Lab Operated by Member of White Supremacist Group," draft HIR report, cancelled 4/23/2010, DHS-HSGAC-16971; "Woman Under Investigation. . . Relocates . . . to Work on Military Base," draft HIR report, cancelled 4/30/2010, DHS-HSGAC-16975. When citing and quoting cancelled reporting in this report, the Subcommittee investigation has removed specific identifying details of individuals wherever possible, including names and locations, and represented those omissions with ellipses and/or bracketed text.

[145] "Possible . . . Gang Smuggling Activity Interrupted . . . " draft HIR, 7/6/2009, DHS-HSGAC-FC-017130.

[146] Id.

[147] Id.

[148] 'Possible Refusal by Mexican Ambulance Services of Transporting Victims of Drug Trafficking Organizations (DTOs) to Mexican Hospitals," draft HIR, cancelled 2/18/2010, INT-3135-09, DHS-HSGAC-FC-017279.

[149] "Possible Drug Smuggling Activity. . ." draft HIR, 2/16/2010, DHS-HSGAC-FC-017375.

[150] Id.

[151] Id.

[152] Id.

[153] TIDE's custodian, the National Counterterrorism Center (NCTC), defines it as containing "identities of individuals known or appropriately suspected to be or have been involved in activities constituting, in preparation for, in aid of, or related to terrorism, with the exception of purely domestic terrorism information." TIDE Fact Sheet,NCTC.gov, http:// www.nctc.gov/docs/Tide_Fact_Sheet.pdf.

[154] "TERRORISM WATCHLIST: [State] Law Enforcement Officials (LEOs) Arrest an Overstay with Terrorist Related Records," draft HIR, cancelled 2/18/2010, DHS-HSGAC-FC-16692.

[155] "TERRORISM WATCHLIST – Encounter with a Jordanian-born U.S. Citizen with Terrorist Related Records,"INT-2611-09, DHS-HSGAC-FC-016740.

[156] Although NCTC describes its TIDE database as holding information on the identities of known and suspected terrorists, DHS officials – who interacted with TIDE data on a daily basis, as they reviewed reporting not only from state and local law enforcement encounters but from encounters by DHS components – said they found otherwise. "Not everything in TIDE is KST," DHS privacy official Ken Hunt told the Subcommittee, using a shorthand term for "known or suspected terrorist."

"Would you buy a Ford?" one DHS Senior Reports Officer asked the Subcommittee staff during an interview, when he was asked how serious it was for someone to be a match to a TIDE record. "Ford Motor Company has a TIDE record."

Ole Broughton headed Intelligence Oversight at I&A from September 2007 to January 2012. In an interview with the Subcommittee, Mr. Broughton expressed the concern DHS intelligence officials felt working with TIDE data. In one instance, Mr. Broughton recalled he "saw an individual's two-year-old son [identified] in an HIR. He had a TIDE record." Mr. Broughton believed part of the problem was that intelligence officials had routinely put information on "associates" of known or suspected terrorists into TIDE, without determining that that person would qualify as a known or suspected terrorist. "We had a lot of discussion regarding 'associates' in TIDE," Mr. Broughton said.

Mark Collier, who served as a Senior Reports Officer and briefly as chief of the Reporting Branch, recalled another case. An HIR was drafted concerning an incident with a TIDE match, but the TIDE record was based on an FBI inquiry. Later on the FBI ended its inquiry and cleared the individual of any connection to terrorism – but because DHS had filed an HIR on the person, the individual's record was kept active in TIDE. Subcommittee interviews of Ken Hunt (2/27/2012), former Senior Reports Officer (3/1/2012), Mark Collier (3/8/2012), and Ole Broughton (4/18/2012).

[157] Memorandum from Matthew L. Kronisch to I&A Reports Officers and Fusion Center Representatives, "Subject: Roles & Functions" (7/29/2008), DHS-HSGAC-FC-047644.

[158] Memorandum from Matthew L. Kronisch to I&A Reports Officers and Fusion Center Representatives, "Subject: Roles & Functions" (7/29/2008), DHS-HSGAC-FC-047644.

[159] Email from Barbara Alexander to James Chaparro, et al., "Subject: Open Source Requirements" (4/1/2009) DHS-HSGAC-FC-059585.

[160] Subcommittee interview of Barbara Alexander (6/22/2012).

[161] Subcommittee interview of Margo Schlanger (5/22/2012).

[162] Principles for Respecting Civil Rights and Civil Liberties in Intelligence Products, Margo Schlanger (3/30/2011),DHS-HSGAC-FC-056639.

[163] With the assistance of a former DHS Civil Rights and Civil Liberties official, the Subcommittee investigation identified two published reports from the period of review which may have included inappropriate information on identified individuals. Subcommittee interview of Timothy Skinner (3/14/2012); DHS-HSGAC-FC-013331, DHS-HSGAC-FC-14519.

[164] For more on TIDE, see footnote 155.

[165] "TERRORISM WATCHLIST: [Organization] Advertises Literature Produced by Persons with Records Related to Terrorism," draft HIR, cancelled 2/26/2010, DHS-HSGAC-FC-16408.

[166] Id.

[167] See "Mongols motorcycle gang members arrested," *Associated Press*, (10/21/2008), http://www.usatoday.com/news/nation/2008-10-21-mongols_N.htm; "U.S. targets bikers' identity," *Los Angeles Times*, Scott Glover (10/22/2008), http://articles.latimes.com/2008/ oct/22/local/me-mongols22.

[168] "Mongols Motorcycle Club (MMC) Chapter . . . Issues Guidelines for Intelligence Collection During Police Encounters," draft HIR, cancelled 2/17/2010, DHS-HSGAC-FC-16551.

[169] Id.

[170] "TERRORISM WATCHLIST—Individual with Terrorist-related Records Speaks at a Seminar . . .," draft HIR, cancelled 7/16/2009, DHS-HSGAC-FC-16303.

[171] "TERRORISM WATCHLIST: Naturalized U.S. Citizen with Records Related to Terrorism is Scheduled to a Lead Seminar [sic],"draft HIR, cancelled 1/11/10, DHS-HSGAC-FC-016339.

[172] "TERRORISM WATCHLIST: U.S. Citizen with Terrorist-related Records Speaks at a Mosque . . . "draft HIR, cancelled 2/17/2010, INT-2483-09, DHS-HSGAC-FC-016644.

[173] Id.

[174] DHS response to Subcommittee inquiry, DHS-HSGAC-FC-059967.

[175] The Subcommittee review of the 386 unclassified HIRs found only 94 had any discernible relationship to terrorism.

[176] "HIR/AZ-0032-09 Law Enforcement Officers Seize Methamphetamine From a Vehicle's Hidden Compartment," published December 22, 2009, DHS-HSGAC-FC-013267.

[177] The investigation noted the potential for duplication between terrorism-related information sharing efforts by fusion centers and FBI-led Joint Terrorism Task Forces (JTTFs), but did not address the issue in its inquiry. At the request of House and Senate Homeland Security Committees, the Government Accountability Office is currently reviewing fusion centers, JTTFs and other information-sharing entities for potential duplication. GAO expects to release its findings in 2013.

[178] "HIR/WA-0001-10 Theft of Explosives from Storage Bunker in Walla Walla, Washington," (3/3/2010), DHS-HSGAC-FC-016082.

[179] Id.

[180] Id.

[181] Id.

[182] "Theft of Explosives in Walla Walla" (7/31/2009), ATF Press Release, http://www.atf.gov/press/releases/2009/07/073109-sea-walla-walla-explosives-theft.html.

[183] "HIR/CA-0078-09 Imam Anwar Nassar Al-Awaki [sic] Praised Fort Hood," (11/13/2009) DHS-HSGAC-FC-014138.

[184] "Fort Hood shooting suspect's ties to mosque investigated," *Los Angeles Times*, Josh Meyer (11/9/2009); (11/9/2009) "Tragedy at Fort Hood: What They Knew," World News with Charlie Gibson, ABC News, Brian Ross(11/9/2009); "Details Emerge About Fort Hood Suspect's Past and His Communications," Fox News, Catherine Herridge (11/9/2009).

[185] To make matters worse, DHS published the report misspelling the Al Qaeda imam's name in the report's title, dubbing him "Al-Awaki."

[186] Performance review provided by DHS (10/26/2010). DHS-HSGAC-FC-004908
[187] Id.
[188] 3/10/2010 "Private Security Firm Claims al-Qaida to Target Tourists in North Africa," HIR/CA-0014-10, DHS-HSGAC-FC-013566.
[189] 4/28/2009 "TAM-C ALERT: MODERATE: NORTH AFRICA," Institute for Terrorism Research and Response,PSI-ITRR-01-0001.
[190] 3/10/2010 "Private Security Firm Claims al-Qaida to Target Tourists in North Africa," HIR/CA-0014-10, DHS-HSGAC-FC-013566.
[191] For more discussion of NCTC, please see the introduction.
[192] Deficiencies in the TIDE database are described earlier.
[193] Subcommittee interview of Senior Reports Officer (3/20/2012). See also, "Standard Operating Procedure for Homeland Intelligence Report Production, v. 1.1," (6/2010) DHS-HSGAC-FC-056483.
[194] Standard Operating Procedure for Homeland Intelligence Report Production, v. 1.1, DHS, 6/25/2010, DHS-HSGAC-FC-056483.
[195] Id.
[196] Subcommittee interview of Joel Cohen (4/16/2012).
[197] Subcommittee interviews of Rick Kopel, DHS/NCTC (4/11/2012), and Cordel James, FBI (6/21/2012).
[198] Subcommittee interview of Joel Cohen (4/16/2012).
[199] Id.
[200] Subcommittee interview of Rick Kopel, DHS/NCTC (4/11/2012).
[201] Subcommittee interviews of Cordel James, FBI (6/21/2012), Rick Kopel, DHS/NCTC (4/11/2012), Joel Cohen (4/16/2012); FBI.gov, "FBI-National Crime Information Center," http://www.fbi.gov/about-us/cjis/ncic/.
[202] Subcommittee interview of Cordel James, FBI (6/21/2012).
[203] Testimony of Timothy J. Healy before the House Judiciary Committee (3/24/10), http://www. fbi.gov/news/ testimony/sharing-and-analyzing-information-to-prevent-terrorism.
[204] Id.; Subcommittee interview of Cordel James, FBI (6/21/2012).
[205] Subcommittee interviews of Rick Kopel, DHS/NCTC (4/11/2012) and Cordel James, FBI (6/21/2012).
[206] Id.
[207] Id.
[208] Subcommittee interview of Rick Kopel, DHS/NCTC (4/11/2012).
[209] At least one DHS I&A official told the Subcommittee that he recalled this duplicative reporting was taking place. Mark Collier, a Senior Reports Officer and one-time reporting branch chief, told Subcommittee staff that NCTC at times "would get the same 'encounter package'" report "through TSC before they got it from us." Subcommittee interview of Mark Collier (3/8/2012).
[210] Subcommittee interview of Caryn Wagner (9/16/2012).
[211] DHS provided the Subcommittee with limited unclassified biographical data on the reporting officials. As a result it was difficult for the Subcommittee investigation to discern whether particular reporting officials were Intelligence Officers (IOs) or Reports Officers (ROs).
[212] Subcommittee interviews of Mikael Johnston (6/18/2012) and Jonathan Wilham (3/6/2012).
[213] DHS response to Subcommittee inquiry, DHS-HSGAC-FC-059967.
[214] DHS personnel spreadsheet, DHS-HSGAC-FC-7154.
[215] General Schedule Salary Tables, 2009 and 2010, U.S. Office of Personnel Management, http://www.opm.gov/oca/10tables/index.asp.
[216] DHS personnel spreadsheet, DHS-HSGAC-FC-7154.
[217] Subcommittee interview of Former Senior Reports Officer (3/21/2012).
[218] Subcommittee interview of Senior Reports Officer (3/20/2012).
[219] Subcommittee interview of Mark Collier (3/8/2012).
[220] Subcommittee interview of Jonathan Wilham (3/6/2012).
[221] Id.
[222] Subcommittee interview of Former Senior Reports Officer (3/21/2012).
[223] Subcommittee interview of Former Senior Reports Officer (3/1/2012).
[224] Subcommittee interview of Harold "Skip" Vandover (3/22/2012).
[225] Subcommittee interviews of Mikael Johnston (6/18/2012), Harold "Skip" Vandover (5/24/2012), Keith Jones (4/2/2012).
[226] DHS response to Subcommittee inquiry, DHS-HSGAC-FC-059967.
[227] Memorandum from James Chaparro to Bart Johnson, "Homeland Intelligence Reports (HIRs)" (1/7/2010), DHS-HSGAC-FC-050742.
[228] Subcommittee interview of Caryn Wagner (9/16/2012).
[229] In August 2012, the department initiated a "pilot" three-week training course for reports officers, but it is a test and has not been instituted as a recurring course. Subcommittee interview of Harold "Skip" Vandover (8/22/2012).

[230] Subcommittee interviews of Harold "Skip" Vandover (3/22/2012); Timeline of Reporting Branch chiefs, DHS-HSGAC-FC-050767.

[231] Subcommittee interviews of Harold "Skip" Vandover (3/22/2012, 5/24/2012).

[232] Subcommittee interview of James Chaparro (6/28/2012).

[233] Memorandum from James Chaparro to Bart Johnson, "Homeland Intelligence Reports (HIRs)" (1/7/2010), DHS-HSGAC-FC-050742.

[234] Subcommittee interview of Caryn Wagner (9/16/2012). "It's a pilot, a proof of concept, to see if we can meet all the requirements," Daylen Heil, a DHS official coordinating the training effort, told the Subcommittee in August, when the course was underway. At that point no further training courses had been scheduled, Mr. Heil said. Subcommittee interview with Daylen Heil (8/22/2012).

[235] DHS is no longer teaching the course, and is piloting a new three-week training. Subcommittee interviews of Harold "Skip" Vandover (8/22/2012), Caryn Wagner (9/16/2012), DHS response to Subcommittee inquiry, DHS-HSGAC-FC-059968.

[236] "Unit 5.2 – Graduation" of the course student guide reads, "Congratulations! After you are briefed on the graduation process, a senior DHS official will offer closing remarks and distribute graduation certificates." It lists "Topics Covered" during graduation to include "The importance of training to the success of the Intelligence Enterprise." DHS Reports Officer Basic Course (ROBC) Student Guide, Rev. 0511, DHS-HSGAC-FC-057117.

[237] Subcommittee interview of Ayn Crawley (6/13/2012).

[238] Id.

[239] Id.

[240] The Subcommittee reviewed resumes for DHS Intelligence Officers at fusion centers and found that most had years of intelligence experience, but few reflected experience collecting intelligence or drafting reports. Mikael Johnston, who oversaw IOs until March 2012, said he believed about a third of IOs had come to DHS with some experience or training in reporting. Subcommittee interview of Mikael Johnston (6/18/2012).

[241] Subcommittee interview of former Senior Reports Officer (3/1/2012).

[242] Subcommittee interview of former Senior Reports Officer (3/21/2012).

[243] Subcommittee interview of Harold "Skip" Vandover (3/22/2012).

[244] Subcommittee interview of Mark Collier (3/8/2012).

[245] Id.

[246] Email from Barbara Alexander to James Chaparro, et al., "Subject: Open Source Requirements," (4/1/2009) DHS-HSGAC-FC-059585.

[247] Memorandum from James Chaparro to Bart Johnson, "Homeland Intelligence Reports (HIRs)" (1/7/2010), DHS-HSGAC-FC-050742.

[248] Subcommittee interview of Amy Kardell (6/5/2012). Ms. Kardell said the HIRWG report was complete before December 2010, but was delayed from being formally submitted to Undersecretary Wagner because of several factors, including Christmas vacation. Concerns from other offices about drafting the report's cover memorandum delayed the report's submission by two months, Ms. Kardell said. See also "Homeland Intelligence Report Working Group (HIRWG) Phase 1 Report and Recommendations," (11/2010) DHS-HSGAC-FC-050770

[249] "Homeland Intelligence Report Working Group (HIRWG) Phase 1 Report and Recommendations," (11/2010) DHS-HSGAC-FC-050770, at 4.

[250] "Homeland Intelligence Report Working Group (HIRWG) Phase 1 Report and Recommendations," (11/2010) DHS-HSGAC-FC-050770.

[251] Memorandum from Caryn Wagner to DHS Homeland Security Intelligence Council, "Subject: DHS Reports Officer Course (ROC)" (4/25/2012), DHS-HSGAC-FC-059035. The "pilot" course is being conducted on a one-time basis with a class of 10 students. There are hopes to improve the training and offer it in 2013 and beyond, but those courses are not yet scheduled. Subcommittee interview of Daylen Heil (8/22/2012).

[252] DHS response to Subcommittee inquiry (9/21/2012), DHS-HSGAC-059968.

[253] Memorandum for Brian Kelly, "SUBJECT: Development of the Reports Officer Course, (ROC)" (2/3/2012), DHS-HSGAC-FC-059023.

[254] Subcommittee interview of Harold "Skip" Vandover (5/24/2012).

[255] 3/2011 Homeland Intelligence Report Working Group (HIRWG) Phase 1 Report and Recommendations, November 2010, DHS-HSGAC-FC-050770.

[256] Subcommittee interview of Harold "Skip" Vandover (3/22/2012).

[257] Memorandum from James Chaparro to Bart Johnson, "Homeland Intelligence Reports (HIRs)" (1/7/2010), DHS-HSGAC-FC-050742.

[258] GAO Report, "Department of Homeland Security: Risk Assessment and Enhanced Oversight Needed to Manage Reliance on Contractors" (10/17/2007), GAO-08-14T, http://www.gao. gov/new.items/d08142t.pdf; Subcommittee interviews of Jonathan Wilham (3/6/2012) and Harold "Skip" Vandover (3/22/2012).

[259] The Subcommittee notes that several DHS officials interviewed for the investigation first joined the Department as contract employees. Subcommittee interviews of former I&A Senior Reports Officer (3/1/2012), Jonathan

Wilham (3/6/2012), former Senior Reports Officer (3/28/2012), former Senior Reports Officer (3/30/2012), and Keith Jones (4/2/2012).

[260] Subcommittee interview of Harold "Skip" Vandover (3/22/2012). Mr. Vandover told the Subcommittee that when he joined the branch in December 2009, it had 10 government employees and between 20 and 25 contractors.

[261] Subcommittee interview of Harold "Skip" Vandover (3/22/2012).

[262] Memorandum from James Chaparro to Bart Johnson, "Homeland Intelligence Reports (HIRs)" (1/7/2010), DHS-HSGAC-FC-050742. Mr. Vandover noted that a Reports Officer in Phoenix, Arizona was a contract employee. Subcommittee interview of Harold "Skip" Vandover (3/22/2012).

[263] Subcommittee interview of Harold "Skip" Vandover (3/22/2012).

[264] Subcommittee interview of former Senior Reports Officer (3/21/2012).

[265] Id.

[266] Subcommittee interviews of Harold "Skip" Vandover (3/22/2012) and former Senior Reports Officer (3/21/2012).

[267] Subcommittee interview of Harold "Skip" Vandover (3/22/2012).

[268] DHS response to Subcommittee inquiry (9/14/2012), DHS-HSGAC-FC-059877.

[269] Subcommittee interview of Mark Collier (3/8/2012).

[270] Email from DHS to Subcommittee staff, "Subj: Request from Wilham interview" (7/26/2012).

[271] DHS Support to Fusion Centers (5/3/2012), PSI-DHS-56-0021.

[272] "I don't recall noting poor reporting in an annual review. It never came up as a black mark against a guy," said Mikael Johnston, who was head of the SLPO in 2009 and 2010. Subcommittee interview of Mikael Johnston (6/18/2012).

[273] DHS provided one personnel review document for a Reports Officer which cited the RO's intelligence reporting reflected "an 80% acceptance rate and 85% error free." "Employee Performance Plan and Appraisal Form for the period 10/1/2011-9/30/2012," (produced 8/17/2012), at 3, DHS-HSGAC-FC-059577.

[274] Subcommittee interview of Jonathan Wilham (3/6/2012).

[275] Mr. Wilham said he had at one time proposed three metrics for assessing the quality of reports officer production centered on whether the intelligence was used by others in the Intelligence Community: first, evaluations submitted by consumers of the reports informing DHS of their value; second, instances in which reports are cited within finished intelligence analysis; and third, instances in which readers have requested further information from the branch about the incident being reported. The branch has never instituted a formal review that incorporated these metrics. The Subcommittee requested and received from DHS a tally of reports which had been the subject of any such evaluation, cite or request for information. In all, 17 percent of published HIRs from fusion centers received any form of recognition identified by Mr. Wilham. Subcommittee Interview of Jonathan Wilham (3/6/2012).

[276] Subcommittee interview of Caryn Wagner (9/16/2012).

[277] To obtain this average, the Subcommittee first identified all HIRs from fusion centers DHS published in June 2009 during the 13-month period underview; and for each, calculated the number of days between its drafting and its date of publication; and then averaged the time periods.

[278] See 12/30/2009 Memorandum from Philip Groven to James Chaparro, "Subject: The Fiscal Year 2009 4th Quarter Management Report," DHS-HSGAC-FC-058860. The Reporting Branch has not been alone in delaying or temporarily halting intelligence reporting. Officials told the Subcommittee that at different times, reporting from certain DHS components, notably U.S. Citizenship and Immigration Services (CIS), and the Transportation Security Administration, has halted or been severely restricted. Subcommittee interviews of Senior Reports Officer (3/20/2012) and Amy Kardell (6/5/2012); HIR Working Group Notes, Meeting July 23, 2010, DHS-HSGAC-FC-056573; Subcommittee interview of Chuck Robinson (7/18/2012).

In a written response to the Subcommittee, CIS stated that between 2008 and 2009 it filed fewer than 100 reports, It noted that it had an I&A reports officer supporting its efforts during the period, whom they asked to be removed "due to poor performance." CIS response to Subcommittee inquiry (9/14/2012), DHS-HSGAC-FC-059878. The Subcommittee received no response from TSA.

[279] Prepared Testimony of Secretary Napolitano before the Senate Committee on Homeland Security and Governmental Affairs, "Eight Years after 9/11: Confronting the Terrorist Threat to the Homeland," (9/30/2009) http://www.dhs.gov/news/2009/09/30/secretary-napolitanos-testimony-eight-years-after-911-confronting-terrorist-threat, accessed 9/18/2012.

[280] Subcommittee interview of Bart Johnson (7/11/2012).

[281] Subcommittee interviews of Harold "Skip" Vandover (3/22/12), Timothy Skinner (3/14/12), and Jonathan Wilham (3/6/12). In addition, a December 2009 memorandum from Philip Groven to James Chaparro suggested a policy dispute between OGC and the Reporting Branch contributed to the virtual shutdown, although that policy dispute was not mentioned by the individuals interviewed. Memorandum from Philip Groven to James Chaparro, "Subject: The Fiscal Year 2009 4th Quarter Performance Management Report" (12/30/2009), DHS-HSGAC-FC-058860.

[282] "Responses to Questions Submitted to Matthew L. Kronisch," (3/22/2012), DHS-HSGAC-FC-047634.

283 Id. Mr. Kronisch acknowledged that OGC and other review offices spent many hours reviewing and revising draft reports that the Reporting Branch had already concluded were the product of unauthorized intelligence efforts."The reviewing offices expended significant effort attempting to perfect these noncompliant nominations, many of which could not be perfected," Mr. Kronisch told the Subcommittee. At one point, he said, over 300 troubled drafts languished in the review process before most of them were eventually cancelled.

284 Subcommittee interview of Curt Heidtke (8/12/2012).

285 Id.

286 Id. Asked if Mr. Heidtke's statements were accurate, DHS said it did not have further comment on the matter, and deferred to Mr. Heidtke's version of events. Email from DHS to Subcommittee, "Subject: RE: Fusion Center questions" (9/7/2012).

287 Subcommittee interviews of Timothy Skinner (3/14/2012), Ken Hunt (2/27/2012), and Margo Schlanger (5/22/12).

288 Memorandum from Charles E. Allen and Matthew L. Kronisch to All Employees, Detailees, and Contractors Supporting the Office of Intelligence and Analysis, "SUBJECT: Interim Intelligence Oversight Procedures for the Office of Intelligence & Analysis," (4/3/2008) DHS-HSGAC-FC-047637.

289 5 U.S.C. Sec. 552a(e)(7)

290 The HIRs were identified by DHS in September 2011, in response to a Subcommittee request for copies of draft HIRs that had been recommended for cancellation. These 40 were recommended for cancellation by the Privacy Office, the Civil Liberties office, or both; or they were cancelled by a reports officer who explicitly cited privacy or civil liberties concerns in his or her recommendation to cancel.

291 Memorandum from Charles E. Allen and Matthew L. Kronisch to All Employees, Detailees, and Contractors Supporting the Office of Intelligence and Analysis, "SUBJECT: Interim Intelligence Oversight Procedures for the Office of Intelligence & Analysis," (4/3/2008) DHS-HSGAC-FC-047637.

292 DHS response to Subcommittee inquiry (6/2012), DHS-HSGAC-FC-57026.

293 CRS memorandum from Jennifer Elsea and Gina Stevens to the Subcommittee, "Subject: DHS'S Intelligence and Analysis Information Collection Practices," (9/26/2012), at 8.

294 Id.

295 Id.

296 "Homeland Intelligence Report Working Group (HIRWG) Phase 1 Report and Recommendations," (11/2010), at 2, DHS-HSGAC-FC-050770.

297 Subcommittee interview of Charles Robinson (7/18/2012).

298 Email from DHS to the Subcommittee, "Subject: Fusion Centers," (7/15/2011) PSI-DHS-72-000001.

299 See "Homeland Intelligence Report Working Group (HIRWG) Phase 1 Report and Recommendations, November2010," DHS-HSGAC-FC-05770; 1/7/2010 memorandum from James Chaparro to Bart Johnson, "Homeland Intelligence Reports (HIRs)," DHS-HSGAC-FC-050742; Memorandum from Philip Groven to James Chaparro, "Subject: The Fiscal Year 2009 4th Quarter Management Report" (12/30/2009), DHS-HSGAC-FC-058860.

300 Subcommittee interview of Charles Robinson (7/18/2012).

301 Memorandum from James Chaparro to Bart Johnson, "Subject: Homeland Intelligence Reports (HIRs)" (1/7/2010), DHS-HSGAC-FC-050742.

302 Subcommittee interview of Charles Robinson (7/18/2012).

303 Id.

304 "Homeland Intelligence Report Working Group (HIRWG) Phase 1 Report and Recommendations, November 2010," DHS-HSGAC-FC-05770, at 2.

305 "2011 Fusion Center Federal Cost Inventory: Results" (6/2012), at 9.

306 Figures are based on FEMA estimates: "Fusion Center Funding Report," Spreadsheet, 6/22/2012, DHS HSGACFC 058336 and "Fusion Keyword Search Solution Area Funding Report," Spreadsheet 2/24/2010, DHS HSGAC FC057017 at 2.

307 For a list of those capabilities, please see Appendix B of this Subcommittee report.

308 Subcommittee interview of FEMA officials (6/14/2012).

309 In 2009, DHS elevated fusion centers to "national priority" status in the grant program guidance; in 2010, 2011,and 2012, DHS identified fusion centers as one of its highest priorities. FEMA response to Subcommittee inquiry; DHS-HSGAC-FC-057115.

310 Subcommittee interview of FEMA (6/14/2012).

311 Id.; Briefing "FEMA Preparedness Grant Funding for Fusion Centers," FEMA/Grants Program Directorate (6/14/2012).

312 "Fusion Keyword Search Solution Area Funding Report," Spreadsheet 2/24/2010, DHS HSGAC FC 057017 at 2.

313 "Fusion Center Funding Report," Spreadsheet, 6/22/2012, DHS HSGAC FC 058336.

314 At the time, DHS said it recognized 72 state and local fusion centers.

315 In some cases, centers' responses did not consistently distinguish DHS funding from other federal sources.

[316] Comparison of June 2011 Biannual Strategy Implementation Report data; DHS HSGAC FC 05833-058340;"Information Sharing and Fusion Center Funding" (12/3/2010); and Vermont Fusion Center response to Subcommittee survey; Vermont Fusion Center 01-0001.

[317] Comparison of June 2011 Biannual Strategy Implementation Report data; DHS HSGAC FC 05833-058340;"Information Sharing and Fusion Center Funding" (12/3/2010); and Minnesota Joint Analysis Center response to Subcommittee survey; PSI-Minnesota Joint Analysis Center 01-0001 at 2.

[318] Subcommittee interview of FEMA (6/14/2012).

[319] Id.

[320] Id.

[321] GAO, *Information Sharing: Federal Agencies Are Helping Fusion Centers Build and Sustain Capabilities, and Protect Privacy, but Could Better Measure Results*, GAO-10-972 (Washington D.C.: September 2010), at 14. In late 2011, DHS attempted to conduct a cost assessment of federal support to fusion centers, however it was unable to include financial figures for FEMA grant funding to fusion centers, which, by FEMA estimates, is a greater federal cost than the operational items (for example personnel, technology, security clearances and network connectivity) in the DHS 2011 cost assessment. 6/2012, "2011 Fusion Center Federal Cost Inventory: Results," DHS; "Fusion Center Funding Report," Spreadsheet, 6/22/2012, DHS HSGAC FC 058336 and "Fusion Keyword Search Solution Area Funding Report," Spreadsheet 2/24/201, DHS HSGAC FC 057017 at 2.

[322] "The Federal Emergency Management Agency's Requirements for Reporting Homeland Security Grant Program Achievements,"OIG-12-92 (6/2012), http://www.oig.dhs.gov/assets/Mgmt/2012/OIG_12-92_Jun12.pdf.

[323] Id. at 9.

[324] Subcommittee interview of Elizabeth Harman, Assistant Administrator, DHS Grants Program Directorate (8/2/2012).

[325] See "Testimony: DHS Improved its Risk-Based Grant Programs' Allocation and Management Methods, But Measuring Programs' Impact on National Capabilities Remains a Challenge" (3/11/2008), prepared by GAO, GAO-08-488T; "Single Audit Improvements" (3/13/2009), prepared by GAO, GAO-09-307R.

[326] The visits and reports have changed over time, and FEMA officials indicated they are preparing to make further changes. Subcommittee interviews of Elizabeth Harman (8/2/2012) and FEMA officials (7/19/2012).

[327] Subcommittee interview of Elizabeth Harman (8/2/2012).

[328] Subcommittee interview of FEMA officials (7/19/2012).

[329] Id.

[330] Id.

[331] "The Federal Emergency Management Agency's Requirements for Reporting Homeland Security Grant Program Achievements," OIG-12-92 (6/27/2012).

[332] "Philadelphia Urban Area FY 2009 Monitoring Report" (9/17/2009), FEMA; "Programmatic Monitoring Report, Pennsylvania – Philadelphia Area, HSGP/UASI," (10/18/2011), FEMA, DHS-HSGAC-FC-059194.

[333] Subcommittee interview of FEMA officials (7/19/2012).

[334] Id.

[335] Id.

[336] "The Federal Emergency Management Agency's Requirements for Reporting Homeland Security Grant Program Achievements,"OIG-12-92, at 9, (6/27/2012),http://www.oig.dhs.gov/assets/Mgmt/2012/OIG_12-92_Jun12.pdf.

[337] DHS Improved its Risk-Based Grant Programs' Allocation and Management Methods, But Measuring Programs' Impact on National Capabilities Remains a Challenge," GAO-08-488T, at 5, http://www.gao.gov/assets/120/119323.pdf.

[338] Subcommittee interview of Elizabeth Harman (8/20/12).

[339] Id.

[340] DVIC Funding Overview, SEPARTF; PSI-PEMA-05-0090.

[341] Response to Subcommittee questionnaire (7/23/2010), Delaware Valley Intelligence Center, PSI-Delaware Valley Intelligence Center-01-0001.

[342] The task force is a subgrantee of the state of Pennsylvania; it receives, allots and spends FEMA grant funds for the Philadelphia region.

[343] "Philadelphia Urban Area FY 2009 Monitoring Report" (9/17/2009), FEMA, at 21; DVIC Funding Overview, SEPARTF; PSI-PEMA-05-0090.

[344] "Philadelphia Urban Area FY 2009 Monitoring Report" (9/17/2009), FEMA, at 21.

[345] Id.

[346] "Programmatic Monitoring Report, Pennsylvania – Philadelphia Area, HSGP/UASI" (10/18/2011), FEMA, DHS-HSGAC-FC-059194; Grant Agreement Between PEMA and SEPARTF for FEMA FFY 2010 UASI funds, (6/10/2011), at 37; "FY2011 HSGP Investment Justification: Fusion Center Addendum," at 2.

[347] "Programmatic Monitoring Report, Pennsylvania – Philadelphia Area, HSGP/UASI" (10/18/2011), FEMA, DHS-HSGAC-FC-059194.

[348] 6 U.S.C. § 609 (b)(4).

[349] Correspondence from Christopher F. Wilson, Pennsylvania Governor's Office of General Counsel, to Edward Atkins, Chair, Southeastern Pennsylvania Regional Task Force (9/15/2011), PSI-PEMA-05-0003. The Subcommittee investigation discovered that a DHS official, Joseph Liciardello, served as one of the DVIC project's managers, outside of his professional capacity as a DHS employee. ("I am the Co-Lead on the [DVIC] Project Management Team." Email from Joseph Liciardello to ISC@DHS.gov, "Subject: Request for documents" (9/23/2010), DHS-HSGAC-FC-020104.) He assisted in crafting documents and providing advice for the project and seemed to be counseling the project on how to recharacterize construction costs they intended to cover using grant funds: ("I . . . am handling the lease negotiations for the DVIC for most of the week." Email from Joseph Liciardello to Kurt Bittner, "Subject: RE: DVIC – Siemens Contact Information," (10/11/10), DHS-HSGAC-FC-022630; "We cannot reference construction so I added 'or additional funding as necessary' to . . . the enhanced lease payment clause." Email from Joseph Liciardello to Evalyn Fisher, "Subject: FW: DVIC Lease" (10/5/2010), DHS-HSGAC-FC-024159; "As to the request for a change from SEPARTF 'construction' to 'requirements[‘], it is necessary because of restrictions found in the grant guidance concerning allowable costs." Email from Joseph Liciardello to Douglas Kubinski, "Subject: RE: DVIC Intergovernmental Cooperation Agreement between the City and Task Force" (2/17/2011), DHS-HSGAC-FC-023663).

In interviews with the Subcommittee, Mr. Liciardello said he never referred to himself as a project lead for DVIC, and that his role was "administrative," and "assistance." He said he was versed in the lease process but only because he was a "referee" between the parties. Subcommittee interviews of Joseph Liciardello (10/31/11 and 11/2/11).

The Subcommittee was unable to confirm the extent of Mr. Liciardello's role in the project, in part because DHS did not produce all emails from his account related to his extra-professional involvement the project. In a written explanation, the Department stated, "our technological representatives were unable to access" emails from May and June 2011. Response to Subcommittee inquiry, DHS, DHS-HSGAC-FC-059294.

[350] "Issues were first raised regarding the construction issue in late February 2011," PEMA officials told the Subcommittee. "They rose to DHS' level . . . we have an April 26, 2011 note from Dennis Donehoo [of FEMA] requiring a [construction] waiver." Subcommittee interview of Pennsylvania Emergency Management Agency officials (11/14/2011).

[351] "The Federal Emergency Management Agency (FEMA) has asked PEMA for the status of the construction/renovation waiver as federal guidance requires such a waiver . . . . PEMA will be unable to reimburse the SEPARTF for any expenditure related to the DVIC until such a time that SEPARTF submits a construction/renovation waiver to PEMA and that waiver is consequently approved by FEMA[.]" Correspondence from Christopher F. Wilson, Chief Counsel, Governor of the Commonwealth of Pennsylvania, to Ed Atkins, Chairperson, Southeastern Pennsylvania Regional Task Force (9/15/2011), PSI-050-0004.

[352] Correspondence from Edward J. Atkins, Chairman, Southeastern Pennsylvania Regional Task Force, to Dennis Donehoo, Program Analyst, FEMA (9/26/2011), PSI-PEMA-05-0012. FEMA did not grant the waiver.

[353] "Programmatic Monitoring Report, Pennsylvania – Philadelphia Area, HSGP/UASI," FEMA, DHS-HSGAC-FC-059194.

[354] Id. at 18.

[355] Letter from Edward J. Atkins, Chairman, SEPARTF to Dennis Donehoo, FEMA (2/23/2012), DHS-HSGAC-FC-05-0796.

[356] Subcommittee interview of Pennsylvania Emergency Management Agency officials (8/1/2012).

[357] PEMA Spreadsheet. (9/20/12)

[358] DVIC Funding Overview, SEPARTF; PSI-PEMA-05-0090; Subcommittee interview of Pennsylvania Emergency Management Agency officials (8/1/2012).

[359] See "2011 National Network of Fusion Centers, Final Report, May 2012," DHS-HSGAC-FC-057027.

[360] Subcommittee interview of FEMA officials (6/14/2012).

[361] See "Report: Tsunami warning funds squandered in American Samoa," CNN.com, Drew Griffin and David Fitzpatrick (10/28/2009), http://edition.cnn.com/2009/WORLD/americas/10/27/asamoa.tsunami.warning system/ index.html.

[362] Subcommittee interview of FEMA officials (6/14/2012).

[363] "OMB Circular A-133 Compliance Supplement 2011," Part 1, http://www.whitehouse.gov/sites/default/files/ omb/assets/OMB/circulars/a133_compliance/2011/pt1.pdf.

[364] See "Single Audit: Opportunities Exist to Improve the Single Audit Process and Oversight," (3/13/2009), prepared by GAO, GAO-09-307R, http://www.gao.gov/new.items/d09307r. pdf.

[365] "Report on National Single Audit Sampling Project" (6/2007), President's Council on Integrity and Efficiency, http://www.ignet.gov/pande/audit/NatSamProjRptFINAL2.pdf.

[366] "The State of California's Management of State Homeland Security Program Grants Awarded During Fiscal Years 2004 through 2006," prepared by DHS IG, (2/2009) OIG-09-33, http:// ipv6.dhs.gov/xoig/assets/ mgmtrpts/OIG_09-33_Feb09.pdf.

[367] Id.

[368] February 2011 "The State of California's Management of Urban Areas Security Initiative Grants Awarded During Fiscal Years 2006 through 2008," prepared by DHS IG, OIG-11-46, http://www.oig.dhs.gov/assets%5CMgmt%5COIG_11-46_Feb11.pdf.

[369] "[T]here is no plan to visit the other three urban areas that received Urban Areas Security Initiative grant funds . .. . The FY 2010 visits would not be timely for the FYs 2006 and 2007 grants since nearly all of these funds would have been spent and reimbursed by the State." "The State of California's Management of Urban Areas Security Initiative Grants Awarded During Fiscal Years 2006 through 2008," prepared by DHS IG, OIG-11-46, at 24, http://www.oig.dhs.gov/assets%5CMgmt%5COIG_11-46_Feb11.pdf (2/2011)

[370] Subcommittee interview of FEMA officials (6/14/2012).

[371] For a complete list of attributes used in the DHS 2011 assessment process, see Appendix B of this Subcommittee report.

[372] Subcommittee interview of Joel Cohen, I&A (7/12/2012).

[373] Subcommittee interview of FEMA (6/14/2012).

[374] Id.

[375] Subcommittee interviews of Joel Cohen, I&A (4/16/2012 and 7/12/2012).

[376] Emergency response and covert surveillance are not key capabilities for fusion centers, as demonstrated in Appendix A and B of this Subcommittee report.

[377] Subcommittee interview of Joel Cohen, I&A (7/12/2012). While Mr. Cohen stated, "I don't know what fusion center needs response vehicles," he confirmed that as long as some portion of the IJ addressed capability gaps, I&A and FEMA would allow the other expenditures as long as they were consistent with FEMA's general guidelines."Okay, so be it," Mr. Cohen said.

[378] Subcommittee interview of FEMA officials (7/19/2012).

[379] Subcommittee interview of FEMA officials (6/14/2012). Specifically, when asked if I&A's State and Local Program Office (SLPO) handled program monitoring of fusion centers, FEMA's Matthew Bower replied, "That's fair to say."

[380] Subcommittee interview of Joel Cohen (7/12/2012).

[381] Id.

[382] Subcommittee interviews of FEMA officials (6/14/2012 and 7/19/2012).

[383] Invoice, Midway Chevrolet-Isuzu, April 14, 2008, PSI-AZDOHS-03-0587 and 2007 State of Arizona Department of Homeland Security, 2007 State Homeland Security Grant Program Project Detail Workbook, Project Justification. PSI-AZDOHS-03-0008. The State of Arizona provided the Subcommittee with the vehicle invoice in response to a request for detailed documentation on its use of homeland security grant funds.

[384] 2007 State of Arizona Department of Homeland Security, 2007 State Homeland Security Grant Program Project Detail Workbook, Project Justification. PSI-AZDOHS-03-0008.

[385] 2007 State of Arizona Department of Homeland Security, 2007 State Homeland Security Grant Program Project Detail Workbook, Project Justification. PSI-AZDOHS-03-0008.

[386] ACTIC, "Intergovernmental Agreement," October 2, 2008, PSI-Flagstaff_Fire_Dept-01-0002.

[387] For a list of fusion center capabilities used by DHS to assess fusion centers in 2011, please see Appendix B of this Subcommittee report.

[388] 1/30/2009 Invoice, Arizona Emergency Products, PSI-AZDOHS-03-0272.

[389] Id.

[390] Subcommittee Interview of Dep. Chief Jerry Bills, Flagstaff Fire Department (2/3/2012). Mr. Bills told the Subcommittee he used the vehicle for his daily commute since receiving it at some point prior to October 2008; he lived 12 miles from his station; and the odometer presently read approximately 27,000 miles. He estimated 15,000 of those miles were from commuting. He did not indicate the truck had ever been used to respond to a CBRNE attack, although he said may have used it to attend and host training sessions in HAZMAT response, terror response and other topics.

[391] "Property Disposal Request and Authorization," March 10, 2010, State of Arizona Surplus Property; also, Midway Chevrolet Invoice, October 27, 2009 PSI-AZDOHS-03-0954.

[392] Subcommittee interview of Cpl. Parker Dunwoody, Arizona State University Police Department (2/2/2012).

[393] Email from Cpl. Parker Dunwoody to the Subcommittee (10/1/2012).

[394] Award letters from Arizona Dept. of Homeland Security (AZDHS) to Arizona Dept. of Public Safety (AZDPS),September 19, 2009, September 18, 2009 and August 6, 2010, PSI-ACTIC-02-0952, PSI-ACTIC-02-0967, PSI-ACTIC-02-0982.

[395] AZDPS lease agreement for ACTIC, July 7, 2009, PSI-AZDOHS-05-0005.

[396] Emails between David W. Nichols, DHS, and Lisa Hansen, AZDHS, February 5-6, 2009, PSI-AZDOHS-03-1312. [Emphasis and emoticon in original.]

[397] For example, "Fiscal Year 2008 Homeland Security Grant Program Guidance and Application Kit," FEMA(2/2008), at 23, B-3; "Fiscal Year 2009 Homeland Security Grant Program Guidance and Application Kit," FEMA(11/2008), at 34, 65; "Fiscal Year 2010 Homeland Security Grant Program Guidance and Application Kit," FEMA (12/2009), at 35, 72.

398 Emails between David W. Nichols, DHS, and Lisa Hansen, AZDHS (2/5/2009 – 2/6/2009), PSI-AZDOHS-03-1312.
399 Id.
400 Id.
401 Id.
402 "Fiscal Year 2009 Homeland Security Grant Program Guidance and Application Kit," FEMA (11/2008), at 63.
403 Subcommittee interview of FEMA officials (7/19/2012).
404 DHS Response to the Subcommittee (8/1/2012), DHS-HSGAC-FC-059232. The states who have been allowed to use grant funds to cover lease costs for fusion centers include California, Arizona, Delaware, Georgia, Massachusetts, Minnesota, Mississippi and Wisconsin; FEMA states it has also allowed fusion center rent costs for Puerto Rico and the city of Jacksonville.
405 Subcommittee interview of Elizabeth Harman (8/2/2012).
406 The program is known as the Urban Area Security Initiative (UASI).
407 2009 Homeland Security Grant Program Award, Grant Agreement Number 555601-05. PSI-ACTIC-02-0907.
408 Wire room list of expenditures, PSI-AZDOHS-08-0047.
409 Id.

410 Email from Maj. Mike Orose, ACTIC, to Subcommittee (2/9/2012), PSI-AZDOHS-08-0001.
411 Id.
412 For the list of Baseline Capabilities for Fusion Centers (2008) and the Critical Operational Capabilities (2008)see Appendix A of this Subcommittee report.
413 "Arizona Counter Terrorism Information Center Baseline Capabilities Assessment," PM-ISE (10/2010), DHS-HSGAC-FC-007497.
414 DHS, "2011 Fusion Center Assessment Individual Report, Arizona Counter Terrorism Information Center," Revised March 2012, DHS-HSGAC-FC-047650.
415 "HSGP Equipment Inventory," NEORFC (7/12/2011).
416 Id.
417 Subcommittee interview of Hugh Shannon, Administrator, Cuyahoga County Medical Examiner's Office (12/15/2011).
418 Northeast Ohio Regional Fusion Center Baseline Capabilities Assessment (October 2010), DHS-HSGAC-FC-010416, at 8, 10.
419 Subcommittee interview of FEMA (7/19/2012).
420 Correspondence from Lee Yoder, SD-LECC Director, to Subcommittee (12/14/2011), at 4, PSI-SDLECC-03-0001; Invoice from ADS to Sherriff's Department of San Diego (4/15/2011), PSI-SDLECC-03-0009.
421 For a list of baseline capabilities for fusion centers, see Appendix A of this Subcommittee report.
422 Correspondence from Lee Yoder, SD-LECC Director, to Subcommittee (12/14/2011), at 4, PSI-SDLECC-03-0001; Invoice from ADS to Sherriff's Department of San Diego (4/15/2011), PSI-SDLECC-03-0009.
423 Memorandum from SD-LECC Director Lee Yoder to Subcommittee (12/14/2011).
424 Memorandum from ADS to HIDTA, Leo Marchand (10/21/2011), PSI-SDLECC-03-0010; Correspondence from Lee Yoder, SD-LECC Director, to Subcommittee (12/14/2011), PSI-SDLECC-03-0001.
425 Subcommittee interview of FEMA (7/19/2012).
426 Id.
427 Dell invoice XCN5467W2M, May 21, 2008, PSI-CalEMA-02-0485; Dell invoice XCNF2T747, May 30, 2008, PSI-CalEMA-02-0411; Dell invoice XCW1P97K1, September 9, 2008, PSI-CalEMA-02-0513; Dell invoice XCW418R32, September 11, 2008, PSI-CalEMA-02-0510; Dell invoice XDRFM3XK7, April 23, 2010, PSI-CalEMA-02-2234; Dell invoice XDRFN8T48, April 23, 2010, PSI-CalEMA-02-2231.
428 Subcommittee interview of SD-LECC officials (11/30/2011).
429 Id.
430 Id.
431 Id.
432 Id.
433 10/2010 "San Diego Law Enforcement Coordination Center – Baseline Capabilities Assessment," PM-ISE, DHS-HSGAC-FC-007893.
434 Id. at 9-12.
435 1FASH8 *Project Concept* MPD-Data Mining, Analytical Software, 1, 4 and 5.
436 FY 2008 DC HSGP Investment 1 Law Enforcement and Information Sharing, 1 and 4. At the time of its application, HSEMA did not know the total amount of funding FEMA would award.
437 Id. at 2, 3.
438 1FASH8 (8SHSP127-01) Award Letter Signed, 1.
439 Id. at 8.
440 1FASH8 Project Plan revised 07152010, 1 and 6.
441 1FASH8 Expenditures; PSI-DCHSEMA-02-0001.

[442] Emails from HSEMA officials to the Subcommittee (6/4/2012).

[443] Subcommittee interview of FEMA (7/19/2012).

[444] Testimony of DHS Secretary Janet Napolitano before the Senate Homeland Security and Governmental Affairs Committee, "Nine Years After 9/11: Confronting the Terrorist Threat to the Homeland" (9/22/2010).

[445] Id.

[446] "The Congressional Research Service (CRS) estimates that there have been 53 homegrown violent jihadist plots or attacks in the United States since September 11, 2001 (9/11)." 11/15/2011 "American Jihadist Terrorism: Combating a Complex Threat," Jerome P. Bjelopera, Congressional Research Service.

[447] See "2010 Baseline Capabilities Assessment," PM-ISE, DHS-HSGAC-FC-007231; "2011 National Network of Fusion Centers, Final Report, May 2012," DHS-HSGAC-FC-057027.

[448] Id.

[449] The need for DHS to gather locally-generated terrorism-related information from fusion centers is an open question. The FBI is the nation's lead federal agency to investigate terrorism cases in the United States, and DHS expects fusion centers to share actual threat-related information immediately with the FBI-led Joint Terrorism Task Forces (JTTFs). ("Domestic Terrorism in the Post-9/11 Era," FBI.gov, http://www.fbi.gov/ news/stories/ 2009/september/domterror_090709/, "Fusion Centers and Joint Terrorism Task Forces," DHS.gov, http://www.dhs.gov/files/programs/gc_1298911926746.shtm). The Department of Justice also leads the National SAR (Suspicious Activity Reporting) Initiative (NSI), which allows personnel at participating fusion centers to relay information about suspicious, potentially terror-linked activity that lacks a clear nexus to terrorism. ("Nationwide SAR Initiative," NCIRC.gov, http://nsi.ncirc.gov/default.aspx). Thus, it is not clear what role exists for DHS to receive terrorism-related information from fusion centers, that is not already being received or coordinated by officials from the Department of Justice. When the Subcommittee asked Undersecretary Wagner what counterterrorism information DHS intelligence reporting at fusion centers shared which was not already being shared via NSI or the JTTFs, Ms. Wagner first suggested reporting on fraudulent documents which had a nexus to a suspected terrorist. Upon consideration, Ms. Wagner said a fusion center would probably share that information with the area JTTF. "There are numerous reasons why IIRs are important," Ms. Wagner then said. "I wish I could come up with a better example." Subcommittee interview of Caryn Wagner (9/16/2012).

[450] Memorandum from Jim Chaparro to Bart Johnson, "Homeland Intelligence Reports" (1/7/2010), at 2, DHS-HSGAC-FC-050743; Email from Chaparro to Johnson, "HIR Backlog" (1/4/2010), DHS-HSGAC-FC-056637.

[451] "2010 Fusion Center Baseline Capabilities Assessment," PM-ISE, (10/2010) DHS-HSGAC-FC-007231; "2011National Network of Fusion Centers, Final Report, May 2012," DHS-HSGAC-FC-057027.

[452] "2010 Fusion Center Baseline Capabilities Assessment," PM-ISE, (10/2010) at 5, DHS-HSGAC-FC-007241.

[453] Id. at 4, DHS-HSGAC-FC-007231. In 2008, the Departments of Justice and Homeland Security devised a list of12 "baseline capabilities" for fusion centers; in 2010, fusion center directors "distilled" that list to eight "National Network priorities." ("Baseline Capabilities for State and Major Urban Area Fusion Centers," September 2008, http://www.it.ojp.gov/ documents/baselinecapabilitiesa.pdf; "National Network of Fusion Centers Fact Sheet," DHS.gov, http://www.dhs.gov/national-network-fusion-centers-fact-sheet).

[454] "2010 Fusion Center Baseline Capabilities Assessment," PM-ISE, (10/2010) at 5, 8, DHS-HSGAC-FC-007231.

[455] September 2008, "Baseline Capabilities for State and Major Urban Area Fusion Centers," http://www.it.ojp.gov/documents/baselinecapabilitiesa.pdf.

[456] "2010 Fusion Center Baseline Capabilities Assessment," PM-ISE, (10/2010) at 17, 18, 24, DHS-HSGAC-FC-007231.

[457] "2010 Fusion Center Baseline Capabilities Assessment," PM-ISE, (10/2010) at 18, 24, 37, DHS-HSGAC-FC-007231 at 37.

[458] "2010 Fusion Center Baseline Capabilities Assessment," PM-ISE, (10/2010) at 3, DHS-HSGAC-FC-007231.

[459] 8/24/2011 "Explanation of Why DHS Did Not Produce the Baseline Capabilities Assessment to Subcommittee Prior to June 24, 2011," prepared by DHS, PSI-DHS-61-0002.

[460] Subcommittee interview of Bart Johnson (6/24/2011).

[461] Id.

[462] Written response from DHS, DHS-HSGAC-FC-059296 (8/1/2012).

[463] Subcommittee interview of PM-ISE officials (9/14/2012); PM-ISE response to Subcommittee inquiry (9/27/2012).

[464] NFCA letter to the Subcommittee (7/1/2011), PSI-NFCA-01-0001.

[465] "About NFCA," http://www.nfcausa.org/; Statement of W. Ross Ashley III, Executive Director, NFCA, before the Subcommittee on Homeland Security, Committee on Appropriations, U.S. House of Representatives, http://appropriations.house.gov/uploaded files/hhrg-112-ap15-rashley-20120307.pdf; Subcommittee interview of Ben Bawden, W. Ross Ashley III (8/21/2012).

[466] Subcommittee interview of Ben Bawden and W. Ross Ashley III (8/21/2012). According to Mr. Ashley, the group receives funds from Microsoft, ESRI, Thomson-Reuters and Mutualink, among other firms. "When you look at why a company's giving money, it's for access," Mr. Ashley said. Mr. Bawden, the group's lobbyist, later clarified that Mr. Ashley meant access to the group's membership. "It's for access to the association's

membership, just like any other professional association," Mr. Bawden said. Email from Ben Bawden to the Subcommittee (10/1/2012).

[467] Subcommittee interview of Ben Bawden and W. Ross Ashley III (8/21/2012).

[468] Id.

[469] Subcommittee interview of Joel Cohen (4/16/2012).

[470] "2011 National Network of Fusion Centers, Final Report, May 2012," DHS-HSGAC-FC-057027, at 5-6. While72 fusion centers participated in the self-assessment, only 60 returned budget and operational cost information, and57 returned data on staff and their products, the report noted.

[471] Id.

[472] Response to Questions for the Record, "Hearing: The Homeland Security Department's Budget Submission for Fiscal Year 2013, March 21, 2012," at 13 (received 6/26/2012).

[473] "2011 National Network of Fusion Centers, Final Report, May 2012," DHS-HSGAC-FC-057027, at 5-6.

[474] Id.

[475] Id.

[476] Subcommittee interview of Joel Cohen (4/16/2012).

[477] Id.

[478] Id.

[479] "2011 National Network of Fusion Centers, Final Report, May 2012," DHS-HSGAC-FC-057027, at vii.

[480] Id. at ix.

[481] Subcommittee of Joel Cohen (4/16/2012). The 2011 report included a section that purported to describe the "maturity" of fusion centers nationwide. A diagram of the "maturity model" showed four stages – "Fundamental," "Emerging," "Enhanced," and "Mature." When 75 percent of fusion centers achieved certain capabilities in each section, according to the model, DHS would judge fusion centers overall at that level. However, the model was not developed until the assessment process was underway, and DHS could provide no objective basis for the thresholds upon which the model relied. "We want to tell a story about the maturity of the network," said Joel Cohen, who developed the maturity model. Explaining how he came up with the 75 percent figure, he said, "We thought two-thirds was too low, and higher than three-quarters was too high. You can have an intellectual debate to your heart's content." Subcommittee interview of Joel Cohen (7/12/2012).

[482] "2011 National Network of Fusion Centers, Final Report, May 2012," DHS-HSGAC-FC-057027, at ix.

[483] "National Network of Fusion Centers," presentation, slide 12, (10/7/2011) DHS-HSGAC-FC-058772

[484] "State and Local Program Office (SLPO) FY 2012 Semi-Annual Briefing," DHS-HSGAC-FC-058809, slide 13(2/8/2012).

[485] Subcommittee interview of Joel Cohen (7/12/2012).

[486] Id.

[487] Id.

[488] Id.

[489] Id.

[490] Id.

[491] Id.

[492] Id.

[493] 10/2010 "2010 Fusion Center Baseline Capabilities Assessment," PM-ISE, at 8, DHS-HSGAC-FC-007231. PM-ISE officials identified the locations of the non-operational centers as Pittsburgh, Philadelphia, South Dakota and Wyoming. Subcommittee interview with PM-ISE officials (9/14/2012).

[494] 10/25/10 Johnson, Bart, "How Fusion Centers Help Keep America Safe," http://www.dhs. gov/blog/2010/10/25/how-fusion-centers-help-keep-america-safe

[495] Testimony of Secretary Janet Napolitano before the House Committee on Homeland Security, "Understanding the Homeland Threat Landscape – Considerations for the 112th Congress" (2/9/2011), http://www.dhs.gov/news/2011/02/09/secretary-napolitanos-testimony-understanding-homeland-threat-landscape.

[496] Testimony of DHS Secretary Janet Napolitano before the Senate Committee on Homeland Security and Government Affairs, "Ten Years After 9/11: Are We Safer?" (9/12/2011), http://www.dhs.gov/news/2011/09/12/testimony-secretary-janet-napolitano-united-states-senate-committee-homeland. DHS has since recognized five more fusion centers, bringing the total of DHS-recognized fusion centers to 77. DHS web site, "Preventing Terrorism Results," http://www.dhs.gov/topic/preventing-terrorism-results, accessed 9/25/2012.

[497] Subcommittee interview of Caryn Wagner (9/16/2012).

[498] 9/4/2009 "State and Local Fusion Center Program: Quarterly Update, Fiscal Year 2009 Report to Congress, Third Quarter."

[499] Id.

[500] "Wyoming FY 2009 Monitoring Report," FEMA (8/18/2009).

[501] Subcommittee interview of Kebin Haller, Deputy Director, Wyoming Division of Criminal Intelligence (9/7/2012).

[502] Id.

[503] "State and Local Fusion Center Program: Quarterly Update, Fiscal Year 2009 Report to Congress, Second Quarter;" (9/4/2009) "State and Local Fusion Center Program: Quarterly Update, Fiscal Year 2009 Report to Congress, Third Quarter." (8/4/2009).

[504] "State and Local Fusion Center Program: Quarterly Update, Fiscal Year 2009 Report to Congress, Second Quarter," (8/4/2009); "State and Local Fusion Center Program: Quarterly Update, Fiscal Year 2009 Report to Congress, Third Quarter;" (9/4/2009); "Fusion Center Locations and Contact Information," DHS.gov, http://www.dhs.gov/fusion-center-locations-and-contact-information, accessed September 27, 2012.

[505] "Philadelphia Urban Area FY2009 Monitoring Report," FEMA (9/17/2009); DVIC Funding Overview, SEPARTF; PSI-PEMA-05-0090.

[506] Response to Subcommittee Questionnaire, Delaware Valley Intelligence Center (7/23/10), at 2, PSI-Delaware Valley Intelligence Center-01-0001.

[507] Subcommittee interview of DVIC officials Walt Smith, Tom Elsasser, and Joseph Liciardello (5/23/2011). Since that interview, Mr. Liciardello has maintained he is not a DVIC official. For more information on Mr. Liciardello's role in the DVIC project, see Chapter V.

[508] Subcommittee interviews of Pennsylvania Emergency Management agency (11/14/2011, 11/30/2011, 8/1/2012).

[509] "2011 National Network of Fusion Centers, Final Report, May 2012," Appendix 5, DHS-HSGAC-FC-057027.

[510] Implementing Recommendations of the 9/11 Commission Act of 2007, Pub. L. No. 110-53, § 511, 121 Stat. 317,318-24 (2007). http://www.gpo.gov/fdsys/pkg/PLAW-110publ53/pdf/ PLAW-110publ53.pdf.

[511] Subcommittee survey of state and local fusion centers (July 2010).

[512] Subcommittee interview of Joel Cohen (4/16/2012).

[513] Michigan Intelligence Operations Center questionnaire response, (7/26/2010) PSI-Michigan Intelligence Operations Center-01-0001.

[514] Michigan Intelligence Operations Center (MIOC) website, http://www.michigan.gov/mioc, accessed Sept. 10, 2012.

[515] Nevada Threat Analysis Center questionnaire response, (7/23/10) PSI-Nevada Threat Analysis Center-01-0001.

[516] "Nevada Threat Analysis Center," Nevada Department of Public Safety website, http://id.dps. nv.gov/programs/Nevada_Threat_Analysis_Center_%28NTAC%29/, accessed Sept. 10, 2012.

[517] John Rollins, "Fusion Centers: Issues and Options for Congress," (1/18/2008) CRS Report RL34070, at 21-22, 87.

[518] Id.

[519] Id. at 68-69.

[520] "Ten Years After 9/11: A Status Report on Information Sharing," before the Senate Homeland Security and Governmental Affairs Committee, testimony of Ronald Brooks (10/12/2011).

[521] NCRIC website, "About NCRIC," https://ncric.org/default.aspx/MenuItemID/122/ MenuGroup/NCRIC+Public+ Contact.htm.

[522] Subcommittee visit to WRTAC, March 16, 2010.

[523] WRTAC Response to Subcommittee Questionnaire, (2/13/2012) PSI-WRTAC-02-0004

[524] "2010 Fusion Center Baseline Capabilities Assessment," PM-ISE, at 3, (10/2010) DHS-HSGAC-FC-007032.

[525] "Fusion Center Success Stories," DHS.gov, http://www.dhs.gov/fusion-center-success-stories, accessed August 21, 2012.

[526] Id.

[527] "Najibullah Zazi Pleads Guilty to Conspiracy to Use Explosives Against Persons or Property in U.S.," press release, Department of Justice, (2/22/2010); See also Sulzberger, A.G., and William K. Rashbaum, "Guilty Plea in Plot to Bomb New York Subway," New York Times, (2/22/2010), http://www.nytimes.com/ 2010/02/23/nyregion/23terror.html; Sulzberger, A.G., "Imam Snared in Terror Plot Admits He Lied to FBI," New York Times, March 4, 2010, http://www.nytimes.com/2010/03/05/nyregion/05terror.html.

[528] "Remarks as Prepared by Secretary Napolitano to New York City First Responders" (9/20/2010), DHS Website, http://www.dhs.gov/news/2010/09/10/remarks-prepared-secretary-napolitano-new-york-city-first-responders, accessed 9/18/2012.

[529] "Fusion Center Success Stories," DHS.gov, http://www.dhs.gov/fusion-center-success-stories, accessed August21, 2012.

[530] "Najibullah Zazi Case," April 2011, Colorado Information Analysis Center.

[531] The CIAC summary notes, however, that two troopers received calls from citizens "reporting concerns and events in-which they deemed suspicious [sic] after the Zazi case became public." The first news stories regarding the Zazi case appeared on Sept. 16, 2009.

[532] "Najibullah Zazi Case," April 2011, Colorado Information Analysis Center.

[533] Id.

[534] Email from Capt. Steve Garcia, CIAC Director, to Subcommittee, "Subject: Follow-up inquiry from PSI"(8/33/2012), PSI-CIAC-03-0001.

[535] "Faisal Shahzad Pleads Guilty in Manhattan Federal Court to 10 Federal Crimes Arising from Attempted Car Bombing in Times Square," Press release, U.S. Department of Justice, June 21, 2010, http://www.justice.gov/ opa/pr/2010/June/10-ag-721.html.

536 "Fusion Center Success Stories," DHS.gov, http://www.dhs.gov/fusion-center-success-stories, accessed August21, 2012.
537 Id.
538 Letter from NY State Police Capt. Douglas R Keyer Jr. to the Subcommittee, Mar. 29, 2011. NYSIC characterized the May 4 AAA call as "an important lead [for the FBI] regarding the second vehicle used by Shahzad."
539 Letter from NY State Police Capt. Douglas R Keyer Jr. to the Subcommittee, Mar. 29, 2011.
540 Subcommittee interview of Timothy Parry, senior investigator, New York State Police (9/6/2012).
541 Id.
542 Id.
543 Correspondence from FFC Director Robert LeFiles to the Subcommittee, March 24, 2011, Florida Fusion Center02-0001.
544 Id.
545 Press release, "Five Arrested for Conspiracy against Troopers, Judges," Alaska State Troopers (3/10/2011), http://www.dps.state.ak.us/pio/docs/Press/2011/ConspiracyArrest_031111.pdf.
546 Press release, "Guilty Verdicts in USA v. Cox, Barney and Vernon," U.S. Attorney for the District of Alaska, (6/19/2012) http://www.justice.gov/usao/ak/news/2012/June_2012/ Francis%20Schaeffer%20Cox.html
547 Subcommittee interview of Lex Leath (9/26/2012).
548 "Speeches put militia leader Schaeffer Cox on FBI radar," Richard Mauer, Anchorage Daily News (5/30/2012).
549 Subcommittee interview of Lex Leath (9/26/2012).
550 Id.
551 "HIR/AK-0001-11, TERRORISM WATCHLIST—Alaska Militia Leader Continues Violent Rhetoric," (1/2011), PSI-AKIAC-01-000001.
552 "Speeches put militia leader Schaeffer Cox on FBI radar," Richard Mauer, Anchorage Daily News (5/30/2012), http://www.adn.com/2012/05/29/2484451/speeches-put-militia-leader-on.html.
553 "Informants aided FBI in militia probe, court documents show," Associated Press, (3/29/2011), http://www.adn.com/2011/03/29/1781500/informants-aided-fbi-in-militia.html.
554 "Militia leader told volunteers to be ready to shoot to kill agents," Richard Mauer, Anchorage Daily News (5/22/2012), http://www.adn.com/2012/05/21/2474525/militia-leader-told-his-squad.html.
555 Letter from Lt. Rex Leath to the Subcommittee (10/1/2012)
556 DHS reponse to Subcommittee inquiry, DHS-HSGAC-FC-059981.
557 Subcommittee interview of DHS (12/13/2011).
558 Statewide Terrorism & Intelligence Center, "Daily Intelligence Notes," November 10, 2011, PSI-Illinois StatePolice-01-0003.
559 "Cyberwar Plan Has New Focus On Deterrence," Wall Street Journal, Julian E. Barnes and Siobhan Gorman(7/15/2011); "Cyber Combat: Act of War," Wall Street Journal, Siobhan Gorman and Julian E. Barnes (5/30/2011)
560 "Foreign hackers targeted U.S. water plant in apparent malicious cyber attack, expert says," Washington Post, Ellen Nakashima (11/18/2011), http://www.washingtonpost.com/blogs/checkpoint-washington/post/foreign-hackers-broke-into-illinois-water-plant-control-system-industry-expert-says/2011/11/18/gIQAgmTZYN_blog.html.
561 "Illinois Water Pump Failure Report," DHS, ICSB-11-327-01, (11/23/2011) DHS-HSGAC-FC-019824.
562 "Working on his vacation in Russia, contractor touches off false report of cyberattack," *Associated Press* (12/1/2011).
563 Id.
564 "NETWORK INTRUSION INTO A SPRINGFIELD, Illinois Public Water District's SCADA system, originated in Russia, resulted in a pump burnout," IIR-4-007-0104-12, Nov. 15, 2011, DHS-HSGAC-FC-019826."HIRs[/IIRs] are not analytic products and should present factual information, rather than theories or conclusions."Standard Operating Procedure for Homeland Intelligence Report Production, 6/25/10, DHS-FC-HSGAC-056474.
565 Subcommittee interview of Anne Wessel, Chuck Robinson (12/13/2011).
566 "NETWORK INTRUSION INTO A SPRINGFIELD, Illinois Public Water District's SCADA system, originated in Russia, resulted in a pump burnout," IIR-4-007-0104-12, Nov. 15, 2011, DHS-HSGAC-FC-019826.
567 Daily Intelligence Highlights, "Illinois: Water System Disrupted by Cyber Intrusion," (11/15/2011)
568 DHS response to Subcommittee inquiry, (9/19/2012) DHS-HSGAC-FC-059955.
569 CERT is part of DHS' National Protection and Programs Directorate, separate from I&A.
570 "ICS-CERT INFORMATION BULLETIN: ICSB-11-327-01—ILLINOIS WATER PUMP FAILURE REPORT," Industrial Control Systems Cyber Emergency Response Team (ICS-CERT), November 23, 2011, DHS-HSGAC-FC-019824.
571 Id.
572 Subcommittee interview of Anne Wessel, Chuck Robinson (12/13/2011).

[573] Id.

[574] "Jared Lee Laughner Pleads Guilty to Federal Charges in Tucson Shooting," Department of Justice press release, (8/7/2012), http://www.justice.gov/opa/pr/2012/August/12-crm-983.html; "Jared Loughner, Ariz. shooting suspect, pleads guilty to 19 counts," CBSNews.com (8/7/2012) http://www.cbsnews.com/8301-504083_162-57488644 -504083/jared-loughner-ariz-shooting-suspect-pleads-guilty-pleads-guilty-to-19-counts/.

[575] "DHS Memo Suggests Shooter May Be Linked to Racist Organization," Jennifer Griffin, FoxNews.com (1/9/2011), http://politics.blogs.foxnews.com/2011/01/09/dhs-memo-suggests-shooter-may-be-linked-racist-organization.

[576] "Jared Loughner's supremacists tie debunked," POLITICO, Kenneth Vogel (1/11/2011), http://www.politico.com/news/stories/0111/47438.html.

[577] Id.

[578] Id..

[579] Harris, Shane, "ANALYSIS: Intelligence File One Bad Apple," Government Executive, Apr. 1, 2011, http://www.govexec.com/features/0411-01/0411-01adif.htm.

[580] "The Modern Militia Movement, MIAC Strategic Report," Missouri Intelligence Analysis Center (MIAC), (2/20/09), http://www.news-leader.com/assets/pdf/DO131242323.PDF, accessed 9/26/2012.

[581] Among other errors, the document reportedly misspelled President Barack Obama's first name, and contained sentences reproduced verbatim from other sources without attribution. See Livengood, Chad, "Top law officials defend embattled MIAC agency," Springfield (Mo.) News-Leader, Sept. 10, 2009.

[582] "The Modern Militia Movement, MIAC Strategic Report," Missouri Intelligence Analysis Center (MIAC), (2/20/09), http://www.news-leader.com/assets/pdf/DO131242323.PDF, accessed 9/26/2012.

[583] Livingood, Chad, "Agency apologizes for militia report on candidates," Springfield (Mo.) News-Leader, March25, 2009.

[584] Id.

[585] The Major Cities Chiefs Association, Global, DOJ, and DHS supported the development of this report, which describes "the all-crimes approach to gathering, processing, reporting, analyzing, and sharing of suspicious activity by the local police agency."

[586] For additional information regarding the ISE Functional Standard for SAR, visit http://www.ise.gov/pages/ctiss.html.

[587] The ISE Shared Spaces concept is a key element of the *ISE Enterprise Architecture Framework* and helps resolve the information processing and usage problems identified by the 9/11 Commission. ISE Shared Spaces are networked data and information repositories used by ISE participants to make their standardized terrorism-related information, applications, and services accessible to other ISE participants. ISE Shared Spaces also provide an infrastructure solution for those ISE participants with national security system (NSS) network assets, historically sequestered with only other NSS systems, to interface with ISE participants having only civil network assets. Additionally, ISE Shared Spaces also provide the means for foreign partners to interface and share terrorism information with their U.S. counterparts. For more information about the ISE Shared Spaces concept, reference the *ISE Enterprise Architecture Framework* and the *ISE Profile Architecture Implementation Strategy* at www.ise.gov.

[588] Additional information regarding CALEA Standard 51.1.1—Criminal Intelligence is available at http://www.calea.org/online/newsletter/no79/criminalintelligence.htm.

[589] LEIU *Criminal Intelligence File Guidelines*—http://www.it.ojp.gov/documents/LEIU_Crim_Intell_File_Guidelines.pdf.

[590] LEIU *Audit Checklist for the Criminal Intelligence Function*—http://it.ojp.gov/documents/LEIU_audit_checklist.pdf.

[591] IALEIA and Global's *Law Enforcement Analytic Standards* booklet is available at http://www.it.ojp.gov/documents/law_enforcement_analytic_standards.pdf.

[592] IALEIA and Global's *Law Enforcement Analytic Standards* booklet is available at http://www.it.ojp.gov/documents/law_enforcement_analytic_standards.pdf

[593] The *Minimum Criminal Intelligence Training Standards for Law Enforcement and Other Criminal Justice Agencies in the United States* is accessible at http://www.it.ojp.gov/ documents/min_crim_intel_stand.pdf.

[594] Those fusion centers utilizing an all-crimes approach that includes gang-related criminal intelligence are encouraged to consult Global's *Guidelines for Establishing and Operating Gang Intelligence Units and Task Forces* to assist in the coordination and/or implementation of their efforts.

[595] These capabilities were developed to ensure that the privacy policies that fusion centers develop are at least as comprehensive as the ISE Privacy Guidelines (see the Methodology section for further background). The achievement of these capabilities will result in a fusion center privacy protection policy that meets the Section 12.d. requirement of the ISE Privacy Guidelines.

[596] The term "protected information" is defined in the ISE Privacy Guidelines, Section 1.b., for both non-intelligence agencies and members of the Intelligence Community. For both federal non-intelligence agencies and SLT agencies, it means, at a minimum, personally identifiable information about U.S. citizens and lawful

permanent residents. States are free to extend this definition to other classes of persons or to all persons (including organizations).

[597] The authorized purpose of the ISE is to share terrorism-related information in a lawful manner that protects the privacy and other legal rights of Americans between and among authorized recipients of such information. (ISE Privacy Guidelines—Section 3)

[598] LEIU *Audit Checklist for the Criminal Intelligence Function*, p. i.

[599] Certified storage environments will either be DHS-certified Open Storage Secret or the equivalent FBI-certified closed storage environment. NOTE: The Open Storage authorization granted by DHS applies only to computer systems and not to document storage.

[600] DHS and the FBI have agreed to allocate the responsibilities for the following support to fusion centers to minimize redundancy: establishing operating classified work environments, getting personnel cleared to be able to access classified information, providing ways to communicate with the federal government, and other technical assistance. See the most recent version of the Federal Coordinated Support Plan for further information regarding these efforts.

[601] See Footnote 594.

[602] IALEIA and Global's *Law Enforcement Analytic Standards* booklet is available at http://www.it.ojp.gov/documents/law_enforcement_analytic_standards.pdf.

[603] See Footnote 587 or the Glossary for more information on the ISE Shared Spaces concept.

In: Fusion Centers
Editor: Art M. Gerardi

ISBN: 978-1-62417-336-3

Chapter 2

INFORMATION SHARING: FEDERAL AGENCIES ARE HELPING FUSION CENTERS BUILD AND SUSTAIN CAPABILITIES AND PROTECT PRIVACY, BUT COULD BETTER MEASURE RESULTS*

United States Government Accountability Office

WHY GAO DID THIS STUDY

Recent terrorist activity, such as the attempted Times Square bombing, underscores the need for terrorism-related information sharing. Since 2001, all 50 states and some local governments have established fusion centers, where homeland security, terrorism, and other intelligence information is shared. The federal government recognizes the importance of fusion centers; however, as GAO reported in October 2007, centers face challenges in sustaining their operations. GAO was asked to assess the extent to which (1) the Department of Homeland Security (DHS) has taken action to support fusion centers' efforts to maintain and grow their operations, and (2) DHS and the Department of Justice (DOJ) have supported fusion centers in establishing privacy and civil liberties protections. GAO reviewed relevant legislation and federal guidance; conducted interviews with 14 of 72 fusion centers, selected on the basis of location and time in operation, among other factors; and interviewed DHS and DOJ officials. The views of fusion center officials are not generalizable but provided insights.

WHAT GAO RECOMMENDS

GAO recommends that DHS define steps to develop and implement standard performance measures for centers and commit to a timeframe for completing them. DHS concurred and described steps it is taking to address the recommendation.

* This is an edited, reformatted and augmented version of the Highlights of GAO-10-972, a report to congressional requesters, dated September 2010.

WHAT GAO FOUND

Fusion centers have cited DHS grant funding as critical to achieving the baseline capabilities—the standards the government and fusion centers have defined as necessary for centers to be considered capable of performing basic functions in the national information sharing network, such as standards related to information gathering and intelligence analysis. However, DHS has not set standard performance measures for the centers. Fusion centers nationwide reported that federal funding accounted for about 61 percent of their total fiscal year 2010 budgets, but DHS's Homeland Security Grant Program (HSGP), the primary grant program through which fusion centers receive funding, is not specifically focused on, or limited to, fusion centers. Rather, states and local governments determine the amount of HSGP funding they allocate to fusion centers each year from among a number of competing homeland security needs. As a result, fusion centers continue to raise concerns about the lack of a longer-term, predictable federal funding source. DHS, in coordination with the Program Manager for the Information Sharing Environment and DOJ, has a nationwide assessment of centers' baseline capabilities under way. To be completed in October 2010, the goal of the assessment is to provide federal agencies and fusion centers with more accurate information on the status of centers' abilities, help identify gaps between centers' current operations and the baseline capabilities, and use this information to develop strategies and realign resources to close those gaps going forward. Recent federal guidance also requires that, by October 29, 2010, DHS should develop an annual reporting process that will document the total operational and sustainment costs of each of the 72 fusion centers in the national network so as to assess the adequacy of current funding mechanisms. If centers are to receive continued federal financial support, it is important that they are also able to demonstrate their impact and value added to the nation's information sharing goals. However, there are no standard performance measures across all fusion centers to do this. DHS has not started developing such measures because the agency is currently focusing on completing the nationwide assessment and compiling its results and, as such, has not defined next steps or target timeframes for designing and implementing these measures. Defining the steps it will take to design and implement a set of measures and committing to a target timeframe for their completion could better position DHS to demonstrate the value and impact of the national network of fusion centers.

To help fusion centers develop privacy and civil liberties policies and protections, DHS and DOJ have provided technical assistance and training, including a template on which to base a privacy and civil liberties policy, and a joint process for reviewing fusion centers' policies to ensure they are consistent with federal requirements. The 14 centers GAO interviewed were at different stages of the policy review process, with 7 completed as of June 2010. Officials from all 14 of the fusion centers GAO interviewed stated that the guidance DHS and DOJ provided was helpful and integral in assisting them to draft their policies.

ABBREVIATIONS

ACLU	American Civil Liberties Union
CLIA	Civil Liberties Impact Assessment

CRS	Congressional Research Service
CRCL	Office for Civil Rights and Civil Liberties
DHS	Department of Homeland Security
DOJ	Department of Justice
FBI	Federal Bureau of Investigation
FEMA	Federal Emergency Management Agency
HSGP	Homeland Security Grant Program
I&A	Office of Intelligence and Analysis
ISE	Information Sharing Environment
NFCA	National Fusion Center Association
PIA	Privacy Impact Assessment
PM-ISE	Program Manager for the ISE
SAA	State Administrative Agency
SLPO	State and Local Program Office

September 29, 2010

The Honorable Mark Pryor
Chairman
The Honorable John Ensign
Ranking Member
Subcommittee on State, Local, and Private Sector
Preparedness and Integration
Committee on Homeland Security and Governmental Affairs
United States Senate

The Honorable Tom Coburn
United States Senate

Recent terrorist activity, such as the attempted Times Square bombing and the attempted bombing of Northwest Airlines Flight 253, emphasizes the importance of developing a national information sharing capability to efficiently and expeditiously gather, analyze, and disseminate law enforcement, homeland security, public safety, and terrorism information. Since 2001, all 50 states and some local governments have established fusion centers to address gaps in terrorism-related information sharing that the federal government cannot address alone and provide a mechanism for information sharing within the state. Although fusion centers vary because they were primarily established to meet state and local needs, under federal law, a fusion center is defined as a collaborative effort of two or more federal, state, local, or tribal government agencies that combines resources, expertise, or information with the goal of maximizing the ability of such agencies to detect, prevent, investigate, apprehend, and respond to criminal or terrorist activity. As of August 2010, there were 72 fusion centers nationwide.[1] Fusion centers are a component of the nation's Information Sharing Environment (ISE), which was established by the Intelligence Reform and Terrorism Prevention Act of 2004 (Intelligence Reform Act) to facilitate information sharing, access, and collaboration in order to combat terrorism more effectively.[2]

The Implementing Recommendations of the 9/11 Commission Act of 2007 (9/11 Commission Act) requires the Secretary of Homeland Security, in consultation with others, to establish a state, local, and regional fusion center initiative within the Department of Homeland Security (DHS) to establish partnerships with fusion centers.[3] Through the initiative, DHS is required to provide to fusion centers operational and intelligence advice and assistance, as well as management assistance, and facilitate close communication and coordination between fusion centers and DHS. In addition, the initiative is to provide training to fusion centers and encourage the centers to participate in terrorism-threat-related exercises conducted by DHS. Accordingly, the federal government has recognized that fusion centers represent a critical source of local information about potential threats for federal agencies and a mechanism for these agencies to disseminate terrorism-related information and intelligence. DHS, the Department of Justice (DOJ), and the Program Manager for the ISE (PM-ISE) have taken steps to partner with and leverage fusion centers as part of the overall ISE. Further, the National Strategy for Information Sharing (National Strategy) states that fusion centers will serve as the primary focal points within states and localities for the receipt and sharing of terrorism-related information. Through the National Strategy, the federal government is promoting fusion centers to achieve a baseline level of capability and to ensure compliance with all applicable privacy laws and standards to become interconnected with the federal government and each other in a national network capable of sharing terrorism-related information.

In January 2005, we designated information sharing for homeland security a high-risk area because the government had continued to face formidable challenges in analyzing and disseminating this information in a timely, accurate, and useful manner. We reported that information is a crucial tool in fighting terrorism and that its timely dissemination is critical to maintaining the security of our nation. This area remained on the high-risk list for our January 2009 update.[4] In 2007, we reviewed the status of fusion centers nationwide and reported that fusion center officials faced challenges in obtaining and maintaining the funding and personnel necessary to conduct their operations.[5] According to the officials, uncertainties in the amount of federal grant funding to be allocated from year to year made it difficult to plan for the future and created concerns about the centers' ability to sustain their capability for the long-term. To improve efforts to create a national network of fusion centers, we recommended that the federal government should articulate its role in supporting fusion centers and determine whether it expects to provide resources to centers over the long-term to help ensure their sustainability. DHS and the PM-ISE concurred with our recommendation, stating that recent efforts to define DHS's, and the federal government's, roles and responsibilities in supporting the development of the nationwide network of fusion centers demonstrates a long-term commitment to helping to ensure their sustainability.[6] However, federal, state, and local entities continue to raise concerns about fusion centers' ability to maintain their operations with limited or uncertain federal grant funding, especially as many state and local governments face near-term and long-term fiscal challenges.

In addition, the 9/11 Commission Act requires the Secretary of Homeland Security, in consultation with the Attorney General, to establish guidelines that include standards for fusion centers related to the privacy of information. For example, these standards are to include that any fusion center shall develop, publish, and adhere to a privacy and civil liberties policy consistent with federal, state, and local law. Because fusion centers collect, analyze, and disseminate information on potential criminal and terrorist threats, some entities have raised concerns that centers are susceptible to privacy and civil liberties violations. For example, according to the American Civil Liberties Union (ACLU), the fusion center concept encourages state and local law enforcement personnel to gather intelligence that could potentially lead to violations of citizens' rights to privacy and civil liberties. According to a senior DOJ official, such violations by fusion centers could lead to a loss of public support or confidence in fusion centers, harm to individuals, proliferation of inaccurate data, or liability. In light of these risks, questions remain about how centers are implementing privacy and civil liberties policies to ensure that centers handle information in a manner that protects citizens' constitutional rights.

Considering these issues and the fusion centers' role in the ISE, you asked us to provide Congress with an assessment of the current status of fusion centers' efforts to maintain and grow their operations and establish privacy and civil liberties protections with support from the federal government. Specifically, this report addresses the following questions:

- To what extent has DHS taken action to support fusion centers' efforts to maintain and grow their operations?
- To what extent are DHS and DOJ supporting fusion centers in establishing privacy and civil liberties protections?

To assess the extent to which DHS has supported centers in their efforts, we analyzed relevant laws and strategies, such as the 9/11 Commission Act and the National Strategy, related to fusion centers' role in the ISE and federal efforts to support centers. We also examined guidance, such as the Baseline Capabilities for State and Major Urban Area Fusion Centers (Baseline Capabilities), which describes the minimum capabilities and operational standards necessary for fusion centers.[7]

We focused our review on DHS's efforts because DHS is the Executive Agent in managing federal interaction with fusion centers and is to coordinate its efforts with DOJ and the PM-ISE. To obtain fusion center views, we conducted interviews with officials from a non-probability sample of 14 of 72 fusion centers.[8] We selected these centers to reflect a range of characteristics, including whether the center is a state or major urban area fusion center; length of time in operation; geographic region;[9] and fiscal year 2010 funding allocations for the centers' states or urban areas from the DHS Homeland Security Grant Program (HSGP), which is the primary federal grant program through which fusion centers may receive funding.

Specifically, we interviewed fusion center directors, or their designees, to obtain information on their centers' approaches and plans to sustain operations, and their perspectives on federal efforts to support these approaches as well as any challenges or issues encountered in sustaining operations. While their comments cannot be generalized to all fusion centers nationwide, the interviews provided a range of perspectives and useful insights on the issue of sustainability.

To assess DHS support provided to fusion centers, we examined guidance, such as for the DHS Fiscal Year 2010 HSGP. We also analyzed documents, such as program descriptions, related to federal efforts to assess fusion centers' baseline capabilities and provide training, technical assistance, and grant funding. We interviewed officials from DHS's Office of Intelligence and Analysis (I&A), which oversees the fusion center program; DHS's Federal Emergency Management Agency's (FEMA) Grant Programs Directorate and Office of

Counterterrorism and Security Preparedness within Protection and National Preparedness, which administer the HSGP and provide support to fusion centers; DOJ's Office of Justice Programs, which provides training and technical assistance to centers; the Federal Bureau of Investigation (FBI), which provides personnel and support to centers; and the Office of the PM-ISE, which oversees management of the ISE. We discussed plans and efforts related to establishing performance measures for fusion centers and compared these plans with criteria in standard practices for program management.[10]

In addition, we conducted interviews with the National Fusion Center Association (NFCA), a nonprofit association that represents the interests of fusion centers, to obtain a broad perspective on fusion center sustainability and the role of DHS, DOJ, and the PM-ISE in supporting centers' efforts. Lastly, we attended the 2010 National Fusion Center Conference to obtain information about federal plans and efforts to support centers and issues and concerns of centers nationwide.[11]

To assess the extent to which DHS and DOJ are supporting fusion centers in establishing privacy and civil liberties protections, we analyzed relevant statutes, including the 9/11 Commission Act and the Intelligence Reform Act, and guidance, such as the ISE Privacy Guidelines, Baseline Capabilities, and DHS HSGP guidance to identify required and recommended actions for fusion centers to take to establish these protections.[12] We analyzed plans and documentation, such as the DHS Privacy Office's 2008 Privacy Impact Assessment of fusion centers and privacy-related training and technical assistance materials.

We also assessed the DHS and DOJ Fusion Center Privacy, Civil Rights, and Civil Liberties Policy Template, which is intended to assist fusion center personnel in developing their privacy and civil liberties policies. We compared this template against the ISE Privacy Guidelines to determine the extent to which the template included components of that guidance. In addition, we interviewed officials from DHS's Privacy Office, DHS's Office for Civil Rights and Civil Liberties (CRCL), DOJ's Office of Privacy and Civil Liberties, and the PM-ISE about efforts to review centers' policies, the status of centers' policy development, privacy-related training and technical assistance, and plans for supporting fusion centers' implementation of privacy and civil liberties protections.

We also interviewed representatives from the Institute for Intergovernmental Research, the DOJ contractor that reviews fusion centers' privacy and civil liberties policies, to obtain additional information about the review process and any challenges encountered related to the development of these policies.[13]

To describe steps fusion centers are taking to establish privacy and civil liberties protections, we included questions in our interviews with officials from 14 fusion centers about the development of privacy and civil liberties policies and procedures; support provided by DHS, DOJ, and the PM-ISE; and any challenges or issues encountered in establishing the protections. Lastly, we included questions in our interviews with NFCA and ACLU officials to obtain a broad perspective on privacy issues in fusion centers.

We conducted this performance audit from March 2010 through September 2010 in accordance with generally accepted government auditing standards. Those standards require that we plan and perform the audit to obtain sufficient, appropriate evidence to provide a reasonable basis for our findings and conclusions based on our audit objectives. We believe that the evidence obtained provides a reasonable basis for our findings and conclusions based on our audit objectives.

BACKGROUND

Fusion Centers

Nationwide, states and major urban areas have established fusion centers to coordinate the gathering, analysis, and dissemination of law enforcement, homeland security, public safety, and terrorism information. After centers had begun to be established around the country, Congress passed the 9/11 Commission Act to require the Secretary of Homeland Security to share information with and support fusion centers. The National Strategy identifies fusion centers as vital assets critical to sharing information related to terrorism because they serve as focal points for the two-way exchange of information between federal agencies and state and local governments. According to DHS, fusion centers are the primary way that DHS shares intelligence and analysis with state and local homeland security agencies. For example, fusion centers typically issue analytical products, such as daily or weekly bulletins on general criminal or intelligence information and intelligence assessments which, in general, provide in-depth reporting on an emerging threat, group, or crime. These products are primarily created for law enforcement entities and other community partners, such as members of the critical infrastructure sectors. In recent years, fusion centers have been credited with being influential in disrupting a planned terrorist attack on the New York City subway system, investigating bomb threats against U.S. airlines, and providing intelligence support to several political conventions and summits. Other fusion centers have been instrumental in providing intelligence and analytical support to assist with securing our nation's borders. For example, the Arizona Counterterrorism Information Center and the New York State Intelligence Center routinely (i.e., either twice a week or quarterly, respectively) issue border-specific intelligence products to enhance the situational awareness of law enforcement agencies in border communities.

While all fusion centers were generally created by state and local governments to improve information sharing across levels of government and to prevent terrorism or other threats, the missions of fusion centers vary based on the environment in which the center operates. Some fusion centers have adopted an "all-crimes" approach, incorporating information on terrorism and other high-risk threats into their jurisdiction's existing law enforcement framework to ensure that possible precursor crimes, such as counterfeiting or narcotics smuggling, are screened and analyzed for linkages to terrorist planning or other criminal activity. Other fusion centers have adopted an "all-hazards" approach. In addition to collecting, analyzing, and disseminating information on potential terrorist planning and other crimes, these fusion centers identify and prioritize types of major disasters and emergencies, such as hurricanes or earthquakes, which could occur within their jurisdiction. In doing so, they gather, analyze, and disseminate information to assist relevant responsible agencies—law enforcement, fire, public health, emergency management, critical infrastructure—with the prevention, protection, response, or recovery efforts of those incidents.

Fusion centers also vary in their personnel composition and staffing levels. Consistent with the statutory definition of a fusion center, these centers typically bring together in one location representatives from several different state or local agencies, such as state and local law enforcement agencies—state police, county sheriffs, and city police departments—homeland security agencies, emergency management agencies, and the National Guard. In addition, as DHS is required to the maximum extent possible to assign officers and intelligence analysts to fusion centers, many centers have federal personnel working on-site, such as DHS intelligence operations specialists and Customs and Border Protection agents, along with others such as FBI intelligence analysts and Drug Enforcement Administration agents. In terms of staffing levels, a 2009 joint DHS and PM-ISE survey of fusion centers reported that the number of personnel working at these centers ranged from under 10 employees to over 75 per center, as shown in figure 1.

Federal Role in Relation to Fusion Centers

Recognizing that DHS had already begun to provide support to fusion centers but needed to play a stronger, more constructive role in assisting these centers, Congress passed the 9/11 Commission Act, which required the Secretary of Homeland Security to create the State, Local, and Regional Fusion Center Initiative.[14] The Act also required the Secretary, in coordination with representatives from fusion centers and the states, to take certain actions in support of the initiative. Specifically, the Act requires that the Secretary take a number of steps to support the centers, including supporting efforts to integrate fusion centers into the ISE, assigning personnel to centers, incorporating fusion center intelligence information into DHS information, providing training, and facilitating close communication and coordination between the centers and DHS, among others. The law also required the Secretary to issue guidance that includes standards that fusion centers shall undertake certain activities. These include, for example, that centers collaboratively develop a mission statement, identify expectations and goals, measure performance, and determine center effectiveness; create a collaborative environment for the sharing of intelligence and information among federal, state, local, and tribal government agencies, the private sector, and the public, consistent with guidance from the President and the PM-ISE; and offer a variety of intelligence and information services and products.

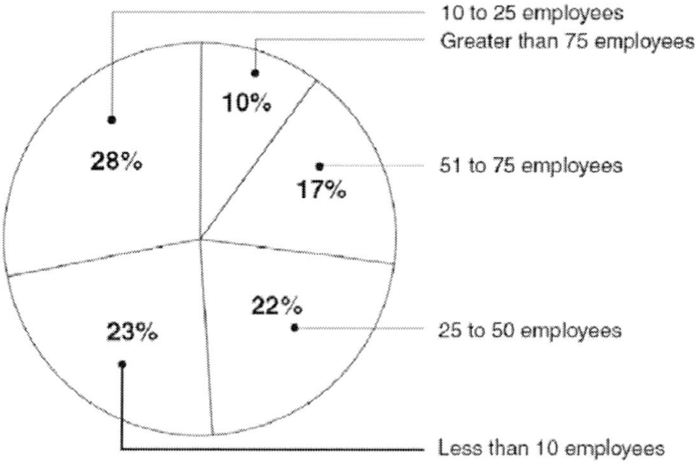

Source: GAO (presentation), PM-ISE (data).

Note: Information was aggregated, but not verified by the PM-ISE or GAO.

Figure 1. Staffing Levels Reported by 62 of 72 Fusion Centers, as of March 2009.

DHS has taken steps to organize and establish a management structure to coordinate its support of fusion centers. In June 2006, DHS tasked I&A with the responsibility for managing DHS's support to fusion centers. I&A established a State and Local Program Office (SLPO) as the focal point for supporting fusion center operations and to maximize state and local capabilities to detect, prevent, and respond to terrorist and homeland security threats.

Consistent with the 9/11 Commission Act and Intelligence Reform Act, DHS, in conjunction with DOJ and the PM-ISE, has issued a series of guidance documents to support fusion centers in establishing their operations. In 2006, through the Global Justice Information Sharing Initiative (Global), DHS and DOJ jointly issued the Fusion Center Guidelines, a document that outlines 18 recommended elements for establishing and operating fusion centers consistently across the country, such as establishing and maintaining a center based on funding availability and sustainability; ensuring personnel are properly trained; and developing, publishing, and adhering to a privacy and civil liberties policy.[15]

To supplement the Fusion Center Guidelines, in September 2008, DHS, DOJ, and Global jointly published the Baseline Capabilities, which were developed in collaboration with the PM-ISE and other federal, state, and local officials. The Baseline Capabilities define the capabilities needed to achieve a national, integrated network of fusion centers and detail the standards necessary for a fusion center to be considered capable of performing basic functions by the fusion center community. For example, the Baseline Capabilities include standards for fusion centers related to information gathering, recognition of indicators and warnings, processing information, intelligence analysis and production, and intelligence and information dissemination. In addition, the Baseline Capabilities include standards for the management and administrative functioning of a fusion center. Among these are standards for ensuring information privacy and civil liberties protections, developing a training plan for personnel, and establishing information technology and communications infrastructure to ensure seamless communication between center personnel and partners. The development of these baseline standards is called for in the National Strategy, which identifies their development as a key step to reaching a national integrated network of fusion centers. By achieving this baseline level of capability, it is intended that a fusion center will have the necessary structures, processes, and tools in place to support the gathering, processing, analysis, and dissemination of terrorism, homeland security, and law enforcement information.

In accordance with the 9/11 Commission Act, DHS, DOJ, and the PM-ISE rely on fusion centers as critical nodes in the nation's homeland security strategy and provide them with a variety of other support.

- Federal Grant Funding: DHS's HSGP awards funds to states, territories, and urban areas to enhance their ability to prepare for, prevent, protect against, respond to, and recover from terrorist attacks and other major disasters.[16] The fiscal year 2010 HSGP consists of five separate programs, two of which are primarily used by states and local jurisdictions, at their discretion, for fusion-center-related funding.[17] These grant programs are not specifically focused on, or limited to, fusion centers. Thus, fusion centers do not receive direct, dedicated funding from DHS; rather, the amount of grant funding a fusion center receives is determined by a state's State Administrative Agency (SAA)—the state-level agency responsible for managing all homeland security grants and associated program requirements—or an urban area's working group, which has similar responsibilities. A fusion center typically contributes to the development of a state's federal grant application by providing information on how it will use the proposed funding needed, called an investment justification.

- Personnel: DHS and DOJ have deployed, or assigned, either part-time or full-time personnel to fusion centers to support their operations and serve as liaisons between the fusion center and federal components. For example, DHS personnel are to assist the center in using ISE information; review information provided by state, local, and tribal personnel; create products derived from this information and other DHS homeland security information; and assist in disseminating these products. As of July 2010, DHS's I&A had deployed 58 intelligence officers and the FBI had deployed 74 special agents and analysts full time to 38 of the 72 fusion centers.
- Access to Information and Systems: DHS and DOJ also share classified and unclassified homeland security and terrorism information with fusion centers through several information technology networks and systems. For example, in February 2010, DHS's I&A reported that it had installed the Homeland Secure Data Network, which supports the sharing of federal secret-level intelligence and information with state, local, and tribal partners, at 33 of 72 fusion centers. DHS also provides an unclassified network, the Homeland Security Information Network, which allows federal, state, and local homeland security and terrorism-related information sharing.
- Training and Technical Assistance: DHS has partnered with DOJ, through Global, to offer fusion centers a variety of training and technical assistance programs. These include training on intelligence analysis and privacy and civil liberties protections, as well as technical assistance with technology implementation, security, and the development of liaison programs to coordinate with other state and local agencies.

Privacy Requirements for Fusion Centers

Fusion centers have a number of privacy related requirements. As provided under the 9/11 Commission Act, DHS is required to issue standards that fusion centers are to develop, publish, and adhere to a privacy and civil liberties policy consistent with federal, state, and local law. In addition, the standards must provide that a fusion center give appropriate privacy and civil liberties training to all state, local, tribal, and private sector representatives at the center and have appropriate security measures in place for the facility, data, and personnel. Because fusion centers are within the ISE when they access certain kinds of information, federal law requires they adhere to ISE privacy standards issued by the President or the PM-ISE under the authority of the Intelligence Reform Act, as amended. Other federal requirements found in 28 C.F.R. part 23, Criminal Intelligence Systems Operating Policies, apply to federally funded criminal intelligence systems, and fusion centers receiving criminal intelligence information must follow these procedures, which also include privacy requirements.

In 2006, the PM-ISE issued the ISE Privacy Guidelines, which establish a framework for sharing information in the ISE in a manner that protects privacy and other legal rights. The ISE Privacy Guidelines apply to federal departments and agencies and, therefore, do not directly impose obligations on state and local government entities. However, the ISE Privacy Guidelines do require federal agencies and the PM-ISE to work with nonfederal entities, such as fusion centers, seeking to access protected information to ensure that the entities develop and implement appropriate policies and procedures that are at least as comprehensive as those contained in the ISE Privacy Guidelines.[18] Among the primary components of these guidelines, agencies are required to, for example, ensure that protected information is used only for authorized, specific purposes; properly identify any privacy-protected information to be shared; put in place security, accountability, and audit mechanisms; facilitate the prevention and correction of any errors in protected information; and document privacy and civil liberties protections in a privacy and civil liberties policy.

FEDERAL EFFORTS ARE UNDER WAY TO ASSESS CENTERS' CAPABILITIES, TARGET FUNDING TO CAPABILITY GAPS, AND ASSESS COSTS, BUT MEASURING RESULTS ACHIEVED COULD HELP SHOW CENTERS' VALUE TO THE ISE

Officials in all 14 fusion centers we contacted cited federal funding as critical to expanding their operations and achieving and maintaining the baseline capabilities needed to sustain the national network of fusion centers. An assessment of fusion centers, led by the PM-ISE, DHS, and DOJ, is under way to obtain data about the current capabilities of centers nationwide, identify the operational gaps that remain, and determine what resources centers may need to close the gaps. DHS is evaluating whether to amend its grant guidance to require fusion centers to use future funding to support efforts to meet and maintain the baseline capabilities. DHS also has plans to assess the costs of the fusion center network to help inform decisions about the extent to which the funding mechanisms in place in support of fusion centers are adequate, or if other funding avenues need to be explored. However, taking steps to implement standard performance measures to track the results of fusion centers' efforts to support information sharing and assess the impact of their operations could help demonstrate center value to the ISE and enable the federal government to justify and prioritize future resources in support of the national network.

Fusion Center Officials We Interviewed Cited Federal Funding as Critical to Sustaining Operations

Officials in all 14 fusion centers we contacted stated that without continued federal grant funding, in particular DHS grant funding, their centers would not be able to expand, or in some instances even maintain, operations. States have reported to DHS that they have used about $426 million in grant funding from fiscal year 2004 through 2009 to support fusion-related activities nationwide, as shown in table 1.

According to a nationwide survey conducted by DHS and the PM-ISE, of the 52 of 72 fusion centers that responded, on average, over half of their 2010 budgets were supported by federal funding.[19] Specifically, as shown in figure 2, these centers reported that federal grant funding accounted for 61 percent of their total current budgets of about $102 million and state or local funds accounted for 39 percent ($40 million), according to information reported to DHS and the PM-ISE.[20] For the 14 centers we contacted, officials in 6 of the centers reported relying on federal grant funding for more than 50 percent of their annual budgets, which ranged from $600,000 to about $16 million.[21]

Officials in all 14 of the centers we contacted stated that federal funding was critical to long-term sustainability and provided varying examples of the impact that not having federal grant funding would have on their fusion centers. Officials in four fusion centers stated that without federal funding, their centers would not be able to continue operations. For example, an official in one of these centers stated that with the state's economic recession, the fusion center does not expect to grow operations over the next 5 years and is struggling to maintain the personnel and funding needed to maintain their current operations, which includes fewer than 10 full-time personnel with an estimated budget of a little over $500,000. Officials in another fusion center stated that while they have a comparatively large budget of about $10 million, they could not maintain their level of operations without the federal grant funding, about $5 million per year, they receive.

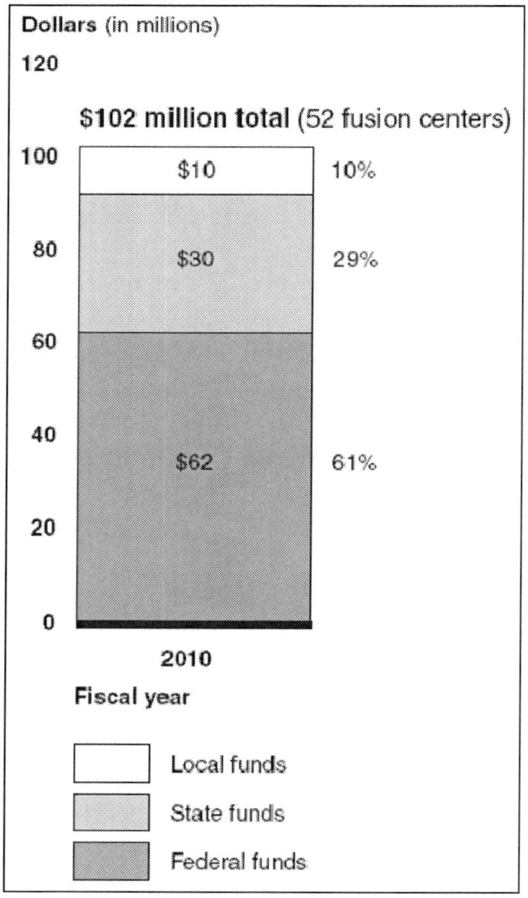

Source: GAO (presentation), PM-ISE (data).

Note: Above amounts rounded to the nearest whole number. Information was aggregated, but not verified by the PM-ISE or GAO.

Figure 2. Average Funding Breakdown for Fiscal Year 2010 Budgets Reported by 52 of 72 Fusion Centers.

Table 1. DHS Funding Reported by Grantees to Support Fusion Center Activities, Fiscal Years 2004 through 2009

Fiscal year	Funding reported by grantees to support fusion center activities
2004	$100,320,799
2005	57,246,542
2006	62,664,343
2007	78,723,783
2008	61,864,080
2009	65,402,360
Total	**$426,221,907**

Source: DHS.

Note: Data are as of June 16, 2010, and include all FEMA preparedness grant programs. Figures represent activities aligned to project types that support fusion center activities, such as the following: establish/enhance a terrorism intelligence/early warning system, center, or task force; establish/enhance public-private emergency preparedness program; and develop/enhance homeland security/emergency management organization and structure. Data are self-reported by grantees every 6 months, and according to FEMA officials, are not validated to ensure that funds were exclusively used to support fusion center activities.

Fusion Centers See Federal Funding as Necessary to Achieve and Maintain the Baseline Capabilities; a Nationwide Assessment to Gauge Gaps in Centers' Capabilities Is under Way

Officials in all 14 fusion centers we contacted stated that without sustained federal funding, centers could not expand operations to close the gaps between their current operations and the baseline capabilities, negatively affecting their ability to function as part of the national network. For example, officials from one fusion center stated that they currently do not have the resources to hire a security officer, which affects the center's development, implementation, maintenance, and oversight of security measures, including ensuring that security measures are in place to provide the proper information protection in compliance with all applicable laws and the center's privacy and civil liberties policy. Officials in another fusion center stated that federal grant funding is essential to expanding their outreach and coordination with other state and local entities—a recommended baseline capability and one of the primary ways that centers maintain partnerships with other entities.

Consistent with fusion center views reported at the 2010 National Fusion Center Conference, officials in all 14 fusion centers we contacted stated that achieving and maintaining the baseline capabilities was key to sustaining their centers. By achieving and maintaining these capabilities, fusion centers should have the necessary structures, processes, and tools in place to support the gathering, processing, analysis, and dissemination of terrorism, homeland security, and law enforcement information as part of the national, integrated network. At the 2010 National Fusion Center Conference, fusion center directors reported that achieving the critical operational capabilities at each fusion center was necessary to ensure an effective flow of information throughout the national network of fusion centers.[22] To do so, these directors cited the importance of performing baseline capability self-assessments, identifying gaps between operations and the baseline capabilities, developing plans to address the gaps, and leveraging existing resources more effectively and efficiently to close those gaps. For example, assessing gaps in centers' current information technology and communication infrastructure and the associated costs of implementing the necessary systems may enable fusion centers to focus resources more efficiently to address these needs and close the identified gaps. Officials in all of the 14 fusion centers we contacted said that, in recognizing the importance of meeting the baseline capabilities, they had taken some steps to review their own operations and identify gaps between their current operations and the recommended baseline capabilities. For example, an official in one center said that he had conducted a systematic gap analysis of the center's current operations against the baseline capabilities and determined that the center still had to achieve an estimated 80 percent of the capabilities, such as developing performance metrics and an outreach program. Gaps identified by officials at the 14 fusion centers included, for example, the need to develop information technology and related tools for analysis; not having a privacy and civil liberties policy in place; not having identified a privacy/civil liberties officer; and not having identified a security officer.

To provide data about the baseline capabilities of fusion centers nationwide, the PM-ISE, DHS, and DOJ are conducting an ongoing systematic assessment of centers' capabilities. The goal of the nationwide assessment, according to DHS senior officials, is to help enable both federal and fusion center representatives to (1) obtain more accurate information on the current status of centers' abilities to meet the baseline capabilities, (2) help identify gaps between centers' current operations and the capabilities, and (3) use this information to develop strategies and realign resources to support centers' efforts to close those gaps going forward. Further, according to both DHS senior officials and fusion center representatives, the results of the assessment are also intended to provide centers with the information needed to develop more accurate and specific investment justifications to their SAAs in competing for DHS HSGP funding.

Table 2. Four Critical Operational Capabilities and Four Enabling Capabilities Identified by Fusion Centers and Federal Personnel at the 2010 National Fusion Center Conference

Operational capabilities
Ability to receive classified and unclassified information from federal partners
Ability to assess local implications of threat information through the use of a formal risk assessment process
Ability to further disseminate threat information to other state, local, tribal, territorial, and private sector entities within their jurisdiction
Ability to gather locally generated information, aggregate it, analyze it, and share it with federal partners as appropriate
Enabling capabilities[a]
Sustainment Strategy
Privacy and Civil Rights/Civil Liberties
Communications and Outreach
Security and Clearances

Source: DHS.

[a] Enabling capabilities are those that support the administrative and management functions of a fusion center.

According to DHS and a senior official from the NFCA, personnel from DHS, the PM-ISE, and DOJ coordinated with state and local government representatives and fusion center officials prior to and during the National Fusion Center Conference in February 2010 to jointly identify four critical operational capabilities and four enabling capabilities to be prioritized in developing the national network of fusion centers.[23] Among the four enabling capabilities are those that relate to establishing a sustainment strategy and establishing privacy and civil liberties protections, as shown in table 2.

The nationwide assessment of fusion centers consists of two phases—a self-report survey followed by onsite validation. First, the PM-ISE sent a self-assessment questionnaire, which was to be completed in May 2010, to all 72 designated fusion centers to use to assess their current operations against all baseline capabilities. Second, starting in June 2010, seven validation teams consisting of federal and fusion center personnel began making site visits to fusion centers to validate centers' responses to the self-assessment.[24] Specifically, the validation teams are to conduct a review of the four critical operational capabilities that were identified collaboratively by federal officials and fusion center directors as being critical to the functioning of the national network. Validation teams are also to review information on the privacy and civil liberties protections established by these fusion centers and to discuss the centers' sustainment strategies. Senior DHS officials stated that this review is to involve discussions on each fusion centers' experiences and related issues, challenges, and associated costs of achieving and maintaining the four critical operational capabilities, as well as the privacy and civil rights/civil liberties enabling capability, to provide additional information on why gaps may exist and how to address them.

According to DHS senior officials, the site visits were completed in September 2010. The results of the assessment, which are to include the aggregate of both the self-assessment and on-site validation data, are expected to be analyzed and shared in a report with the participating fusion centers by the end of October 2010. Further, according to DHS senior officials, they are planning to conduct the assessment on a recurring basis. Thus, this initial assessment is expected to serve as a baseline against which to measure the development of the baseline capabilities in individual fusion centers, as well as across the national network.[25]

DHS Has Efforts under Way to Link DHS Grants to Filling Baseline Capabilities Gaps and Plans to Assess Costs of the Fusion Center Network

DHS has opportunities to better target federal fusion center funding to fill critical baseline capability gaps and is taking steps to do so. Both the National Strategy and DHS emphasize that federal agencies are to play an active role in addressing the challenge of sustaining fusion centers by ensuring that they are able to achieve and maintain the baseline capabilities. Specifically, the National Strategy states that federal agencies are to assist fusion centers in incorporating the baseline capabilities into their operations by amending and modifying grants and grants guidance, and other applicable funding programs, to ensure that centers are able to meet and sustain the baseline capabilities and operational standards. In its fiscal year 2010 HSGP grant guidance, DHS encourages, but does not require, that fusion centers prioritize the allocation of HSGP funding they receive through their SAAs to meet and maintain the baseline capabilities. Further, senior DHS officials stated, generally, that the results of the nationwide assessment will be used to address future fusion center funding and that the office will determine how it may leverage DHS's HSGP to ensure that centers have access to grant funds and assist with putting these mechanisms in place for the future.

Senior officials from DHS as well as all 14 of the fusion centers we contacted stated that linking, or tying, future HSGP grant funding to achieving and maintaining the baseline capabilities may better enable fusion centers to obtain the resources needed to address the gaps in baseline capabilities by allowing them to more specifically detail how grant funding is to be used in their investment justifications. For example, by tying future grant funding to developing fusion centers' ability to gather information, aggregate it, analyze it, and share it as appropriate, centers may be more likely to obtain the funding necessary to develop the specific information systems and analytical tools needed to enable them to achieve these capabilities. An Acting Director with FEMA's Office of Counterterrorism and Security Preparedness stated that, as part of developing the Fiscal Year 2011 HSGP guidance, FEMA is currently working with DHS and fusion center stakeholders to evaluate the potential for amending the guidance to accomplish two goals. Specifically, they are working to (1) require, rather than encourage, that fusion centers use 2011 grant funding allocated from SAAs to achieve and maintain all of the baseline capabilities; and (2) focus funding to specifically address gaps in baseline capabilities identified during the assessment process. For example, the official said that they are exploring options such as requiring centers to include in their investment justifications the results of the nationwide assessment and indicating how the center would use funding to fill any identified gaps. Further, this official added that FEMA has also begun collaborating within DHS and with DOJ to discuss current grant programs and possibilities for future interagency coordination on the support specifically for fusion centers. Directives such as these could help ensure that capabilities are met by enabling fusion centers to provide specific data about operational gaps and needs in their investment justifications.

While DHS could ensure that fusion centers target the federal funding they receive on filling baseline capabilities gaps, fusion centers have called on the federal government to establish a dedicated funding stream for them. DHS's HSGP is the primary grant program through which fusion centers receive funding, but these grants are not specifically focused on, nor limited to, fusion centers. As such, fusion centers compete with other state homeland security, law enforcement, and emergency management agencies and missions for a portion of the total amount of HSGP funding awarded to the SAA, which decides what portion of the total funding centers will receive. This process has generated long-standing concerns by the fusion center community about the lack of a longer-term, predictable funding source for the centers. For example, we reported in October 2007 that fusion centers reported challenges with funding, that these issues made it difficult to plan for the future, and that fusion centers were concerned about their ability to sustain their capability for the long term.[26] The Congressional Research Service (CRS) similarly reported in January 2008 that the threat of diminished or eliminated federal or state funding, such as a decrease in DHS grant funding programs, poses a risk to the development of fusion centers.[27] The DHS Office of Inspector General subsequently reported in December 2008 that fusion center officials they spoke with remained concerned with sustainability and funding, emphasizing that sustainment planning and funding from the federal government is essential for the success of fusion centers.[28]

Officials from 13 of the 14 centers we contacted cited a number of challenges with obtaining funding and the lack of a dedicated funding source, which affected their ability to plan long term or expand their operations.[29] For example, officials in 9 of these centers stated that uncertainty around the amount of federal grant funding the fusion center will receive from their states each year made it difficult to plan and expand operations. For instance, an official from a fusion center stated that the center relies on federal funding for 80 percent of its annual operating budget, but has to compete with several other state agencies and about 75 counties for a portion of HSGP funding each year. Officials in another fusion center stated that competition for limited federal grant funding has made getting the necessary funding more difficult and, as a result, they have had to scale back part of their outreach efforts to state and local entities, which is one of the four critical enabling capabilities.

In referring to the role fusion centers are to have in the national information sharing network, officials from all 14 fusion centers stated that there should be a federal grant funding stream or program dedicated specifically to support fusion centers. For example, officials from 6 centers stated that, since the National Strategy has identified fusion centers as a key component of the success of the ISE, the federal government should recognize the importance of providing dedicated funding support so that centers with varying missions and resources can continue to close baseline capability gaps and function as key partners in the national network. An official from one of these fusion centers stated that while centers are owned and operated by state and local entities—and should thus be supported by state and local resources—centers are also expected, as members of the ISE, to support a national information sharing, homeland security mission. Moreover, this official said that if fusion centers, as the primary focal points of information sharing between state and local and federal governments, are to support this mission, there should be a targeted federal funding source to support centers' efforts to meet and achieve the baseline capabilities, which have been identified as being essential for centers to function in the national network.

Senior I&A and FEMA officials said that they understood the fusion centers' concerns and recognized the challenges centers faced in competing for funding. However, these FEMA officials stated that they do not have the authority to create a fusion-center-specific grant within the HSGP and that doing so would require congressional action. These FEMA officials said that, in addition to the nationwide assessment that is underway to identify gaps in baseline capabilities, within the HSGP, they have broadened the allowable costs for which fusion centers can use HSGP funding and prioritized funding on achieving the baseline capabilities. However, DHS has not directed that a certain percentage of HSGP funding be used for fusion centers out of concern that other state agencies, such as emergency management agencies, would likewise lobby for such specific funding. These officials added that this would not be possible because they are trying to balance ensuring that SAAs have flexibility in administering HSGP funds while ensuring that federal fusion center requirements are supported and met.

Further, senior DHS officials stated that DHS has recognized the need to conduct extensive research on funding options for fusion centers, stating that, after the nationwide assessment is completed, the SLPO is to assess key budgetary processes to determine how support to fusion centers can be affected and determine DHS's ability to identify additional funding options for centers. In addition, Fiscal Year 2012 implementation guidance for the ISE requires that, by October 29, 2010, DHS should develop and promulgate an annual common reporting process that will document the total operational and sustainment costs of each of the 72 fusion centers in the national network. Senior DHS officials stated that, while not yet completed, the SLPO has begun to develop this reporting process and that it is to be based in part on surveys implemented in previous years at fusion centers. These officials added that the goal of the guidance is to develop annual data on the costs to sustain fusion centers, and that these data are a necessary first step to assessing the adequacy of current funding mechanisms.

Taking Steps to Implement Standard Performance Measures to Track the Results of Fusion Centers' Efforts to Support Information Sharing Could Help Demonstrate Centers' Value to the ISE

If fusion centers are to receive continued financial support, it is important that centers are also able to demonstrate that they are providing critical information that is helping the federal government and state and local agencies protect against terrorist and homeland security threats. We have previously emphasized the importance of performance measures as management tools to track an agency's progress toward achieving goals and to provide information on which to base organizational and management decisions.[30] Performance data allow agencies to share effective approaches, recognize problems, look for solutions, and develop ways to improve results.

The Fusion Center Guidelines recommend that individual fusion centers develop and use performance measures as an ongoing means to measure and track performance and determine and evaluate the effectiveness of their operations to make better decisions and allocate resources. The Baseline Capabilities expand on these guidelines and recommend that fusion centers develop measures that allow them to, among other things, track their performance and results against the centers' individual goals and objectives. Officials from 5 of the 14 centers we contacted stated that one of the gaps they identified between their current operations and the baseline capabilities was development of methods to monitor and evaluate their fusion center's performance.[31] Officials from these 5 fusion centers stated that it was a challenge to develop performance measures to monitor their operations and demonstrate results because their mission was to prevent crimes, and it is difficult to know how many crimes were averted due to their efforts. Additionally, officials from 3 of these 5 fusion centers stated that their ability to develop performance measures was also affected by the fact that, due to limited personnel, addressing other operational work responsibilities, such as analyzing intelligence information and developing related reports, was the priority. A senior official from NFCA said that these challenges are similarly experienced across the broader network of fusion centers, and that centers would welcome a collaborative process in developing these measures to involve participation from, among others, federal agencies such as DHS, DOJ, and the PM-ISE.

According to DHS senior officials, the nationwide assessment currently under way is to gauge whether or not each fusion center has developed methods to monitor and evaluate its own performance. For example, the assessment results are to indicate to what extent a center has developed mechanisms to receive feedback on the value of its products or to determine the effectiveness of its operations in achieving identified goals and objectives. DHS senior officials stated that the results will be used to help federal agencies assess to what extent there are gaps in this baseline capability across the national network of fusion centers and to make decisions about where to allocate resources to support centers' efforts to develop these individual performance measures.

However, while federal guidance recommends that individual fusion centers develop and use performance measures as a baseline capability, currently there are no standard measures to track performance across fusion centers and demonstrate the impact of centers' operations in support of national information sharing goals. According to PM-ISE and DHS senior officials, the results of the nationwide assessment are not intended to provide standard measures for fusion centers to demonstrate the results they are achieving in meeting broader information sharing goals as part of the national network. For example, the assessment results are not intended to provide information about how well centers disseminated federal information to local security partners or how useful federal agencies found the information that centers provided them.

The PM-ISE and DHS have recognized the value of implementing standard performance measures across fusion centers. In its 2009 annual report to Congress, the PM-ISE stated that among the activities the office would undertake in 2009 and 2010 would be designing a set of performance measures to demonstrate the value of a national integrated network of fusion centers operating in accordance with the baseline capabilities. Senior PM-ISE officials stated that the PM-ISE had not begun this effort and is no longer planning to develop these performance measures however, because DHS, as the lead agency in coordinating federal support of fusion centers, is now responsible for managing development of these performance measures. Further, in response to a requirement under the 9/11 Commission Act, DHS stated in its 2008 fusion center Concept of Operations that it will develop qualitative and quantitative measures of performance for the overall network of fusion centers and relevant federal entities, such as DHS and DOJ.[32] According to senior DHS officials, the agency recognizes that developing these measures is important to demonstrate the value of agency efforts in support of the ISE. However, these officials stated that, while DHS has started collecting some information that will help in developing such measures, the agency is currently focusing on completing the nationwide assessment to gauge the capabilities and gaps across fusion centers.[33] As such, these officials said that they have not defined next steps or target timeframes for designing and implementing these measures. Standard practices for program and project management state that specific desired outcomes or results should be conceptualized, defined, and documented in the planning process as part of a road map, along with the appropriate steps and time frames needed to achieve those results.[34] By defining the steps it will take to design and implement a set of standard measures to track the results and performance across fusion centers and committing to a target timeframe for completion, DHS could help ensure that centers and federal agencies demonstrate the value of fusion centers' operations to national information sharing goals and prioritize limited resources needed to achieve and maintain those functions deemed critical to support the national fusion center network.

Federal Agencies Are Providing Technical Assistance and Training to Centers to Help Them Develop Privacy and Civil Liberties Policies and Protections, and DHS Is Assessing the Status of These Protections

DHS and DOJ are providing technical assistance to assist fusion centers in developing privacy and civil liberties policies, and fusion centers nationwide are in varying stages of completing their policies. Additionally, fusion center officials we interviewed reported taking steps to designate privacy/civil liberties officials and conduct outreach about their policies. Further, DHS and DOJ are providing training to fusion centers on implementing privacy and civil liberties policies and protections that officials in the 14 centers we contacted found helpful and wanted to be continued. DHS also has several efforts underway to assess the status of fusion centers' privacy and civil liberties protections, including updating the privacy and civil liberties impact assessments to help ensure centers' protections are implemented.

DHS and DOJ Are Providing Technical Assistance to Help Fusion Centers Develop Privacy and Civil Liberties Policies, and Centers Nationwide Are in Varying Stages of Completing Their Policies

Because fusion centers are collecting and sharing information on individuals, federal law establishes requirements and federal agencies have issued guidelines for fusion centers to establish policies that address privacy and civil liberties issues. Consistent with the 9/11 Commission Act, the Fusion Center Guidelines call for fusion centers to develop, publish, and adhere to a privacy and civil liberties policy. Further, the Baseline Capabilities provide more specific guidance on developing such a policy and contain a set of recommended procedures for fusion centers to include in their policies to ensure that their centers' operations are conducted in a manner that protects the privacy, civil liberties, and other legal rights of individuals according to applicable federal and state law. According to federal guidance, if centers adhere to the Baseline Capabilities, they in turn will be in adherence with the ISE Privacy Guidelines. Further, DHS's fiscal year 2010 HSGP funding guidance stipulates that federal funds may not be used to support fusion-center-related initiatives unless a fusion center has developed a privacy and civil liberties policy containing protections that are at least as comprehensive as the ISE Privacy Guidelines within 6 months of the grant award. According to senior DHS Privacy officials, the fiscal year 2010 grants were awarded in September 2010, so fusion centers will have until March 2011 to have their policies reviewed and certified by the DHS Privacy Office. If a fusion center does not have a certified privacy and civil liberties policy by March 2011, according to DHS guidance, DHS grants funds may only be used to support the development or completion of the center's privacy and civil liberties protection requirements.

To facilitate fusion centers meeting federal requirements for their privacy and civil liberties policies, DHS and DOJ have published a template and established a process to review and certify the policies. The template incorporates the primary components of the ISE Privacy Guidelines and provides sample language for the center to use as a starting point when drafting procedures for a privacy and civil liberties policy. To ensure fusion centers comply with the certification requirements in DHS's grant guidance, DHS and DOJ have established a joint process to review and certify fusion centers' privacy and civil liberties policies. First, a fusion center sends its draft policy to a team of attorneys contracted by DOJ's Bureau of Justice Assistance to provide a detailed review of the policy and compare its language and provisions against language in the template. After its review, DOJ submits the center's completed draft policy to the DHS Privacy Office for a final review. This office reviews the policy specifically to determine whether it contains protections that are at least as comprehensive as the ISE Privacy Guidelines. If the policy satisfies the ISE Privacy

Guidelines, the DHS Chief Privacy Officer sends written notification to the fusion center director stating that the policy has been certified.

Using this guidance and technical assistance, fusion centers nationwide are in varying stages of completing their privacy and civil liberties policies. Specifically, 21 centers had certified policies; 33 centers had submitted policies; and 18 centers, while they have not yet submitted their policies, were currently receiving technical assistance, as of August 2010.[35] Senior DHS Privacy officials stated that they expect that all 72 fusion centers will have submitted their policies and the federal agencies will be able to review and certify them by the March 2011 deadline to avoid any limits on grant funding. The 14 centers we contacted were at different stages of the review process and reported that they found the template and technical assistance to be helpful. Specifically, 7 centers had certified policies, 6 had policies in the review process, and 1 center was crafting its policy. Officials from all 14 of the fusion centers stated that they used or were using the template to write their policies, and that the template was a helpful guide to developing their policies. In addition, officials in 13 of these centers that had submitted their policies for review stated that the technical assistance and guidance DHS and DOJ provided was integral in assisting them draft their policies, especially a tracking sheet the DOJ review team used to document comments, feedback, and recommendations.

Consistent with Recommended Federal Guidance, Fusion Center Officials We Interviewed Have Taken Steps to Designate Privacy/Civil Liberties Officials and Conduct Outreach

The Baseline Capabilities recommend that fusion centers designate a privacy/civil liberties official or a privacy committee to coordinate the development, implementation, maintenance, and oversight of the fusion center's privacy and civil liberties policies and procedures. Furthermore, the Baseline Capabilities recommend that if the designated privacy/civil liberties official is not an attorney, fusion centers should have access to legal counsel with the appropriate expertise to help clarify related laws, rules, regulations, and statutes to ensure that centers' operations are adhering to privacy and civil liberties protections. Officials from all 14 fusion centers we contacted stated that they have taken steps to designate privacy/civil liberties officials or form privacy committees. For example, officials in 12 of these centers said that they designated a single individual to serve as the privacy/civil liberties official; officials in 1 fusion center selected two officials—attorneys from the state's bureau of investigation and the state's department of safety; and officials in 1 center created a privacy committee. For more information on the qualifications of privacy/civil liberties officials and the challenges associated with designating them, see appendix I.

In addition to developing a privacy and civil liberties policy and designating a privacy/civil liberties official, the Baseline Capabilities recommend that fusion centers facilitate public awareness of their policy by making it available to the public. Officials in 7 of 14 fusion centers we contacted described taking steps to make the public aware of their fusion center's privacy and civil liberties protections.[36] For example, officials in 3 centers said that they met with privacy and civil liberties advocacy groups to elicit feedback about the centers' policies. For instance, one official said that his fusion center shared its policy with a local chapter of the ACLU, which reviewed it and made suggestions for revisions, some of which the center implemented. Additionally, officials from 6 of 14 fusion centers we interviewed said that they posted their policies on their centers' Web sites or planned to post them once they are certified. To assist centers with their outreach efforts, DHS and DOJ officials stated that they are developing a communications and outreach guidebook that will include information on how fusion centers can communicate their mission, operations, and privacy and civil liberties protections to state and local governments, privacy advocacy groups, and the general population. These officials added that this guidebook will recommend that fusion centers post their privacy and civil liberties policies online to help centers achieve the baseline capability of promoting transparency and public awareness of their privacy and civil liberties protections.

Fusion Center Officials We Interviewed Reported That DHS's and DOJ's Training on Privacy and Civil Liberties Protections Was Helpful and Would Like It Continued after Their Policies Are Developed

The 9/11 Commission Act requires DHS to establish guidelines for fusion centers that include standards for fusion centers to provide appropriate privacy training for all state, local, tribal, and private sector representatives at the fusion center, in coordination with DHS's Privacy Office and CRCL. To support fusion centers in this effort, DHS, in partnership with DOJ and Global, has implemented a three-part training and technical assistance program for fusion center personnel consisting of (1) a "Training the Trainers" Program, where representatives from DHS's Privacy Office and CRCL provide instruction to fusion center privacy/civil liberties officials with the intent that these officials then implement and teach the material to personnel at their centers; (2) a Web site "Tool Kit" or Web portal, which provides a single point of access to federal resources on privacy training and contains training material and video resources for state and local personnel on privacy topics; and (3) an On-site Training Program, where representatives from DHS's Privacy Office and CRCL travel to fusion centers, upon request, to provide training on privacy, civil rights, and civil liberties issues. Appendix II discusses this training program in greater detail.

Officials from all 14 fusion centers we contacted stated that DHS's and DOJ's three-part training and technical assistance program was helpful and expressed a need for continued training or guidance as they continue to establish their privacy and civil liberties protections. Fusion center officials cited several reasons why they wanted continued training and updated guidance, including evolving privacy laws, and the recognition that some privacy/civil liberties officials may lack privacy-related expertise or backgrounds. In addition to training, six fusion center officials expressed a need for continued privacy guidance, such as briefings on examples of fusion center privacy violations and how they were corrected. For example, an official from one of these centers expressed a need for federal guidance on how centers should deal with certain groups who make threats against state or local governments, as these groups can span across multiple states. Recognizing that fusion centers would like continued federal training and guidance on privacy, senior officials from DHS's Privacy Office and CRCL stated that they plan to continue the DHS-DOJ joint three-part training and technical assistance program over the next several years and to tailor its privacy, civil rights, and civil liberties instruction to the needs of individual centers. Further, senior DHS Privacy officials stated that a goal of the training program is to develop multiyear relationships with privacy/civil liberties officials in each center, helping to establish a professional cadre of trained privacy/civil liberties officials across the national fusion center network.

DHS Has Efforts under Way to Assess the Status of Fusion Centers' Privacy and Civil Liberties Protections

Senior DHS Privacy officials stated that the review of fusion centers' privacy and civil liberties policies is a first step in providing ongoing federal oversight of the development of privacy and civil liberties protections across fusion centers. These officials stated that continued assessment and oversight—by the federal government and by fusion centers themselves—is necessary to ensure that the protections described in centers' policies are implemented in accordance with all applicable privacy regulations, laws, and constitutional protections. For example, a Director with DHS's Privacy Office noted that a fusion center can, in theory, have a model privacy and civil liberties policy but not correctly implement its protections, increasing the risk of potential violations such as the proliferation of inaccurate data. The 9/11 Commission Act requires that the Secretary issue guidelines that contain standards that fusion centers shall not only develop and publish a privacy and civil liberties policy, but also that they adhere to it. Further, the Baseline Capabilities recommend that fusion centers, as part of their privacy and civil liberties protections, identify methods for monitoring the implementation of their privacy and civil liberties policies and procedures to incorporate revisions and updates. While the 9/11 Commission Act does not dictate specific oversight mechanisms for fusion center privacy and civil liberties protections, DHS, in coordination with DOJ and the PM-ISE, has two efforts under way to assess the status of these protections across fusion centers and is taking steps to encourage centers to assess their own protections going forward to identify any existing privacy and civil liberties risks and develop strategies to mitigate them.

First, the nationwide assessment asks fusion centers to provide information on each of the privacy-related baseline capabilities, including information on the centers' designated privacy/civil liberties officials, components of their privacy and civil liberties policies and related protections, policy outreach efforts, and training. Following that, validation teams are to review the self-reported information in detail with each fusion center. According to senior DHS officials, this information may help to identify any critical gaps in privacy and civil liberties protections across the national network of fusion centers. Senior DHS Privacy officials stated that this information will be an important tool in developing a longer-term oversight and assessment strategy to ensure that resources are aligned to address these gaps.

Second, the 9/11 Commission Act, enacted in August 2007, requires, among other things, that DHS submit (1) a report within 90 days of the enactment of the Act containing a Concept of Operations for the Fusion Center Initiative that includes a privacy impact assessment (PIA) and a civil liberties impact assessment (CLIA) examining the privacy and civil liberties implications of fusion centers, and (2) another PIA and CLIA within 1 year of enactment.[37] In general, these assessments allow agencies to assess privacy and civil liberties risks in their information sharing initiatives and to identify potential corrective actions to address those risks. DHS published a PIA in December 2008[38] that identified several risks to privacy presented by fusion centers, explained mitigation strategies for those risks, and made recommendations on how DHS and fusion centers can take additional action to further enhance the privacy interests of the citizens in their jurisdictions.[39] CRCL similarly published a CLIA in December 2008 that evaluated fusion centers' impact on the civil liberties of particular groups or individuals, outlined procedures for filing a civil liberties complaint with DHS, and highlighted the importance of training fusion center personnel on civil rights and civil liberties.

DHS has not completed the second PIA or CLIA, which were to be issued by August 2008. However, according to senior DHS Privacy officials, the DHS Privacy Office is currently beginning to develop the updated PIA. These officials said that they identified two key milestones when determining when to begin work on the updated PIA. First, the officials said that they wanted to complete the "training the trainers" program for designated fusion center privacy/civil liberties officials, which they did in July 2010. Second, officials said that they delayed the start of the updated PIA to allow time for fusion centers to develop their privacy and civil liberties policies—which are to be certified by DHS by March 2011. Ensuring that centers had completed, and were beginning to implement, their policies would help in assessing updates to any risks identified in the initial PIA, according to these officials. Senior DHS Privacy officials stated that they have begun planning for the updated PIA, and that the assessment will be published in 2011.

These officials stated that the updated PIA will be comprehensive in its scope, and include an assessment of the steps fusion centers have taken to address the recommendations of the 2008 PIA, an analysis of federal and state government involvement in fusion center privacy and civil liberties protections, a description of what federal agencies have done and are doing to assist fusion centers in establishing these protections, and a discussion about related initiatives. These officials added that the updated PIA will be a useful tool in assessing where fusion centers are in implementing protections and addressing the 2008 PIA recommendations, and that the information will be used to inform decisions on where to focus their training and oversight efforts going forward.

Further, senior officials from CRCL stated that they have also begun to develop the updated CLIA, and plan to publish the assessment in 2011.

According to these officials, the updated CLIA will address topics such as oversight of fusion centers, common issues and challenges that fusion centers face in establishing civil rights and civil liberties protections, examples of civil rights and civil liberties complaints directed at fusion centers, and key issues brought up during fusion center trainings. Given the assessments' proposed scope and content, completing the updates to the PIA and CLIA as required will help provide critical information to help ensure that fusion centers are implementing privacy and civil liberties protections and that DHS, and other federal agencies, are supporting them in their efforts.

In addition to the nationwide assessment and updated PIA and CLIA, DHS is also taking steps to encourage fusion centers to conduct their own PIAs once their privacy and civil liberties policies are reviewed and certified by the DHS Privacy Office as a means to oversee their own privacy and civil liberties protections going forward.

According to senior DHS Privacy officials, individual PIAs are integral for a fusion center's development and promote transparency by describing fusion center activities and authorities more fully than the policies can alone. To assist fusion centers in developing their own PIAs, DHS and DOJ jointly published a guide to conducting PIAs specific to state, local, and tribal information sharing initiatives, including a template to lead policy developers through appropriate privacy risk assessment questions.[40] In addition to the template itself, according to senior DHS Privacy officials, the importance of conducting a fusion center PIA is conveyed through the three-part training and technical assistance program where the steps the office took to conduct its own PIA in 2008 are covered.

CONCLUSION

Fusion centers—as the primary focal points for the two-way exchange of information between federal agencies and state and local governments—play a critical and unique role in national efforts to combat terrorism more effectively.

In light of their reliance on fusion centers as critical components in the ISE, DHS, in collaboration with DOJ and the PM-ISE, provide fusion centers with a variety of support, including DHS grant funding, personnel, and technical assistance. However, centers remain concerned about their long-term sustainability and ability to meet and maintain the baseline capabilities given the current federal funding sources and fiscally constrained state and local economic environments.

DHS's efforts to require, rather than encourage, centers to target HSGP funding to achieving and maintaining the baseline capabilities are aimed at enabling fusion centers to close gaps in capabilities and develop more accurate and specific investment justifications in competing for DHS HSGP funding within their respective states. Further, by completing the nationwide assessment and the required cost assessment of the fusion center network, DHS can begin to address long-standing concerns and questions about sustaining the fusion center network.

If fusion centers are to receive continued financial support, it is important that centers demonstrate that they are providing critical information that is helping the federal government protect against homeland security and terrorist threats through a set of performance measures. The PM-ISE and DHS have recognized the value of developing such performance measures, but defining the steps it will take to design and implement them and committing to a target time frame for completion could help ensure that fusion centers and federal agencies track fusion center performance in a manner that demonstrates the value of fusion center operations within the ISE.

RECOMMENDATION FOR EXECUTIVE ACTION

To enhance the ability to demonstrate the results fusion centers are achieving in support of national information sharing goals and help prioritize how future resources should be allocated, we recommend that the Secretary of Homeland Security direct the State and Local Program Office, in partnership with fusion center officials, to define the steps it will take to design and implement a set of standard performance measures to show the results and value centers are adding to the Information Sharing Environment and commit to a target timeframe for completing them.

Agency Comments and Our Evaluation

We requested comments on a draft of this report from the Secretary of Homeland Security, the Attorney General, and the Program Manager for the ISE on September 13, 2010. DHS, DOJ, and the PM-ISE did not provide official written comments to include in our report. However, in an email received September 23, 2010, a DHS liaison stated that DHS concurred with our recommendation. DHS and DOJ provided written technical comments, which we incorporated into the report, as appropriate. In its technical comments, DHS stated that the agency has recently started to develop a performance management framework to demonstrate the value and impact of the national network of fusion centers and is using the nationwide assessment data to support the development of specific performance measures. With regard to target timeframes, DHS stated that it is planning to (1) collaborate with fusion center directors and interagency partners on the development of these performance measures throughout the remainder of 2010 and (2) provide performance management resources at the next National Fusion Center Conference in March 2011. If properly implemented and monitored, developing these standard performance measures should enhance the ability to demonstrate the results fusion centers are achieving in support of national information sharing goals and help prioritize how future resources should be allocated.

DHS also noted that while the report emphasizes the importance of sustainment funding for fusion centers, it does not recommend that DHS develop a sustainment strategy to assist fusion centers in getting the critical federal support they require. In our 2007 report, we recommended that the federal government articulate such a sustainment strategy for fusion centers—a recommendation with which DHS agreed and that we consider to still be current and applicable. Specifically, we recommended that the federal government define and articulate its role in supporting fusion centers and determine whether it expects to provide resources to centers over the long-term to help ensure their sustainability. During our review, DHS described actions that it plans to take that begin to build this strategy. More specifically, DHS said that it plans to collect and assess cost data from centers—a necessary first step to assessing the adequacy of current funding mechanisms and level of the resources that DHS provides to fusion centers. While a positive start, it will be important for DHS to follow through on these plans and develop a sustainment strategy for fusion centers. This would in turn be responsive to our recommendation.

Eileen Regen Larence
Director, Homeland Security and Justice Issues

Appendix I. Qualifications of Fusion Center Privacy/Civil Liberties Officials and Challenges Associated with Designating Them

According to our interviews with officials in 14 fusion centers, the individuals designated to be privacy/civil liberties officials varied in terms of their position and legal experience. For example, in the 13 fusion centers with privacy/civil liberties officials, 3 of these officials were center directors and 6 were analysts. The remaining 4 fusion centers designated attorneys from other bureaus or agencies within their respective state or local governments, such as state attorneys' general offices, as their privacy/civil liberties official. These officials stated that because they either did not have the appropriate legal expertise within the fusion center or had an existing working relationship with a state bureau or agency, designating officials outside their center as the privacy/civil liberties official was the best option available in achieving this baseline capability.

Among the 9 centers that had designated fusion center personnel as the privacy/civil liberties official, none of these personnel was an attorney; however, officials in 3 of these centers stated that their privacy/civil liberties officials had access to other legal counsel within the state police agency or city police department, for example, to help clarify laws and regulations governing privacy and civil liberties protections and to assist with the development of the centers' policies.

Fusion center officials we interviewed reported several challenges in designating privacy/civil liberties officials, including concerns that some officials had other operational duties at the fusion center or may not have sufficient legal expertise to ensure implementation of privacy and civil liberties protections. For example, of the nine fusion centers with directors or analysts serving as the privacy/civil liberties official, two had officials whose sole duty was to oversee development of the center's privacy and civil liberties policy and implementation of privacy and civil liberties protections. The other seven privacy/civil liberties officials had other operational duties at the fusion center. For instance, one fusion center's privacy/civil liberties official also served as the center's critical infrastructure and key resources analyst, which according to the center officials, slowed the development of the center's privacy and civil liberties policy.

According to a Director with DHS's Privacy Office, it is difficult to assess the effect of fusion center privacy/civil liberties officials having responsibilities outside of their privacy-related duties because the position is relatively new and this is common. The official added that, in general, it is better to have the designated privacy/civil liberties official be able to focus exclusively on privacy-related duties. Additionally, officials in two fusion centers were concerned that their privacy/civil liberties officials may not have sufficient legal expertise to effectively monitor privacy and civil liberties protections at the centers. For example, one official stated that it was difficult to identify personnel who, in addition to legal expertise, had experience in both intelligence analysis and standard law enforcement practices which, in his experience, were necessary skills for a center's privacy/civil liberties official. Senior DHS Privacy officials said that, in recognizing that fusion center privacy/civil liberties officials have multiple duties and vary in terms of their experience and legal expertise, DHS is committed to training and has taken steps to train centers' designated officials and tailor DHS's privacy instruction to the needs of individual fusion centers to help centers achieve this baseline capability.

Appendix II. Privacy/Civil Rights and Civil Liberties Training and Technical Assistance Program

DHS, in partnership with DOJ and Global, has implemented a three-part training and technical assistance program in support of fusion centers' efforts to provide appropriate privacy, civil rights, and civil liberties training for all state, local, tribal, and private sector representatives at the fusion center:

- A "Training the Trainers" Program: In this 2010 program, representatives from the DHS Privacy Office and CRCL provided instruction to fusion center privacy/civil liberties officials at four regional fusion center conferences that are held annually. These 1 1/2-day classes were intended to provide privacy/civil liberties officials with instruction on the requirements of a fusion center in implementing privacy and civil liberties protections, the general privacy law framework of the ISE, and instruction on how privacy/civil liberties officials can best teach the material to fusion center personnel at their centers. According to senior officials from CRCL, privacy/civil liberties officials from 68 of 72 fusion centers have received the training as of August 2010.[41] According to directors with the DHS Privacy Office and CRCL, the training delivered at the conferences is specialized and tailored based on feedback the offices receive from fusion center staff on key issues they would like covered. Officials added that they obtain feedback at each training session to also identify the privacy, civil rights, and civil liberties-related subject areas in which privacy/civil liberties officials may need more training. Participants in this program are asked to teach the material to other fusion center personnel within their centers within 6 months.
- A Web site "Tool Kit:" This tool-kit, or Web portal, provides a single point of access to federal resources on privacy, civil rights, and civil liberties training. The portal contains training material and video resources for state and local personnel on a broad range of privacy, civil rights, and civil liberties topics. The public Web portal can be found at www.it.ojp.gov/PrivacyLiberty. Furthermore, the Web portal provides access to training resources on the requirements in 28 C.F.R. part 23, which contains guidelines for law enforcement agencies operating federally grant-funded criminal intelligence systems.[42] DHS HSGP guidance states that in fiscal year 2010, all fusion center employees are expected to complete the online 28 C.F.R. part 23 certification training. Officials from all 14 fusion centers we contacted stated that fusion center staff have completed the requisite online certification training, and that it was helpful in making their staff aware of the regulations governing their criminal intelligence systems. Furthermore, officials from 5 of these 14 fusion centers stated that they plan to require that fusion center personnel complete the 28 C.F.R. part 23 certification training on an annual basis to ensure that staff are well-versed on privacy requirements.
- An On-site Training Program: For this program, representatives from the DHS Privacy Office and CRCL travel to fusion centers, upon request, to provide a full day of training on privacy, civil rights, and civil liberties issues in the following core areas: civil rights and civil liberties basics in the ISE, privacy fundamentals, cultural competency, First Amendment issues in the ISE, and "red flags" when reviewing or creating intelligence products. Additionally, fusion centers have the option of selecting topics from a list of available training modules, such as a civil rights and civil liberties case scenario or an intelligence analysis product review exercise, and receiving customized instruction based on the training needs of their fusion center. Prior to the training, representatives from CRCL conduct interviews with fusion center officials to learn about their specific privacy, civil rights and civil liberties

questions or issues, review state constitution and relevant state law, and research local media to identify the types of issues related to the work of the fusion center that have raised concerns among citizens in their jurisdictions. According to senior officials from the DHS Privacy Office and CRCL, as of August 2010, 21 of 72 fusion centers have received this on-site training. Officials we contacted in 3 fusion centers stated that they had requested and received on-site training on privacy, civil rights, and civil liberties protections from DHS personnel at their fusion centers and that the training was helpful.

End Notes

[1] All 50 states have designated a primary fusion center to serve as the focal point for information sharing. In general, these fusion centers are statewide in jurisdiction and are operated by state entities, such as the state police or bureau of investigation. In addition, 22 major urban areas have established their own fusion centers, which are regional centers that usually cover large cities with substantial populations and numerous critical infrastructure sites and may be operated by city or county law enforcement or emergency management agencies. For purposes of this report, "fusion centers" is used to refer to both state and major urban area fusion centers.

[2] Pub. L. No. 108-458, 118 Stat. 3664, as amended This act also required, among other things, that the President designate a Program Manager with governmentwide authority to manage the ISE, oversee its implementation, assist in the development of ISE standards and practices, and monitor and assess its implementation by federal agencies. § 1016(f), 118 Stat. at 3667-68. The President was also required to issue guidelines, in consultation with the Privacy and Civil Liberties Oversight Board, which protect privacy and civil liberties in the development of the ISE, and submit a report to Congress describing the means that privacy and civil liberties will be protected in the ISE. § 1016(d)(2)(A), (e)(8), 118 Stat. at 3665-67.

[3] Pub. L. No. 110-53, § 511, 121 Stat. 266, 317-324.

[4] GAO, *High-Risk Series: An Update*, GAO-09-271 (Washington, D.C.: January 2009).

[5] GAO, *Homeland Security: Federal Efforts Are Helping to Alleviate Some Challenges Encountered by State and Local Information Fusion Centers*, GAO-08-35 (Washington, D.C.: Oct. 30, 2007).

[6] DOJ did not provide comments on our recommendation.

[7] Global Justice Information Sharing Initiative, *Baseline Capabilities for State and Major Urban Area Fusion Centers, A Supplement to the Fusion Center Guidelines* (September 2008).

[8] We interviewed officials from the following 14 centers: Arkansas State Fusion Center; Boston Regional Intelligence Center; Delaware Information and Analysis Center; Georgia Information Sharing and Analysis Center; Kansas City Regional Terrorism Early Warning Group, Inter-Agency Analysis Center; Los Angeles Joint Regional Intelligence Center/Los Angeles Regional Terrorism Threat Assessment Center; New York State Intelligence Center; Northern California Regional Intelligence Center; Oklahoma Information Fusion Center; Southern Nevada Counterterrorism Center; Southeastern Wisconsin Threat Analysis Center; Tennessee Fusion Center; Virginia Fusion Center; and the Wisconsin Statewide Information Center.

[9] Specifically, we selected fusion centers whose directors were identified as the chair or co-chair of a regional fusion center group. DHS and DOJ established regional groups (i.e., western, central, southeast, and northeast) in order to facilitate interaction among fusion centers in the same area and communication with federal partners.

[10] Program management standards we reviewed are reflected in the Project Management Institute's *The Standard for Program Management* © (2006).

[11] The 2010 National Fusion Center Conference was sponsored by the PM-ISE, DHS, and DOJ, among others. The conference brought together close to 1,000 state, local, tribal, territorial, and federal partners involved in state and major urban area fusion centers across the country, including fusion center directors and senior leadership.

[12] In 2006, the PM-ISE issued the ISE Privacy Guidelines, which outline guidelines and steps for ISE members to implement to protect the information privacy rights and civil liberties of Americans.

[13] The Institute for Intergovernmental Research is a nonprofit research and training organization that specializes in law enforcement, juvenile justice, criminal justice, and homeland security issues.

[14] In consultation with the PM-ISE and the Attorney General, as well as the department's Privacy Officer, Officer for Civil Rights and Civil Liberties, and Privacy and Civil Liberties Oversight Board.

[15] Global serves as a Federal Advisory Committee and advises the U.S. Attorney General on justice information sharing and integration initiatives. Global was created to support the broad exchange of justice and public safety information and consists of organizations and federal, state, and local agencies from a range of law enforcement, judicial, and correctional disciplines.

[16] DHS's FEMA, specifically the Grant Programs Directorate within Protection and National Preparedness, manages the grant process and allocates these funds to state and local entities.

[17] The State Homeland Security Program supports the implementation of State Homeland Security Strategies to address planning, organization, equipment, training, and exercise needs to prevent, protect against, respond to, and recover from acts of terrorism and other catastrophic events. Each state receives a minimum allocation under this program and additional funds are allocated based on the analysis of risk and anticipated effectiveness. The Urban Area Security Initiative program addresses the planning, organization, equipment, training, and exercise needs of high-threat, high-density urban areas, and assists them in building an enhanced and sustainable capacity to prevent, protect against, respond to, and recover from acts of terrorism. These funds are allocated on the basis of risk and anticipated effectiveness to about 64 candidate areas.

[18] Protected information is information about U.S. citizens and lawful permanent residents that is subject to information privacy or other legal protections under the U.S. Constitution and federal laws.

[19] This figure is based on information reported to the PM-ISE by 52 of 72 fusion centers. Information was aggregated, but not verified, by PM-ISE or GAO.

[20] While the average overall current fiscal year fusion center budget was just under $2.1 million, the centers' budgets varied in size. For example, 52 percent of the centers reported current fiscal year budgets of $1 million or more, while 48 percent reported current fiscal year budgets of less than $1 million.

[21] These figures are based on estimated annual operating budgets as reported to us by officials from the 14 fusion centers we interviewed. We did not independently verify the accuracy of these estimates.

[22] This information was reported to PM-ISE, DHS, and DOJ by fusion center directors at the 2010 National Fusion Center Conference.

[23] Senior DHS officials stated that while these eight capabilities have been identified as the most critical of the baseline capabilities to achieve and maintain, the remaining capabilities are also to be accomplished and will be subsequently prioritized.

[24] Each validation team consists of personnel from DHS, DOJ, and the PM-ISE, as well as one fusion center director.

[25] According to a senior DHS I&A official, they have not determined how often (e.g., annually or every other year) the assessment will be conducted. They will make a determination using an after-action review of the results of the assessment and the related costs of administering it.

[26] GAO.

[27] CRS, *Fusion Centers: Issues and Options for Congress*, RL34070 (Washington, D.C., Jan. 18, 2008).

[28] DHS OIG, *DHS' Role in State and Local Fusion Centers Is Evolving*, OIG-09-12 (Washington, D.C., Dec. 10, 2008).

[29] An official from the remaining fusion center stated that, while obtaining federal funding has not been challenging for his center, he believed that funding across the national network of centers is a big challenge and stated that, in his opinion, not having a dedicated funding program has negatively affected fusion centers efforts to effectively plan their operations.

[30] GAO, *Executive Guide: Effectively Implementing the Government Performance and Results Act*, GAO/GGD-96-118 (Washington, D.C.: June 1996).

[31] Because we asked fusion center officials about baseline capability gaps in general, not about gaps in performance metrics specifically, not all fusion center officials provided information on their status of developing performance measures.

[32] Ninety days after enactment of the 9/11 Commission Act, and before it implemented the fusion center initiative, DHS was required, in consultation with others, to submit a concept of operations for the fusion center initiative that contained a developed set of quantitative metrics to measure program output and a developed set of quantitative instruments to assess the extent to which stakeholders believe their needs are being addressed, among other things. Pub. L. No. 110-53, § 511(d). The plan submitted did not contain the developed set of metrics and acknowledged the Baseline Capabilities was the framework from which measures of effectiveness for fusion centers could be developed.

[33] For example, one senior DHS official stated that the agency has begun collecting and aggregating information on fusion center "success stories" as examples of the contributions centers provide to the ISE.

[34] Project Management Institute, *The Standard for Program Management* © (2006).

[35] The 21 centers are: Ohio Strategic Analysis and Information Center; Louisiana State Analytic & Fusion Exchange; Vermont Fusion Center; Indiana Intelligence Fusion Center; Nevada Threat Analysis Center; Austin Regional Intelligence Center; Iowa Fusion Center; Georgia Information Sharing and Analysis Center; Statewide Terrorism and Intelligence Center (Illinois); Oklahoma Information Fusion Center; Washington State Fusion Center; Florida Fusion Center; Kansas City Regional Terrorism Early Warning Group Interagency Analysis Center; Houston Regional Information Sharing Center; Wisconsin Statewide Information Center; Southern Nevada Counter-Terrorism Center; California State Terrorism Threat Assessment Information Center; Northern California Regional Intelligence Center; San Diego Law Enforcement Coordination Center; Central California Intelligence Center; and Los Angeles Joint Regional Intelligence Center.

[36] Because we asked fusion center officials about outreach and training in general in establishing privacy and civil liberties policies, protections, and plans, not about outreach to the public specifically, not all fusion center officials provided information on steps they may have taken in this particular area.

[37] According to DHS, the purpose of the State and Local Fusion Center Concept of Operations (CONOPs) was to establish a framework for a comprehensive, coordinated and consistent approach for outreach by DHS to fusion centers. DHS published its CONOPs in December 2008.

[38] DHS, *Privacy Impact Assessment for the Department of Homeland Security State, Local, and Regional Fusion Center Initiative* (Dec. 11, 2008).

[39] According to a Director with DHS's Privacy Office, the PIA was not published within the 90-day time period stated in the 9/11 Commission Act because the CONOPs, in which the initial PIA was required to be included, was itself not published until December 2008. This official added that, in addition, within this 90 day time period, many fusion centers were just beginning to establish their operations and, similarly, federal efforts to support and provide guidance to fusion centers on their privacy and civil liberties protections were also in the early stages. By delaying issuance of the initial PIA until December 2008, this official stated the DHS Privacy Office had more time to assess the privacy implications of the fusion center initiative.

[40] DHS and DOJ (Global), *Guide to Conducting Privacy Impact Assessments for State, Local, and Tribal Information Sharing Initiatives.*

[41] To train privacy/civil liberties officials from the fusion centers who were not able to attend the regional conferences, CRCL scheduled a fifth "Training the Trainers" session, which was held in August 2010.

[42] The standards contained at 28 C.F.R. part 23 apply to federally funded criminal intelligence systems. As described by the regulations, because the intelligence data collected and exchanged could pose potential threats to the privacy of individuals to whom the data relates, guidelines are required. 28 C.F.R. § 23.2. Accordingly, criminal intelligence sharing systems may only disseminate criminal intelligence information to law enforcement agencies that agree to follow procedures consistent with enumerated principles, such as sanctions against unauthorized access and storing information such that it cannot be modified without authorization, among others. 28 C.F.R. § 23.3.

INDEX

D

E

F

G

M

N

O

P

Q

R

S

T

U

V

W

Y